Adventurous Alliance

BOOKS BY LOUISE HALL THARP

Champlain: Northwest Voyager

Company of Adventurers
The Story of the Hudson's Bay Company

The Peabody Sisters of Salem

Until Victory
Horace Mann and Mary Peabody

Three Saints and a Sinner
Julia Ward Howe
Louisa, Annie and Sam Ward

Tory Hole

Adventurous Alliance
The Story of the Agassiz Family of Boston

Adventurous Alliance

The Story of the Agassiz Family of Boston

BY LOUISE HALL THARP

WITH ILLUSTRATIONS

Little, Brown and Company

BOSTON · TORONTO

The author wishes to thank the following for permission to quote from copyrighted material:

Charles P. Curtis for MEMORIES OF FIFTY YEARS by Caroline Gardiner Curtis, and for THE CARY LETTERS edited by Caroline Gardiner Curtis.

Howard Doughty for the Parkman letters published in the *Harvard Library Bulletin*.

Harvard University Press for quotations from MICHIGAN COPPER AND BOSTON DOLLARS by William B. Gates, Jr.; THREE CENTURIES OF HARVARD by Samuel Eliot Morison; EDWARD SYLVESTER MORSE, A BIOGRAPHY by Dorothy G. Wayman. Copyright 1951, 1946, and 1942 by the President and Fellows of Harvard College.

Houghton Mifflin Company for illustrations from LETTERS AND RECOLLEC-TIONS OF ALEXANDER AGASSIZ edited by George Agassiz; excerpts from THE HEART OF EMERSON'S JOURNALS by Bliss Perry.

Charles B. Newhall, executor of the will of Gabriella Shaler Webb, for THE AUTOBIOGRAPHY OF NATHANIEL SOUTHGATE SHALER. Copyright 1909 by Sophia P. Shaler, copyright 1937 by Gabriella Shaler Webb.

Miss Margaret Perry for LIFE AND LETTERS OF HENRY LEE HIGGINSON by Bliss Perry.

Radcliffe College for ELIZABETH CARY AGASSIZ by Lucy Paton.

Published simultaneously in Canada
by Little, Brown & Company (Canada) Limited

PRINTED IN THE UNITED STATES OF AMERICA

In
Affectionate Remembrance
Amey Willson Hart
Radcliffe 1906

Contents

Illustrations appear between pages 210 and 211

Principal Characters
Arranged by Families

THE PERKINS FAMILY

Colonel Thomas Handasyd Perkins, 1764–1854

Maternal grandfather of Mrs. Louis Agassiz
Married Sarah Elliot

James Perkins

Brother of Col. Perkins (great-uncle of Mrs. Agassiz). Escaped slave insurrection in West Indies with his family

Children of Thomas Handasyd Perkins and Sarah Elliot Perkins:

Mary Ann Cushing Perkins (Cary)

Mrs. Louis Agassiz's mother
Married Thomas Graves Cary

Eliza Perkins (Cabot)
Caroline Perkins (Gardiner)
Sarah Perkins

Mrs. Agassiz's maternal aunts living on Temple Place

Nancy Perkins (Cary)

Married William Cary of New York

George Perkins

Sailed with Captain Charles Cary, as passenger

Thomas Handasyd Perkins, Jr.

Associate in father's business

Children of Samuel Cabot and Eliza Perkins Cabot:

James Elliot Cabot
Elizabeth Cabot (Lee)
Edward Clarke Cabot

Among 8 Cabot cousins of Mrs. Louis Agassiz

THE CARY FAMILY

Samuel Cary, 1742–1812

Paternal grandfather of Mrs. Louis Agassiz
Married Sarah Gray

Among the 14 children of Samuel Cary and Sarah Gray Cary:

Thomas Graves Cary, 1796–1859

Mrs. Agassiz's father
Married Mary Ann Cushing Perkins

Samuel Cary

Uncle in charge of sugar plantation owned by Carys at time of slave insurrection in the West Indies

Captain Charles Cary

Uncle who was master of Perkins ship Levant *and refused to carry opium*

Robert Cary
Henry Cary
William Cary

New York merchant uncles

Margaret Cary
Harriet Cary
Anne Cary

Chelsea maiden aunts

Edward Cary

Died at 19 of tuberculosis

Children of Thomas Graves Cary and Mary Ann Cushing Perkins Cary:

Mary Louisa Cary (Felton)
1821–1864 ("Mollie")

Oldest sister of Mrs. Louis Agassiz
Married Professor Cornelius Conway Felton of Harvard 1846

Children of Thomas Graves Cary and Mary Ann Cushing Perkins
Cary (cont'd)

ELIZABETH CABOT CARY (AGASSIZ)   *Married Louis Agassiz 1850*
1822–1907

Thomas Graves Cary Jr. 1824–
1888
Caroline Cary (Curtis) 1827–
1917 ("Carrie")   *Younger brothers and sisters of*
Sarah Gray Cary 1830–1898   *Mrs. Agassiz*
("Sallie")
Emma Cary 1833–1918
Richard Cary 1836–1863

THE AGASSIZ FAMILY

Louis Benjamin Rodolphe Agassiz   *Swiss clergyman, father of*
                                    Louis Agassiz
                                    Married Rose Mayor

Children of Louis Benjamin Rodolphe Agassiz and Rose Mayor Agassiz:

JEAN LOUIS RODOLPHE AGASSIZ,   *Scientist, explorer and teacher*
1807–1873 ("Louis")   *Married (1) Cécile Braun 1833*
                                    (2) Elizabeth Cabot
                                    Cary 1850

Auguste Agassiz   *Brother and sisters of Louis*
Cécile Agassiz   *Agassiz*
Olympe Agassiz

Children of Louis Agassiz and Cécile Braun Agassiz:

Alexander Agassiz   *Scientist. Developed Calumet &*
                                    Hecla mines
                                    Married Anna Russell

Ida Agassiz (Higginson)   *Married Major Henry Lee*
                                    Higginson, who founded Bos-
                                    ton Symphony Orchestra

Pauline Agassiz (Shaw)   *Married Quincy Adams Shaw,*
                                    financier (cousin of Robert
                                    Gould Shaw, Civil War hero)

Children of Alexander Agassiz and Anna Russell Agassiz:

George Agassiz
Maximilian Agassiz
Rodolphe Agassiz   *Married Maria Dallas Scott*

Among 5 children of Quincy Adams Shaw and Pauline Agassiz Shaw:

Pauline Shaw ("Paunie")
Robert Gould Shaw ("Rob-   *Married (1) Nancy Lang-*
bie")   *horne, later Lady*
                                                     Astor
                                             (2) Mrs. Dorothy
                                                   Converse

Children of Rodolphe Agassiz and Maria Scott Agassiz:

Marie Agassiz
Anna Agassiz   *Married Gordon C. Prince*

THE FELTON FAMILY

Cornelius Conway Felton, 1807–   *Married (1) Mary Whitney*
1862   *(2) Mary Louisa Cary*
                                                         1846
                                             President of Harvard 1860–1862

Children of Cornelius Conway Felton and Mary Whitney Felton:

Mary Felton, 1839–1896 (Niece
"Mollie")
Julia Felton, 1842–?

Children of Cornelius Conway Felton and Mary Louisa Cary Felton:

Louisa Felton, 1849–1915   *Niece with whom Mrs. Louis*
("Lisa")   *Agassiz was living at the time of*
                                               her death

Cornelius Conway Felton,
1851– ("Con")
Thomas Graves Felton, 1855–
1898 ("Tom")

THE CURTIS FAMILY

Charles Pelham Curtis, 1824–1906   *Married Caroline Cary 1851*

Children of Charles Pelham Curtis and Caroline Cary Curtis:

Margaret Pelham Curtis (Russell), 1858–1924

Assisted Mrs. Louis Agassiz on Board of Directors of Radcliffe Married Robert Shaw Russell (1850–1924) in 1883

Charles Pelham Curtis,
1860–1948 ("Charlie")

In charge of Mrs. Louis Agassiz's financial affairs in her later life. Married Ellen Amory Anderson.

Among the children of Charles Pelham Curtis and Ellen Amory Anderson Curtis:

Charles Pelham Curtis, 1891–
Lawyer-Author

See Acknowledgments

Adventurous Alliance

CHAPTER ONE
To Meet Mr. Agassiz

TURNAGAINE ALLEY they called Temple Place [1] when Boston was a village in Massachusetts Bay Colony. The alley led out of Tremont Street opposite Boston Common and ended in a stone wall and a flight of steps which led down into the high road — now Washington Street. When Thomas Handasyd Perkins, Boston's leading merchant prince, bought land on each side of the alley, Boston had become a city; the year was 1832, and Turnagaine Alley had become Temple Place.

In 1834, Colonel Perkins built himself a mansion [2] just beyond the Masonic Temple from which the street took its new name, and he built brick houses for each of his three sons-in-law. The Perkins family, the Cabots, the Gardiners and the Carys made Temple Place, or "The Court," as it was sometimes called, the height of fashion for the next twenty years. Here Elizabeth Cary Agassiz and her brothers and sisters grew up, in an atmosphere of wealth but in a home where ideals predominated.

Temple Place was not cut through to Washington Street until 1865, and so no heavy-footed cart horses and scarcely a hired carriage invaded these exclusive precincts in the heart of Boston.

All seven of the Cary children soon learned to recognize the different sounds of carriages belonging to members of their clan. There was the rumble of their Grandfather Perkins's coach, of English make. It had an awe-inspiring sound, in keeping with the dignity of Thomas Handasyd Perkins — "Colonel" and "Honorable," the benevolent despot of his neighborhood. Their Uncle Samuel Cabot also had an English carriage which rumbled with almost as much authority. He had married Eliza, the Colonel's eldest daughter; he was a member of the Perkins firm and devoted his entire talents to making money. Uncle William Gardiner, a lawyer, liked the latest thing in barouches, broughams or cabriolets. His wife was Caroline, younger daughter of the Colonel, and a lady who had her heart set on the things of this world. When it came time to divide the Perkins heirlooms, she made it quite clear that she must have the best. Aunt Caroline disapproved of her sister, Mary Perkins Cary, who, in her opinion, "left out the ornamental" in bringing up her family.

The Carys lived next door to Colonel Perkins, and in many ways they were nearest his heart. Their father, Thomas Graves Cary, came of a merchant family as distinguished as the Perkinses but less keenly acquisitive. Mary, their mother, had been the prettiest of the Perkins daughters. All seven of the Cary children long remembered the sound of family carriages in Temple Place, but they had none of their own. Their father hired a chaise when necessary; the girls took an omnibus and sometimes found the trip exciting. They all walked, and they enjoyed walking.

Eventually it devolved upon a Cabot cousin to eulogize Thomas Graves Cary.[3] "Never brilliantly successful as far as his own fortune was concerned," J. Elliot Cabot apologized, "his purity of character and unselfishness of conduct gave him an honored place in the community." This was true, but it did little to recall the quiet man with the twinkle in his eyes, who spoke seldom but always to the point. His appearance, especially in later life, was that of a stern Puritan, but his letters to his children were full of affectionate understanding. He was the kind of man to whom his daughter Elizabeth would instinctively turn for advice.

In speaking of their mother, the Cary children often referred to her "elastic, sunshiny temperament." They also said that she showed the gift of prophecy — on a Sunday in October, at King's Chapel. The Carys had climbed to the balcony of their church, where they owned pew Number 85. It was almost directly over the pulpit, and next to it on the right was pew Number 83, belonging to Mr. John Amory Lowell.

Mrs. Cary had looked with pride at her long line of children — Elizabeth, Tom, Caroline, Sallie, Emma and Dick; they were all there except Mollie, the eldest daughter. In the autumn of the previous year, Mollie had married Cornelius Conway Felton, Professor of Greek at Harvard, in this same King's Chapel. Mrs. Cary was pleased with her first son-in-law. He had a jovial personality, a fondness for music, good talk and good food. He was older than his bride, a widower with two little girls — but Mollie was the motherly sort. Now Mrs. Cary would like to see her second daughter, Elizabeth, married to some equally attractive man.

Lizzie, as Elizabeth Cabot Cary was always called, was pretty, like her mother. She wore her hair "in soft ringlets," in the latest style, and her eyes "looked like the water of a brook running over a bed of autumn leaves." She had a beautiful, carefully trained voice, and her duets with her sister Mollie had been the feature of many a musical evening on Temple Place before Mollie was married. Lizzie Cary was almost twenty-four on this October Sunday in 1846, and it occurred to her mother that there was no better place to find a suitor for her than in church.

From her vantage point in the balcony, Mrs. Cary looked over the congregation. Mr. John Amory Lowell had arrived. He was trustee of the Lowell Lecture Foundation and he had a stranger with him — probably a lecturer. With astonishment, Mrs. Cary observed that the stranger actually resembled Professor Felton! The unknown gentleman was handsomer, however, and something about the cut of his clothes gave him a foreign air. The similarity was mostly in the fine Roman nose, the curling hair and the creases beside the eyes suggesting easy laughter. The stranger had a cleft chin, his mouth was full and generous, and his brilliant dark eyes had a compelling quality.

Back home on Temple Place, the Carys sat down to their Sunday dinner with the enthusiasm of a family whose duty has been well done. And in one of those silences which come upon even the most voluble group, Mrs. Cary spoke. "I wonder who it was who sat in Mr. Lowell's pew today. He was the first person I ever saw whom I would like Lizzie to marry." [4]

Before the rest could recover from their surprise, Lizzie spoke up. "You must not set your hopes on him, Mother. It was Mr. Agassiz, and he has a wife and three children in Switzerland."

Mrs. Cary joined in the laughter at her expense. The story of her choice of husband for Lizzie was later often told, and with variations, but it was her daughter Caroline, nineteen at the time, who wrote it down. Carrie gave no definite date, but if Mrs. Cary did not already know Louis Agassiz by sight, then Agassiz had not been long in Boston. He arrived the first week in October, 1846; left for New York on October 16; and gave his first Lowell Lecture in Boston in December.

That Elizabeth Cary knew more about Louis Agassiz than her mother did was not surprising. One of Agassiz's earliest and most devoted friends was Professor Felton, Lizzie's brother-in-law. The Swiss naturalist Jean Louis Rodolphe Agassiz was already famous in Europe for his studies of fish, fossil and otherwise, and for his support of the new and controversial glacial theory. Lecture-loving Boston went mad about him and newsboys shouted his name on the street corners when he was to speak. Tickets to the Lowell Lectures, which were free, were engaged far in advance, and soon everybody was talking about Agassiz, whether they had managed to crowd into Tremont Temple to hear him or not.

"Plan of the Universe," Agassiz called his first course of lectures, and the title was typical of the man, whose imagination and enthusiasm were boundless. As time went by, he would have his enemies, and there is no enmity more bitter than that of one scientist for another. But people who really knew him loved him dearly. Emerson, listing "My Men" in his journal, put Agassiz second after Carlyle, with Thoreau, Alcott and Oliver Wendell Holmes following him.

Longfellow spoke of Agassiz's "bright, beaming face." Thoreau sent Agassiz some fish, some turtles and a black snake from Walden Pond. "How wild it makes the pond and the township!" Thoreau wrote when Agassiz told him that some of these specimens had yet to be described and named.

Alcott's was something of a dissenting voice. Agassiz's broad forehead, his square jaw offended Alcott, who felt that Phrenology proved the narrow British type of head to be superior.[5] "Such breadth of brain and horizontal overcapping of the ears . . . takes temperamentally to mundane subjects" was Alcott's pronouncement, and he considered fish, snakes and even glaciers too mundane to be worthy of attention.

One of the younger and more perceptive of Agassiz's students was William James. He was puzzled by a man who had the fire and love of drama commonly ascribed to the French together with a passion for meticulous, patient investigation associated with Germans — or, in other words, a man who came from Switzerland. "There is more charlatanerie and humbug about him and solid worth too, than you often meet with," said James. Agassiz's "charlatanerie . . . seems of an unconscious, childish kind that you can't condemn him for, as you would most people. He wishes to be omniscient, but his personal fascination is very remarkable."

Louis Agassiz appeared on the American scene at exactly the right time. The struggle for mere survival in the United States was now over for a large number of people. The machine age had produced a new leisure class with money for the education of their children, but the old idea that the law and the ministry were the only occupations for a gentleman was rapidly going out of date. Young men flocked to Rome with a slice of their father's hard-earned cash in their pockets only to discover that the arts required talents which they lacked. William James himself, and J. Elliot Cabot, Elizabeth Cary's cousin, had been for some time in process of learning that painting lessons do not necessarily make an artist. And now came Louis Agassiz to say that the physical world around them was full

of wonders and undiscovered secrets; that it was not literally created in six days, but that by weighing and measuring, by observation and deduction, a man might discover a "Plan of the Universe."
This was just the thing that practical young Americans were looking
for — something you could touch and see as well as dream about, a
new frontier for the adventurous with mountain peaks to scale,
ocean depths to plummet — as well as theories to promote or de-
molish.[6]

J. Elliot Cabot joined Agassiz's Great Lakes expedition as geological illustrator. And William James wrote his parents, ". . . I want
you to become familiar with the notion that I *may* stick to science." [7]
Neither of these boys managed to "stick to science" to the extent
Agassiz hoped, but a whole generation of scientific men were
Agassiz-trained and all over the country Agassiz-inspired museums
were founded and flourished. Many scientific schools owed their
start to the Swiss naturalist with his gift of enthusiasm, his "personal
fascination."

As soon as the Lowell Lectures began, Agassiz found himself a
social lion in a society supposed to be cold and exclusive. Dating his
journal entry January 9, 1847, Longfellow wrote: "In the evening
a reunion at Felton's to meet Mr. Agassiz, the Swiss geologist and
naturalist." So began a round of dinners and tea parties, the guests
from Boston, from Cambridge and from the Harvard faculty. Longfellow told of "Agassiz lounging in his chair" when a faculty dinner
party was over, "pricking up his ears and eagerly listening to what
was said at table." Longfellow pricked up his own ears to hear
"Agassiz extolling my description of the Glacier du Rhone in *Hy-
perion* which is pleasant in the mouth of a Swiss who has a Glacier
Theory of his own."

In February Agassiz visited Cambridge, accepting the invitation
of Edward Everett, President of Harvard. Everett was not just then
popular with the Harvard faculty, as Longfellow related in his journal. So it was said that the chilly atmosphere at Everett's house would
be just the thing "by way of preparation for Agassiz's lecture on
glaciers," and Longfellow gave credit to Pierce, Professor of Mathematics, for the joke, which he thought was a good one.

It occurred to Mollie Cary Felton to give a supper party for the Cambridge visitor, inviting only her husband's Harvard associates but asking her sisters, Elizabeth and Caroline Cary, to come out from Boston to help entertain the men in the evening. Whatever anxieties the bride may have had about her meal, she knew the music that followed would go well. She and Lizzie would sing some of their duets — sad, sentimental ballads which were so much the fashion.

> Sister, since I saw thee last,
> O'er thy brow a shade has passed . . .

That was sure-fire. Or

> Love not, love not —
> The thing you love will die . . .

Mollie played the accompaniment and sang contralto. Lizzie carried the air, and the girls confidently expected to "melt their audience to tears."

Elizabeth Cary met Louis Agassiz for the first time in her sister Mollie's parlor. If her mother had already made her famous choice of husband for her, then the sisters could hardly keep their faces straight when Lizzie and Louis Agassiz were introduced. No one took the matter seriously, of course, but the laughter in her eyes would have added to Lizzie's attraction. "Agassiz seems to be a great favorite with the ladies," Longfellow noted. Soon it seemed that Miss Lizzie Cary was a great favorite with Agassiz.

Agassiz loved music, Elizabeth discovered. He liked "humming along all out of tune" whenever she sang to him and, to the exceptionally musical Miss Cary, this seemed a charming trait. It was said that he used to yodel, "but not after he came to the United States" — and certainly not in Cambridge.

CHAPTER TWO

The Indies, the Orient and Boston

THE fact that John Amory Lowell invited Louis Agassiz to share his pew in church amounted to a social accolade. Mrs. Cary could be sure the stranger was a gentleman. For generations, every member of both the Cary and the Perkins family had had a British background and it might be argued that it was time for a change. But perhaps even the remarkably open-minded Mrs. Cary did not know that Agassiz was European when she chose him for a son-in-law.

Of course the Carys were not really Bostonian. They came from Chelsea. Every Sunday afternoon, Thomas Graves Cary drove fifteen miles by hired chaise back to his old homestead while his wife attended on her mother in Temple Place. A chaise held two adults comfortably — or a parent and two or three children lucky enough or well behaved enough to go with their father. "It was no afternoon call and away again, but a drawing up of chairs around the fire, answering of questions, giving of advice, going back to old times and ending with a wonderful tea." The "Chelsea aunts," Margaret, Harriet and Anne, together with their shy, white-haired brother Charles, were all that was left of a once large family. From Cambridge, in later years, it was a long, slow trip by omnibus to Chelsea, but as long as the Chelsea aunts lived — and Aunt Margaret lived to be ninety-two — their niece Elizabeth went regularly to see them.

The Cary homestead stood on a little hill and once it had been surrounded by three hundred and sixty acres of farm and woodland. The gradual selling-off of the acres for city house lots kept the aunts in modest comfort all their lives. Aunt Margaret, the eldest, remembered the day when she first saw "The Retreat," as the Chelsea place was called. "We went in at a gate and through rows of cherry trees to the house." The family, after nineteen years of self-imposed exile in the West Indies, had come home. It was July 2, 1791, and the "Boston bells were ringing for eleven o'clock — as they did then and for years afterward, instead of at noon." [1]

The Carys had landed on Long Wharf and "filled two cabs," for they had brought seven of their children with them and three Negro servants. Two little children had died on the Island of Grenada. Charles, the second son, had been sent alone to England to school, while Sam, the eldest, remained in Grenada in charge of his father's sugar plantation. The sugar plantation was expected to maintain the family in affluence here in the United States, for the rest of their lives.

Samuel Cary, born in Charlestown, Massachusetts, of English country gentry descent, had gone as a young man to the West Indies to make his fortune. And in spite of heavy mortgages on his plantation, he felt in 1791 that he had done just that. He returned and set about beautifying the Chelsea property, which had come to him through his wife, remodeling the old farmhouse built in 1629, planting "elms, oaks, chestnuts and Lombardy poplars." He bought saddle horses — doing everything required to turn a productive farm into a gentleman's estate. There was no need to improve the view from the Chelsea hilltop. Nearby a wide, empty sea beach glittered with white sand, and Elizabeth Cary used to hear her father tell of many an early morning gallop beside the green rollers with the deep blue of ocean beyond.

That beach is now Revere, with its roller coasters, "Tunnels of Love" and shooting galleries — the playground of very different peo-

ple in a different world. Yet amid smoke-grimed city buildings, the
Cary homestead still stands, with a sign posted beside the door: OPEN
THURSDAYS FROM 2 TO 5.

During the summer of 1791, Thomas Graves Cary was born at
The Retreat in Chelsea. He was the first of four more sons of Samuel
and Sarah his wife — a whole new family born in America. The year
1791 saw also the beginning of slave insurrections in the West Indies.
The country had been "in perfect peace," but "The coming of the
French Revolution brought tumult and disorder." A society in France
called *Les Amis des Noirs* demanded abolition of slavery, and universal emancipation was pronounced in 1793 — but not until hundreds of plantations lay in ruins and "such of the inhabitants as had
fallen into the hands of former soldiers and slaves had been sacri-
ficed."

The Cary sugar crop was burned in the fields, sugar-making machinery was wrecked and the plantation house burned to the ground.
The Cary slaves remained loyal, but four of them were killed by the
insurgents. Young Sam helped the rest to escape to another island.
He was sure that when order was restored he could make a new
start.

In Chelsea, Massachusetts, life went on in a generous, happy style.
Refugees from Grenada drifted in and were made welcome. The
Negro butler, who had a way with a fiddle, played for square dancing, and Miss Margaret, who had been educated in England, tinkled
the harpsichord. She taught music to her younger brothers and sisters, and Tom Cary, as soon as he was old enough, learned to play
the flute.

Pompey the butler and his wife Nancy eventually grew homesick
for Grenada, and when order was restored they were sent home to
their island. But Fanny, the childrens' nurse, remained. She had arrived in Grenada aboard a slave ship when she was about seven years
old, and Mrs. Cary had bought the frightened African child whom
nobody else wanted. Fanny lived all the rest of her life "in her little
red cottage" on Cary land in Chelsea with "her cat, her parrot and
her pipe." Elizabeth Cary and her sisters used to go to see her, and if

they found favor with her she would give them a parrot's feather. In old age she came to live at the big house, where "her children," Miss Margaret, Miss Harriet and Miss Anne, took care of her.

In 1797, Samuel Cary senior went back to Grenada. It had finally been borne in upon him that he had paid too much for his plantation, had mortgaged it too heavily. Young Sam, eighteen at the time of the insurrection, had been unable to raise capital to hire field hands, replant, buy machinery and rebuild.

Before reaching Grenada, Cary senior was taken prisoner by a French privateer. He reached port under guard, but Pompey, his former servant, saw him, managed to talk to him and sent word home — one of those cheerful messages telling the family not to worry. When Cary was released, he went out to the plantation and wrote of boarding up an old mule pen to make himself a place to live. Pompey's wife Nancy he found "keeping shop in St. George's and doing very well," but when she heard how her former master was living she insisted on going out to the plantation to look after him lest he be taken ill. In fact, illness now became the family enemy. Irrigation ditches had been blocked by the insurgents and were breeding places for malarial mosquitoes. The Carys, father and son, returned to Chelsea much broken in health.

Now came the realization that the fortune Samuel Cary senior thought he had made was gone. The Chelsea farm was rented out on shares. Plans for the children's education in Europe were given up, and Margaret set up a little school for her younger brothers and sisters. Elizabeth Cary was shown the table where her father used to sit to learn his lessons. She heard about the essays the whole family wrote each week and read aloud on Sunday mornings at the breakfast table. To have a school in your own home — this was an idea worth remembering.

With the help of his older brother Sam, Thomas Graves Cary went to an academy after his sister Margaret had taught him all she could. When he was sixteen, he passed his entrance examinations and entered Harvard. He then prepared his younger brothers, Robert and William, and when Robert was "particularly correct in mathematics," the President of Harvard, who gave entrance examinations personally, quite rightly "congratulated Thomas." The whole family was proud when Tom began reading law.

By 1814, Thomas Graves Cary was referred to in his mother's letters as "our young attorney." His sister Margaret was less respectful. On September 7 of that year she wrote, "Our young cadet, twenty-three yesterday, and in high spirits because he knows nothing, fears nothing, talks and laughs as if his company were invulnerable." Tom had joined the Massachusetts Militia and considered himself ready almost singlehanded to protect Boston against invasion — for the War of 1812 was still in progress. The Cary women were sure that a landing force from the British fleet would come ashore at Revere almost any night. "Tom tries to persuade us females that we shall certainly have at least ten hours warning of the approach of the enemy," his sister Margaret said — but she had her doubts. She and her mother had packed a small box of valuables — some of the Cary silver with the family crest, brought over from England by the first American ancestor, the crest being "a swan proper, charged on the breast with an anchor, sable . . ." to indicate a younger branch. Mrs. Cary hoped she had "secured from a neighbor the use of a team upon emergency," for their own horses and carriages had long since been sold.

The British did not land on Revere Beach, and Tom Cary had no chance to prove himself a hero. His children's children were to look wonderingly on silver pieces with the "swan proper," but there was no story of a midnight ride to go with it. A handsome uniform was no hindrance to Tom, however. Thomas Handasyd Perkins was a Colonel in the Massachusetts Militia and Cadet Cary found himself welcome when he came calling on the Colonel's five daughters. It was Mary, the third one, who soon pleased him best. She was dark-haired, vivacious, and looked so well in "red Canton crape [*sic*] without any ornaments."

By February, 1818, Thomas Graves Cary and Mary Perkins were engaged. William Cary, describing his future sister-in-law, said, "Mary was handsome in white satin . . . I can't tell you how charmed I was with her voice which is really divine." He was also "charmed with her conversation, with her manner. Then her little laugh is killing, absolutely."

William commented upon Caroline Perkins, youngest of the five: "Miss Caroline is a lovely, animated girl, and I admire her soft blue eyes and long eyelashes, but she talks at too great a speed for me." There was also Nancy, and William Cary mentioned her not at all. But she was the one he was to marry.

William was pleasantly surprised by the cordiality with which he was received by Boston's leading merchant: "Col. Perkins gave me his hand in a handsome easy manner and at several times during the evening made occasional observations to me which entirely eradicated from my mind the idea which I had always maintained of his extreme coldness and reserve." William Cary was in Boston only on a visit for he had established himself as a commission merchant in New York and was doing quite well. But it did not seem to occur to him that any man with five daughters, four of them unmarried, would be reasonably cordial to a well-born young man with good prospects.

The Perkins and the Cary families were alike in some ways and very different in others. Both were of Colonial stock descended from British landed gentry. Both families had been much involved in the West Indies. But the Perkins family might be said to have had all the luck, and most certainly they had better business judgment than the Carys. There was also a ruthless streak in the Perkinses missing in the Carys. Although it was truthfully said of Colonel Perkins at his death that he was a philanthropist, he had never indulged his conscience until he could afford it.

There were three Perkins brothers in the West Indies at one time or another — James, Thomas and Samuel. It was the James Perkins family who were the West Indies residents, however, Samuel and Thomas returning home when the climate proved impossible for them. Thomas, during a short residence, also bought a slave out of pity — as did Mrs. Cary. "Moussa," the Perkins slave was called, a man sold for only thirty dollars because he was thought to be in a dying condition. Thomas Handasyd Perkins sent him to a hospital and, on leaving the islands, gave him to Mrs. James Perkins. The name "Moussa" was probably a West Indian corruption of "Monsieur" and the Perkins children always thought it was given by the other slaves because of Moussa's elegant manners.

At the time of the insurrection, James Perkins, his wife and child, with Moussa to drive their carriage, had gone on a series of visits to neighboring plantations. They were on their way home when they "engaged to dine with the Marchioness de Rouvry." According to Perkins tradition, Moussa discovered that the de Rouvry slaves planned to kill their masters and the guests that night. At the risk of his life, Moussa gave warning.[2] There is a tradition of a midnight stealing-forth of Moussa with his mistress and the child to a flat-bottomed boat in an irrigation canal; of the lady and the child lying hidden under sugar cane as Moussa poled the boat to safety. An equally exciting version tells of three coachloads of guests and plantation owners tearing madly down the highway, slipping through a hamlet full of carousing insurrectionists, Moussa in the lead coach, whipping up the horses. In any case, Moussa somehow saved the lives of his masters and later drove the James Perkins carriage in Boston. In old age he "sat on the door" at the Brookline house in a handsome mahogany chair awarded to his use. He greeted guests ceremoniously and by name in most cases, until his death in 1831 when he was buried in the Perkins family vault under St. Paul's Church in Boston.

Like the Carys the James Perkins family suffered severe loss as a result of the West Indies insurrection — but with this vast difference: two Perkins brothers were in Boston doing well. While Samuel Cary and his son were unable to make a fresh start, the firm of J. and T. H. Perkins traded profitably in the West Indies during and after the insurrection. Their fortune was founded on merchant ships, most of which could sail away when disaster struck — while the Cary land, labor and sugar presses were lost. Also Perkins interests were not concentrated entirely in the West Indies as were the Carys' — in fact as Thomas G. Cary was to write, the "main business" of Colonel Perkins and his various associates was "on the northwest coast and in China."[3]

Thomas Handasyd Perkins made his first voyage to the Orient in 1789 as supercargo aboard the *Astrea*, Elias Haskett Derby of

Salem, owner. Perkins was twenty-five and had been married not quite a year to Sarah, only daughter of Major General Simon Elliot. The Stuart portrait of Elizabeth Cary's maternal grandmother shows a striking, black-haired, black-eyed young lady looking quite capable of managing the large family she was to produce and of upholding the dignity of the large fortune her young husband was determined to provide.

Elizabeth Cary's grandfather kept a diary of his early adventures which her own father, Thomas Cary, edited after Colonel Perkins's death.

"Malayan women dress their hair, which is long and coal black, with a most refined degree of taste," young Perkins thought. "It is combed all to the back of the head and after being twisted is fastened in a circular form with long pins. The juice of the cocoanut tree which is used in lieu of pomatum, gives it a gloss like japanned ware, and makes it appear very agreeably." The girl Perkins left behind him wore her hair in short ringlets under a white muslin turban. It seemed her husband liked variety. He also liked painted fingernails: "Many natives have their fingernails tinged with a vermillion color and this color gives them a very pretty appearance."

The diary of young T. H. Perkins was by no means a fashion manual, however. It dealt for the most part with the art of negotiation. At Batavia, the Dutch refused permission for the *Astrea* to trade but gave the necessary papers to a British ship. "Whatever I thought of the partiality, I very respectfully took my leave," said Perkins. Then he "dined with the governor," "supped with high officials," "making interests" for the *Astrea* till leave to trade was granted.

J. and T. H. Perkins kept "two or three ships in the West Indies . . . shipping coffee and sugar to Europe," as Elizabeth Cary's father wrote at the time of her grandfather's death in 1854. The statement was true so far as it went.[4] But in the Perkins letter books there were 147 letters concerning West India slave-trading vessels. Among the ships were the *Willing Quaker* and the *Delight*, surely sardonic-sounding names for slavers. Letters to captains contained advice against buying too many women and children and disposing of such as must be taken in any deal as quickly as possible because they might sicken and die. There was information about the latest laws against the importation of slaves in certain ports and suggestions as to the best ways of outwitting law enforcement.

Increasingly severe French and British laws against slavery finally made the trade unprofitable, however, and Perkins ships headed for the northwest coast, where they traded for otter skins which they sold in China, picking up a cargo of tea, silks, ceramics — whatever would sell best back home. It was polite to speak of these ships as bearing spices from the Orient; there usually was some pepper aboard. But by far the best-paying cargo was opium.

The Cary children never dreamed that there were letters from their Grandfather Perkins's firm to their Uncle Charles — that gentle, white-haired man who tried to run the Chelsea farm for his sisters and who should have been addressed as "Captain Cary." In 1821, Captain Cary had been twice to the Columbia River — his "observations of the entrance" from aboard the *Levant* were of great value to the firm. It was Captain Cary who was entrusted with the safety of Colonel Perkins's son George, who was being sent to the Orient, and it is plain that Colonel Perkins held Captain Cary in high regard.

In the discreet memoirs of the Cary family, Captain Cary's early retirement was explained this way: ". . . In those days, opium entered largely into the trade with China, whither his voyages had been made, and there came a time when he was called upon to choose between receiving the appointment to a new ship or obeying his conscientious scruples." He refused to carry opium and his retirement was a typical Cary choice, probably completely inexplicable to a Perkins. But "a much respected old Canton merchant" said that "Charles Cary was a moral hero."

In some passages in his journals, Colonel Perkins seemed to be deliberately educating himself in hardness of heart. He was in Paris during the last days of the French Revolution and he went to see some public executions. He had been afraid his nerve might desert him as he watched the guillotine from a balcony close to the scaffold. Far from it, however; when the time came, he took out his watch. "The entire proceedings" from the moment the "prisoners descended from the carts until their heads were all in long baskets" took exactly fourteen minutes. Mr. Perkins thought of a way in which two minutes could have been saved. They should have placed "all the remains in one basket."

Thomas Handasyd Perkins was learning to be hard. And yet, in Paris, he got in touch with Madame Lafayette, and was able to send her son secretly to the United States aboard an American ship. Lafayette senior was in prison — it would have gone hard with Perkins if he had been caught in a conspiracy to save the son. Perkins liked to tell his grandchildren of being later summoned to Mount Vernon by Washington to receive thanks for his aid to young Lafayette.

As a father and a husband, Colonel Perkins was decidedly human. "Save my letters," he wrote his wife. "Do not let the girls use them for curl papers." He instructed a clerk to write to a merchant in Baltimore: "Please send 2 more such shawls as you sent our Mr. T. H. P. They are wanted for his daughters and although rather an extravagant article of dress, he is disposed to gratify them." The letter was written in 1819, and one of the shawls was doubtless for Mary's trousseau, for she was married to Thomas Graves Cary in 1820 after an engagement of nearly three years.

They spoke of Tom Cary's "office on State Street" at the time of his engagement. Evidently he was dissatisfied there, for he immediately took his nineteen-year-old bride to Brattleboro, Vermont, then a frontier town where there might be opportunity for a young lawyer. Perhaps he wisely decided to begin married life away from the domination of his wife's formidable family. In this, he was not entirely successful — since the decree went forth that Mary's first child must be born in Boston. Tenderhearted to a degree, Tom Cary could not insist for a moment that his wife should bear her child in a small town on the edge of the wilderness when the Perkins mansion — the one on Pearl Street — was waiting for her. Mary Cary made the long journey back on roads that scaled mountainsides and plunged into valleys where there were streams to ford, since as yet few bridges had been built. The journey could have proved more dangerous to her than a midwife's efforts in primitive Brattleboro. But Mary Perkins Cary was strong and healthy, and her little daughter "Mollie" was born in Boston in 1821.

On December 5, 1822, Elizabeth Cabot Cary was born and she too was a Bostonian by Perkins decree. She was named for her aunt, Elizabeth Perkins Cabot, but just as the aunt was always called "Eliza," so the new little Cary daughter must be called something other than her real name. "Lizzie" was the popular diminutive and considered very sweet and pretty. She was "Lizzie Cary" — often called by this combination of her first and last names.

Like her mother, Lizzie Cary was a happy, friendly person. She had a great deal of common sense about money, which was a Perkins trait, to put it mildly. But she had no urge to shine in the world of fashion where money counts — she would follow her heart and judge the world well lost. She had her father's touch of humor. In the many letters she later wrote from far places — the Amazon, the Strait of Magellan — she would tell of scenes where she herself was the object of her own ridicule. And now and then, it must be admitted, she walked serenely through the scenes that were funny, had she but known it.

CHAPTER THREE
Schooling without School

PERHAPS the Brattleboro farmers and trappers were too law-abiding to need a lawyer. Perhaps they had so little cash with which to pay a lawyer that they preferred to settle their differences with their own hard fists. Whatever the reason, Thomas Graves Cary found his practice growing less rapidly than his family. Meanwhile three of his brothers had established themselves in New York, Henry being listed as "merchant" as early as 1815 with William joining him the following year and Lucius in 1820. "Cary and Company" urged Tom to become a partner and easily convinced him that New York had already begun to grow and that it would be foolish to wait for Brattleboro. Thomas Graves Cary pulled up stakes and Elizabeth Cabot Cary, though Boston-born, became a New Yorker for the next ten years.

Longworth's *American Almanac and New York Directory* for the years 1822 and 1823 carried the name of Thomas G. Cary and the address, "29 Laight Street." Beginning at the Hudson River, Laight Street ran west, crossing Hudson, Varick and Canal Streets. Between Hudson and Varick, Laight Street formed the northern boundary of Hudson Square.

The exit to the Holland Tunnel now spews forth its stream of traffic at Hudson Square and solid pavement with a confusion of route-markers now replaces shade and dappled sunlight on green lawns. Gone is the ornamental iron fence with gates hospitably open and the great trees under which the Cary children played. St. John's Chapel, a handsome Greek Revival building with high pillared portico and graceful steeple, has long since disappeared. It stood on Varick Street overlooking the park in the Carys' time, and lent an air of peace and dignity to the scene. Residents, who strolled top-hatted, tail-coated or in bonnet and shawl, called this place "St. John's Park" instead of Hudson Square.[1]

At the Hudson River end of Laight Street there was a wharf where stone had been landed, and a yard where the stone was dressed for the building of Castle Clinton (later Castle Garden) during the feverish days of "Mr. Madison's War." Laight Street was then definitely on the edge of town and ended in "Lespinard's Swamp" — which people with house lots for sale hopefully called a "meadow." Lots at this upper end of the street had an unhappy faculty of disappearing under water, and residents were forever petitioning the city to "fill the upper end of Laight Street." In 1824, a lot cost thirty-four dollars and perhaps under the circumstances the price was high.

The Cary brothers wisely chose the most desirable part of Laight Street, the block opposite St. John's Park. Thomas G. Cary's brick house was almost in the center of the park block. It looked like all its neighbors, with a fanlight over the door and recessed stone columns at each side of the entrance, but the plot was deep with a garden at the back — and also a privy. Indoor plumbing had yet to be introduced. There was a public well with a pump only half a block away, which doubtless made the park vicinity a still more choice location. In 1824, Nancy Perkins came to visit her sister Mary Cary and promptly got engaged to Mary's brother-in-law, William Cary. They bought a house three doors east on Laight Street.

There were gay doings in New York for the young married Carys.[2] In September, 1824, they made up a theater party to catch a glimpse of Lafayette on his return visit to the United States. The play was called *Laugh When You Can* but nobody paid any attention to it when Lafayette came in during the first act. The audience rose and cheered. "Proceedings on the stage came to a standstill but afterwards the general seemed to enjoy the play and the people enjoyed his pleasure."

Then there were the boat races in New York Harbor. Tom Cary dutifully escorted his mother-in-law, Mrs. Thomas Handasyd Perkins, to Castle Garden to see "two elegant light-boats with three men each" that "skimmed over the water to a close finish." They watched, at the same time, "a ship in full sail setting out for London." In the evening, the grownups could all go back to see Castle Garden "lighted by gas."

Perhaps encouraged by their success in marrying off Nancy Perkins to bachelor brother William, the young Thomas Carys invited Tom's sister Margaret to stay in New York for a long visit. The prim Margaret "had the amusement to see her brother William do the waltz" at a party her brother Henry gave. "It was not so objectionable in reality as it had been in my imagination," Margaret admitted. But she could not be induced to learn the step. She helped Henry's wife, who had an incompetent cook, to give a nine-course dinner, and made "cherry pie, custard, almond pies and Sunderland pudding" with her "own hands." But when a gentleman guest asked her for her recipe for "stewed calf's head" and "penned it down," Margaret was so completely flustered she could hardly speak. Although she once "could not help smiling" at a young man, she remained too hopelessly shy for romance, a maiden lady till the end of her days.

Margaret soon began to excuse herself from parties and, taking brother Henry's little boy Hal by the hand, she went to spend the afternoon and evening with Tom's children. Aunt Margaret "took her work," usually knitting of an intricate pattern, "and sat in the nursery till the children had completely gratified their inclination for noise and play, and ate their supper on a little deal-board table just like the one" their father and his younger brothers had gathered around in Chelsea — when Margaret taught them their A B Cs.

The two little Boston-born Carys, Mollie and Lizzie, were joined in 1824 by Thomas Jr., the first New Yorker. Then came Caroline, in 1827, and Sarah in 1830. The elder Perkinses were becoming resigned, apparently, to having grandchildren born outside of Boston. In 1829, "Thomas G. Cary and his wife Mary P." [3] bought, of

Moses Henriques and his wife and of Preserved Fish and his wife, a house and land at 129 Hudson Street. They were not leaving peaceful St. John's Park, they were only moving to the opposite side. There would be new cousins to play with, for the William Carys had twin girls.

Elizabeth Cabot Cary remembered her New York childhood. Her nursery windows on Hudson Street overlooked the Park and when she was kept indoors by some childhood illness, she remembered enviously watching her brother and her sisters playing below. She remembered the street hawkers crying "fresh strawberries" and she saw the nurse wheeling her twin cousins in their double perambulator.

In their enthusiasm for the city, the Cary brothers overextended themselves in real estate and it was probably no accident that Colonel Perkins chose a time when Cary fortunes were at a low ebb to offer his son-in-law, Thomas, a partnership, on condition that he would leave New York. Elizabeth was not quite ten years old when she returned to her birthplace and became a Bostonian.

The year was 1831, and the Masonic Temple at the corner of Tremont Street and Temple Place had just been built, its towers of gleaming white Quincy granite rising ninety feet in air. It was one of the first Neo-Gothic buildings in Boston, in a new era of white and pink, before Quincy granite grew gray and brownstone turned from pale rose to rusty-black. "Turnagaine Alley" had become "an avenue 40 feet wide" but its "handsome mansion houses" were not yet completed and the Thomas Carys went to live with Grandfather Perkins on Pearl Street. Here Emma, one more Cary daughter, was born.

In 1833 the "mansion houses" were ready. Colonel Perkins bought the Carys' New York property and Thomas Cary paid for his own Temple Place house rather than taking it as a gift from his father-in-law. This was a touch of independence typical of the Carys. The Colonel gave his Pearl Street house, valued at thirty thousand dollars, to be used as a school for the blind. "Perkins Institution," he stipulated that it be called, in his honor, and he had a director all picked out. As far back as 1826, Colonel Perkins had been interested in a young doctor, Samuel Gridley Howe of Boston. After Dr. Howe went off to help the Greeks in their war against oppression, Colonel Perkins put a hundred dollars "at the service" of the young man "in case he had to leave Greece with a Turkish sabre at his heels." Dr. Howe had easily outdistanced the Turks whenever necessary, and he was now again in Boston — head of "Perkins Institution."

By the end of 1833, the Carys were established on Temple Place, next door to Grandfather Perkins. From now on, Elizabeth Cary lived in the shadow of her grandfather's house until she had a home of her own. People came to speak of her poise, her elegance, her gracious dignity. And this was not surprising. The wonder of it was that she could break completely with her environment, taking with her everything of value but tossing aside as useless all the conventions that might have bound her.

Her younger sisters were afraid of their grandfather. Elizabeth was not. He was a handsome, stern old man who had built a huge house, but it was only his butler who tried to keep the younger children out of it — and then only when his master's back was turned. Colonel Perkins built his house for his children and grandchildren, and when they no longer wanted to fill it for him he hated the place. He loved to hear music from the concert grand piano in the double parlors, and as he came down the great marble spiral stair, he loved to find Lizzie ready and willing to sing to him. The chaos which the Temple Players would make of his parlors was at his own suggestion and the crowd of people coming to the plays would be his welcome guests.

From the marble-floored vestibule, steps led to a circular hall where statues, ill-clad for Boston's winter climate, stood in niches. Thomas Crawford, among other sculptors, had reason to be glad that Colonel Perkins liked statuary. Painters were not so lucky. The Colonel, on a trip to Europe, decided that copies of popular paintings were just as good as originals but much cheaper. He liked engravings, however; collected quantities of them and papered the billiard room with them.

To the right of the entrance was a dining room "large enough for a state dinner" but not large enough for a Perkins Thanksgiving dinner when sixty members of the clan sat down to tables placed end to end in the double parlors.

On the second floor, the side whose bulging bay window looked toward Boston Common belonged to Grandmother Perkins. She had a sitting room with bedroom behind it and the Colonel had rooms to correspond across the hall. The Colonel's furnishings were new, built of oak and carved monstrously. He had carved cases for his curios — a shell collection and a collection of skulls which one of his sea captains had obligingly turned graverobber to get for him in the name of science. There were closets smelling of sandalwood where Chinese kites and puzzles were kept for the early crop of grandchildren like Lizzie and Tom Cary and Elliot Cabot, who knew better than to be afraid of a fearsome old man.

In her rooms, Madame Perkins had stubbornly kept old furniture — just "plain mahogany." Her tea tray, when it was brought up to her and her grandchildren, was anything but plain, however. She liked fancy cakes, preserves and Canton ginger. It always puzzled the Perkins women but they accepted it as the will of God that they should be overweight.

Grandmother Perkins was formidable too — especially to the younger children such as Emma Cary and her little brother Richard, born on Temple Place in 1836. If a child appeared alone at her sitting room door, Grandmother Perkins always said, "Where's your mother?" It was "disconcerting," Emma remembered.

Upward wound the staircase to a third floor where the two unmarried Perkins children lived. The Colonel still hoped that one more sea voyage would help George, the second of two sons. He had been such a healthy, promising lad before a fall from his horse "affected his nerves." His mind was increasingly disturbed till "every two or three years he became strange" and was "shut up for some months." When Colonel Perkins was away it was Mr. Cary, gentle, firm and reliable, who was responsible for George.

Sarah was the only unmarried daughter. She had grown enormously fat and it was said that her only suitor had been a "Chinese gentleman" to whom her poundage was a form of beauty. She ran the house for her mother but was never given any money of her own beyond a sort of schoolgirl allowance. She was particularly fond of the Cary nieces, who had less spending money than some of their cousins, and she used to ask the girls up to her room to choose for themselves a length of China silk or an embroidered shawl from a great camphorwood chest of hers which could no longer be termed a "hope chest."

Every night in the week, the three married daughters with their husbands assembled at Colonel Perkins's house. His front door was made of "black oak" taken from the ship *Constitution,* and "the thud of its closing" could be heard throughout the Court. This was curfew for the younger grandchildren. "There goes your Aunt Caroline," Mrs Cary would say. And "There goes your Aunt Eliza." Living next door, Mrs. Cary could afford to be last — but she must not be late. The sons-in-law went "to smoke with Grandfather" while the daughters sat with their mother across the hall.

Colonel Perkins held a sort of Star Chamber session each evening where Perkins interests were discussed and policy determined upon. The family business was no longer confined to merchant ships but included real estate, textile mills and railroads. Colonel Perkins was senior partner, and his associates included his son, T. H. Perkins, Jr., Samuel Cabot and, after 1831, Thomas Graves Cary. In 1835, when Colonel Perkins went to Europe, he left an informal inventory listing such assets as bank stock worth $28,550; shares in insurance companies coming to around $140,000, plus such miscellaneous holdings as "the Boston Steamboat," the "Tremont Theater," and "coal lands in Pennsylvania." Cabot was to "see about rents" on wharves and loft buildings. T. G. Cary was to "do the best he can" with "the hotel in Quincy" and the one in Nahant. Where human relations were involved, tact necessary, Cary was the man for it. He was to "manage . . . domestic concerns" for his father-in-law.

Colonel Perkins retired in 1838 and the firm was broken up. He was "Boston's wealthiest merchant." He was called a philanthropist, and so he was. But he was never easy to get along with, and it could have been with a sigh of relief that Thomas G. Cary became Treasurer of the Appleton and Lowell Mills.

Mr. Cary's change of business made little difference to his family. His office was in Boston at the corner of Pemberton Square, close to Temple Place, and every morning after a leisurely breakfast, and after reading his strictly Whig newspaper, he walked to work. He came home to dinner at three in the afternoon. The Carys lived simply — there were only three-course dinners served on week days. Then it was back to the office and home for tea. This meal was called "tea," but it was really supper and not afternoon tea — which was only for ladies and their friends and clergymen on pastoral calls. Any other man appearing at afternoon tea did so under suspicion of having no proper business to attend to.

Then there was "the pleasant custom" of having food laid out on the sideboard in the dining room late in the evening. Cary young people were free to bring their friends — although of course their father never went to bed until the last young man had left.

On Monday, Wednesday and Friday afternoons, beginning in 1834, Mollie and Lizzie Cary and their cousin Lizzie Cabot, with Miss Lyman, the Cary girls' governess, emerged from Temple Place, entered the Masonic Temple on the corner and climbed the staircase in the Temple tower.[4] They were going to the room where Bronson Alcott had his school. But they were not going to Mr. Alcott's Temple School, although some of the younger Gardiner cousins were his pupils. The Cary girls and Lizzie Cabot were members of Miss Peabody's "Historical School."

Elizabeth Peabody, a woman in advance of her time, considered history to be well within the grasp of the female intellect. She gave Mollie and Lizzie Cary *Ferdinand and Isabella* by Prescott — but also Combe's *Constitution of Man*, which had much to say about rules of health along with the theory that the bumps on a man's skull indicated regions of developed intellect. Mrs. Cary insisted that her daughters read these two books on alternate days because the girls showed too much devotion to Prescott. Obediently, Lizzie complied, admitting Combe was "perhaps a better exercise for the mind than such interesting histories."

Miss Peabody's "Historical School" was the only school of any sort that Elizabeth Cary ever attended! [5] To say that Miss Peabody's school was unusual would be an understatement. She used Alcott's Socratic method of question and answer, teaching her pupils to think and to express their ideas orally and fluently. Elizabeth Peabody's own personal gift to her pupils was her way of stimulating a lifelong intellectual curiosity. Lizzie Cary learned to keep her mind awake, to study under her own volition and never to imagine that she had finished her education.

There was of course a governess in each family of Perkins grandchildren on Temple Place. In the Cary household it was Martha Brewster Lyman, who came to them when they moved to the Court and remained a friend long after her charges had grown up and married. She was only six years older than Mollie Cary, her eldest pupil, and when the Cary girls had children of their own it was "dear Miss Lyman" to the rescue in case of illness or the sudden need of a chaperone. When she died, at the age of seventy-five, she was buried in the Cary family plot in Mt. Auburn cemetery.

Besides Miss Lyman, there were special tutors for "music, drawing, languages and dancing." It was a foregone conclusion that the boys would go to school to prepare for Harvard, but it was a sign of an advanced viewpoint when Mollie, Sallie and Emma Cary were sent to George Barrell Emerson's day school for girls. They were sufficiently silly schoolgirls — Mollie was thirteen — to thrill over a pirate captain,[6] "handsome in the highest degree," one of thirteen being tried in the Masonic Temple because the new courthouse was not finished. The pirates came "to the Court, chained two and two," and the captain, noticing the girls, exclaimed over the "beautiful señoritas." The girls promptly decided he was "Conrad-like," and got themselves into "a very agitated state" lest he be condemned. But Lizzie Cary was not a member of the whispering, giggling group "upon the sidewalk" at the time. She could only read Byron's *Corsair* over again and wish her parents would let her go to school with the others — and be noticed by a "Conrad-like" pirate. It was her cough that kept her at home and indoors for several winters.

Years later, Elizabeth realized that her parents must have feared that she had tuberculosis — which had carried off an uncle, Edward Cary, at the age of nineteen. She had missed the schoolgirl friendships that were a part of education and she studied much harder than the girls at school, making good progress in both Greek and Latin — lest her friends outstrip her. Realizing, at last, the cause of her parents' anxiety, she was glad that they never let her imagine herself an invalid nor frightened her with the dread word "consumption."

Out of the five Cary daughters, Lizzie, the one who never went to school, became the pioneer in education for women. As she gave out diplomas to Radcliffe's successive graduating classes, she valued them the more for never having received one herself. Her own habit of studying without benefit of school bells stayed with her all her life. German classes, French classes, lecture courses and concert series — her diary was full of them, with a record of faithful attendance despite the snow and ice of the New England climate and the unaccommodating schedule of the horse-drawn omnibus. Social engagements never took precedence over these lessons, which she really loved.

Lizzie Cary studied alone with her governess while her youngest sister Emma and still younger brother Dick were allowed to go to a primary school. Through the gate in their own back fence they went, and then across the yard behind it. They came out on West Street, where there was "a row of small brick houses." In one of them, Miss Mary Peabody, sister of Elizabeth Peabody, kept school. There was a "purple carpet" on the floor and "maps and tables" for the children, but the little girls "learned to sew principally," for which they were "grateful" afterwards. Some of the older children told the little ones that "Dr. Peabody was a dentist and that, if they didn't behave, they would be put in the same room with him." Doubtless this seemed a good joke to the pupils, who knew that the gentle old man would never hurt anyone if he could help it.

By the time the girls on Temple Place were sixteen, their schooling was finished, regardless of what they might or might not have learned. Some sort of effort had been made to teach them to cook. "Mollie and Lizzie made a cake while I laughed and played with the cat," wrote Caroline in her diary. None of the Cary girls equaled their Aunt Margaret with her pies and puddings and "stewed Calf's head." But they were all accomplished in the art of receiving and paying calls, of going to and giving parties. Even Elizabeth, for many years, thought of higher education for women as something of interest only to girls who must earn a living.

Parties were in private homes, which were built with double parlors: the front one stiff and formal, the back parlor a family gathering place with its center table covered with books and sewing baskets. Sliding doors could make the two rooms one, and when Thomas Graves Cary gave a dancing party for Mollie and Lizzie the "small rooms looked very spacious with all the furniture removed and the carpet covered with a white cloth." There were flowers from Grandfather Perkins's greenhouse in Brookline, where he had taken up horticulture and planned, after retirement, to win all the first prizes away from his neighbors.

It was the thing "to hire Shaw's band of five or six pieces" and the Cabot boys, just back from their European grand tour, had brought home music by men named Strauss. Temple Place young people had been "dancing quadrilles mostly" but the boys taught the girls the Viennese waltz. It was fifteen years since William Cary had waltzed in New York, but Lizzie twitted her young cousin Sam Cabot on having too "sober legs" for "the whirling dance."

Lizzie Cary was nineteen when her father gave her a dancing party. She was "a very pretty girl . . . in the style of beauty that belonged to the day — graceful, gentle, rather languid in her movements but bright and animated in conversation." It was her sister Emma, ten years younger than she, who wrote the description when they were both grown women. With the painful honesty peculiar to younger sisters, Emma added: "I would never have predicted a career that would have given her a wide reputation."

CHAPTER FOUR
The Temple Place Players

THERE was a legend that the walls of a New England meeting house would give out "Old Hundred" if you rapped on them — and people said that the walls of the Cary house on Temple Place would do the same except that the music would not always be a hymn tune. Emma, the youngest of the girls and one of Boston's most accomplished pianists, learned her first piece at about the age of five so as to "accompany father on his flute." Mollie had "a heavenly voice" and Lizzie's voice was as sweet and true as her father's flute when she sang to his obbligato. Sallie, by the time she was seventeen, had developed a mezzo-soprano which was perhaps the loveliest of them all.

Young people could become very well acquainted by means of music, even in a strictly chaperoned era. The only trouble was that few outsiders broke into the charmed circle of Temple Place. Richard Greenough managed it, however. He was twenty-three when Lizzie Cary was nineteen — a guest at her dancing party. His brother Horatio was already in Florence studying sculpture, his "Chanting Cherubs" eventually ordered by J. Fenimore Cooper and shocking the prudish but bringing him fame. Henry, another brother, would soon set up a studio in Florence — and eventually become the architect of the Agassiz Museum. But Richard, who longed to try his hand at portrait sculpture, was in Boston attempting to unscramble his late father's affairs. Richard had a fine voice, one that blended nicely with Lizzie's.

Then there were the brothers Frank and Harry Lee. They could sing, and no one thought better of their ability than themselves. Harry Lee was five years older than Lizzie Cary. He had a sharp wit, but he was his own leading man in every situation and manufactured limelight for himself out of parlor lamps or even broad daylight. The only stage he did not care for was his office in his father's firm of Lee and Bullard, where he was expected to make at least an occasional personal appearance after 1836, when he graduated from Harvard. Of course he considered his appearance on the business stage a success like all his other performances so it was no surprise to him to become a member of the subsequent firm of Lee, Higginson, where he said that his idea of introducing "safety vaults" was the "crowning effort of his career."

If it is true that opposites attract, then it is not surprising that of all the young men who came calling at the houses on Temple Place Harry Lee was the one that Lizzie Cary liked best. She saw a great deal of him, because he was a member of the troupe giving amateur theatricals on the Court — a troupe of which she and most of her sisters, brothers and cousins were members. Harry Lee said that he "inaugurated" the "Tremont Players." The Carys and the Cabots had an idea that they did, and Tom Cary, who kept a running account of the Players, had proof that they were right.[1]

Musical comedies were given — by no means new ones, but with new words lampooning contemporary Boston and written, more often than not, by Tom Cary. *Bombastes Furioso* was the first play, with Harry Lee well pleased with his part of Bombastes, a homecoming victorious general in the manner of Rhadames in *Aïda*. But the troupe ran into trouble choosing another play to fill out a double bill. "Harry didn't show much fraternal feeling whether Frank had a good part or a bad one," commented Tom Cary. "This gave us a first insight into a trait of Harry's character. . . ."

Harry got the leading part in both plays, but he and his brother Frank "fought so much at one time" that Tom "thought all hopes of the play were at an end." By dint of much patience on the part of everybody else, however, the first plays were given — "in Uncle Cabot's parlor." The comment "Harry quarrelled with Frank" ran like a refrain through Tom's account of the rehearsals, but Tom was fair when it came to reporting the results. "Harry played with more system than any of us. . . . He played with much spirit and well deserved the praise he received."

Tom criticized himself severely. His part was "injured by want of self confidence," he said, and he knew this "to be one of" his "troubles, if others do not." Emma, for example, thought him "a very elegant young man and quite aware of the fact." A great deal was expected of an eldest son with his father's name and Tom was hopeful, hard-working and never quite able to do himself justice.

The audience for the Temple Place Plays consisted of the family, with friends asked in by special invitation. Colonel Perkins had the largest, most comfortable chair right up front in the Cabot's parlor. "Grandfather was so much pleased" with the first performance that "he said we played too well for gentlemen and ladies," according to Tom. It was a much-quoted comment. Colonel Perkins also said that he wanted the Temple Players at his own house.

"We, of course, were delighted," Tom wrote. He talked the matter over with his cousin, J. Elliot Cabot, and came to the conclusion that if Grandfather wished for music, he must pay the piper. "I sent mother in to attack him and she, putting her figure lower than we wished, obtained $50.00 — but my making appropriate thanks induced him to double the amount," Tom said. The brothers Elliot and Edward Cabot painted scenery and built a more or less portable stage complete with candles for footlights.

The plays at Colonel Perkins's house began in February, 1847, and on the twenty-fifth they gave *The Waterman* with Lizzie Cary as leading lady — and Harry Lee with the best male part, of course.

The play was a sufficiently silly affair by Charles Dibden — about an ambitious mother, a beautiful daughter and two suitors; the daughter choosing, in the end, the simple Thames boatman with the heart of gold. It had been played in London at the Drury Lane Theatre as early as 1776 and shared a bill with *Pinafore* as late as 1887. The part of the heroine, "Wilelmini," was a pleasant one, with some pretty tunes to show off Lizzie Cary's voice to good advantage.

Elizabeth had not wanted to be in any of the plays. She very much preferred helping with the costumes and making herself useful behind the scenes. Between acts, she gladly came out to entertain with a song or two while the amateur scene-shifters stumbled and bumped about behind the green curtain. But she always hated to stand on a stage and let silent rows of people stare at her while she talked or sang for what seemed to her long periods of time.

Tom wrote in his journal what he thought of his sister Lizzie's acting. ". . . The debutante, Lizzie, being new, deserves a word. Her whole performance was one of great merit, correct without being stiff, and very easy on the stage without being familiar with the audience. She was much admired by all and won the hearts of the old gentlemen, generally." It did not seem to occur to Tom that old gentlemen's hearts were not the ones Lizzie would have liked best to win.

Lizzie played in *The Rivals*, but her part was much cut, as Tom regretfully remarked. Harry Lee played Sir Anthony Absolute in *The Rivals*, and played it so much to his own satisfaction that he often repeated it, getting up other troupes to support him — for this was one of the last plays given by the Temple Players. Finally, on a private stage of his own which he built in Brookline, Harry Lee played Sir Anthony to Fanny Kemble's Lydia Languish. On this occasion, the great Miss Kemble forgot her lines for the first time in her life — a story Harry was never tired of telling.[2]

The Temple Place plays were a welcome change from most Boston forms of entertainment. According to the prevailing rules of etiquette, a really nice girl never got her name in the paper except on the day she was married and when she died. But the Temple Players were reported — although with names discreetly suppressed. "A correspondent of a Philadelphia newspaper" gave an account of "Private theatricals . . . at the 'West End' in Boston." The play commented upon was *Bombastes Furioso*, in which the name of the heroine was "Distaffina." "The gem of the piece," said the correspondent, "was 'Distaffina,' which was taken by a young lady of great personal beauty and, we understand, of rare accomplishment." The "young lady" was Sallie Cary.

And the correspondent "could not but mention in conclusion, the dark-eyed damsel who came out as 'orchestra,' then presiding at the piano, and in the course of the evening sang several songs and ballads. There was in this young lady's performance a combination of exquisite taste and purity of style that we have rarely seen." And this "dark-eyed damsel" was Lizzie.

The Temple Plays continued for several winters, sometimes with a new bill, sometimes repeating an old success with new songs added by Tom. At one point he sang a song he composed himself. As players dropped out others took their places, for on Temple Place there were eight Cabots, six Gardiners, seven Carys — and at number one Joy Street five children of "young" Tom Perkins — almost all of them willing to take a part. Even so, Tom Cary visualized the end when he said that "Gus Perkins" was "so taken up with his studies that he could not attend to his part." In March, 1847, the players gave their last performance in Grandfather Perkins's house. It was *Bombastes Furioso,* "which was received with roars of laughter from beginning to end. . . . Nothing could have been more satisfactory . . . for a finale."

Next day Tom and two of his cousins dismantled the stage. They stored "scenes, skies, hangings" on the floor of their grandfather's billiard room at the top of his house. Heavy properties such as the king's throne in *Bombastes* went out to the Perkinses' stable. And then Tom came back once more, with Frank Lee.

"I should hardly have known him or myself or the room," Tom wrote. "Frank was changed. He had cut off the mustache and beard," which he had grown for his part. "The room was changed, there were no scenes, no green benches and no old candle ends lying on the floor. I was changed, there was to be no rehearsal. I looked out of the window and felt as if the world had been to the barber's and had its hair cut too short. I wondered if I should ever get used to it."

The plays were not quite over, after all. The following December, Uncle William Gardiner "proposed about three weeks before Christ-

mas that the actors of the previous winter should perform at his
house on Christmas night as it would save him the trouble of giving
a stupid family party." And Tom agreed that "a dramatic performance well supported throughout is one of the best and most satisfactory amusements, when there is no charge for admission and supper
is served gratis."

Tom was "stage manager" for the performance at his uncle's
house. He was "desirous to keep Harry quiet" and was successful
because "Sallie [Cary] and Mary Gardiner kept him in a constant
state of fume and worry and thereby diverted his attention" from
Tom. He would have been astounded if he had known how much
his sister Lizzie liked Harry Lee. Twenty years later, Elizabeth saw
Harry in another amateur play and she went up to him and told him
he was "as fascinating as ever he was in the days of our Temple
Theater. The same kind of feeling I used to have . . . comes over
me — a dangerous kind of sentiment," she said.

But on Temple Place, one of fourteen first cousins was Lizzie
Cabot, almost the same age as Lizzie Cary. As children, the two had
been constant playmates and were called "the Lizzies." It was Lizzie
Cabot that Harry Lee married.

Harry Lee's witty sayings were much quoted as the years went
by. "The Lowells, the Higginsons and the Jacksons came up from
Salem and Newburyport, social and kindly spoken people inclined
to make acquaintances and mingle with the world pleasantly," Harry
said. "But they got some Cabot wives who shut them up." [3] Of
course the Lees came from Salem, too; but Lizzie Cabot never quite
managed to shut Harry up.

Colonel Perkins was not the only patriarch who gathered his family about him in a favorite neighborhood. "Lees, Jacksons and Put-
nams, all related to one another, congregated about Chauncy Place
and Bedford Street; Lawrences and Masons in Colonnade Row; El-
liots in Park and Beacon . . . Curtises and Lorings were in Somerset
Place." And Caroline Cary, who told in later years of these neigh-
borhoods, wondered if "the clannish way in which Boston families
settled down near each other, and . . . the closeness of the intimacy
it produced . . . brought a certain narrowness of spirit." Carrie

need not have wondered — narrowness was inevitable. Her two older sisters were in luck when the Greenoughs moved to Cambridge. Richard Greenough was the youngest of eleven children, seven of whom were girls more or less the same age as the five Cary sisters, but just which ones and how many of them were meant by the term "the Greenoughs" nobody ever bothered to say. In any case, it was a large, hospitable family, and as calls must go on, the Cary girls began to take the "hourly" — the omnibus which ran from Scollay Square to Cambridge once an hour. The Greenoughs made new friends in Cambridge whom they willingly shared, and by 1845 they had helped Mollie and Lizzie to break out of the tight little circle centered on Temple Place.

The "omnibus crossed a long causeway," then a bridge over the Charles, and proceeded "for about two miles between houses and gardens along a rather solitary road to Harvard College." As for Cambridge, it was "so scattered that there is really nothing that can be called a street in it" — or so said Lord Acton while visiting this country in 1851. "Surrounded by few trees, appear a couple of red brick buildings of rather tumbledown appearance and two small edifices of stone. This is Harvard College."

Mollie and Lizzie Cary saw Harvard in a different light — that of unreserved admiration. Either to the countinghouse or to Harvard had gone all their male relatives on both sides of the family and for several generations. If any other college existed, they seemed not to have heard of it. They were pleased that Cambridge should have no proper streets because they were tired of pavement, and unlike Longfellow, who complained bitterly of the mud in Cambridge, they never seemed to notice it. They liked a town where formal gardens gave way to open fields and "a black schooner" might be seen lying in the river, as though "at anchor . . . among the haycocks." [4]

The Greenoughs' parlor was the scene of musical parties just as their home in Boston had been, but with this improvement: Harvard men were to be met with, both professors and undergraduates. By the second of October, 1845, Longfellow wrote in his journal, "We accuse Felton of walking as in a dream and think he visits the Carys often." Professor Felton had met Mollie Cary in the Greenoughs' parlor and he was now calling on her regularly on Temple Place.

Mollie was twenty-four and the professor was fourteen years her senior. His first wife had died in April of the same year; but if it seems that he was rather soon in the market for another, it should be remembered that Mary Whitney, the first Mrs. Felton, had been "in a state of dualism" and mentally out of touch with reality at intervals and for some time. She left two little girls: Mary, aged six, and Julia Ward, three years old.

On the 14th of April, 1846, there was "a party at the Greenoughs" which Longfellow attended. "The Carys were there, father, mother and sisters three," Longfellow said. "Felton likewise, radiant, on the brink of marriage." Longfellow liked Mollie Cary, and the engagement, in his opinion, was "good — very good."

The wedding was on September 28, 1846, just a little less than a year from the date when Longfellow noticed that Felton must have lost his heart. Longfellow's account of the wedding said merely that "the church looked pleasantly, darkened by the gathering shades of afternoon." Further details were contributed by the bride's aunt, Eliza Cabot. The bridal party arrived at the church exactly on time, but "it was somewhat awkward from the sexton not being there to open the doors," said Aunt Cabot.[5]

"An immense crowd gathered in the entry . . . while a blacksmith was sent for to open the lock." This the blacksmith did, but the door proved to be bolted on the inside. John Gardiner, a young cousin, "was hoisted into a window," climbed down inside the church and opened the door. Meanwhile a crowd of decidedly uninvited guests had collected in the street. Colonel Perkins, waiting in his carriage, "was very much disturbed."

Less than three months after Mollie's wedding, her sister Lizzie met Agassiz in Mollie's parlor. At the time, no one thought of the encounter as significant, although they may have laughed about it because of Agassiz's married status and Mrs. Cary's strange prophecy. But Professor Felton was an ardent matchmaker, and he thought he, not Mrs. Cary, knew just the man for Lizzie. It was his friend Charles Sumner.

There was a group of mutually admiring, intellectual young men calling themselves the "Five of Clubs." They were, originally, Longfellow, Felton, Hillard, Sumner and Cleveland. Elizabeth Cary knew Henry Cleveland very well, for he had married her cousin "Lilly" Perkins — but he had died, and the fifth member was now Dr. Samuel Gridley Howe. Felton, who had loved "running off to New York for mirth and oysters," had tried his best to marry off some of his fellow club members to the "Three Graces of Bond Street," the Ward heiresses. Dr. Howe had married the bewitching Julia Ward, to be sure, but Longfellow had at last been accepted by his long-loved Fanny Appleton and Sumner had never cared for Annie Ward after all. Felton could not be said to be a great success as a matchmaker, but he never stopped trying. Sumner was the only bachelor left in this charmed circle and at Felton's suggestion he was often asked to dinners as Lizzie Cary's partner.

Sumner seemed to enjoy the society of Miss Cary. He talked brilliantly, as always, and his subject was Abolition. Miss Cary's father was an ardent Whig interested in cotton mills. Her grandfather, for all his giving up of slave running and his increasing reputation as a philanthropist, was anything but an Abolitionist. Longfellow, observing Sumner and Lizzie Cary at a dinner at his own house, remarked, "Miss C. pleasant but rather taciturn."

Agassiz had expected to return to Europe as soon as his course of Lowell lectures was finished, and as soon as he had explored a few choice areas in the United States and Canada, collecting "marine animals" and observing evidences of glacial action. His idea of what territory he might hope to cover was typical of his boundless optimism: "This summer I hope to explore the lower lakes of Canada and also the regions lying to the eastward as far as Nova Scotia; in the autumn I shall resume my excursions on the coast and in the Alleghanies and shall pass part of the winter in the Carolinas." he wrote. If he could get the Jardin des Plantes to finance an expedition, he would go in 1848 to "a zone thus far completely neglected by naturalists, the region namely of the small lakes to the west of Lake Superior, where the Mississippi takes its rise, and also of that lying between this great basin of fresh water and the southern arm of Hudson Bay." After this simple little journey there would be "the autumn" for "exploring the great valley of the Mississippi and" he would "pass the winter on the borders of the Gulf of Mexico."

After that, Agassiz would be ready to go home. "Notwithstanding the interest offered by the exploration of a country as rich as this is, notwithstanding the gratifying welcome I have received here, I feel, after all, that nowhere can one work better than in our old Europe. . . ."

No money was forthcoming from Paris, however, and Agassiz confessed that he would "soon be at the end of the subsidy granted . . . by the King of Prussia." He had the happy faculty of making grandiose plans and then being able to put them aside, confident that the day would yet come when they would all be realized. Meanwhile, he rejoiced in what came to hand — trips on board the Coast Survey steamer *Bibb* — for salt water excited and delighted him. His first explorations were confined to Boston Harbor, but he declared: "I learn more here in a day than in months from books . . ."

During the summer of 1848, Louis Agassiz's wife died in far off Freiburg. He sent for his children, for he had accepted the chair of Zoology and Geology at Harvard's newly created Lawrence Scientific School. He began his first course of lectures in April, 1848.

If Lizzie Cary kept a diary during her girlhood, it would seem not to have survived. Her sister Carrie's diary remains, however, and during the following spring it was full of such entries as, "Went to Cambridge with Mother and spent the day." "French exercises etc. Went out to Cambridge." Mollie's first child, named Louisa and called "Lisa," was three months old when her young Aunt Carrie thought she began "to look less inhuman." On May 12, she wrote, "Lizzie has gone to Cambridge to stay."

It was a long visit during which Lizzie Cary took care of Felton's two little girls. It was a time when Agassiz dropped in often to see Felton, who was his most intimate Cambridge friend. In the early evening, when the little girls were in bed and Mollie was upstairs with the baby, Lizzie had the habit of sitting down at the piano to play and to sing softly, as Agassiz soon discovered. To a man so full of nervous tension as Agassiz, the atmosphere of peace and friendliness was like a gift from Heaven. He rarely spoke of personal matters — he was surrounded by people who spoke a foreign tongue. But Elizabeth Cary understood French perfectly, although she was shy about speaking it. He could talk to her — or just sit and listen to her music — or he could "hum along all out of tune." "*Leezie*," he called her. And in her ears it sounded like a new and beautiful name.

CHAPTER FIVE
The Rare Comet

IN Europe they believed in giving a boy a number of names, then choosing one by which to call him. Jean Louis Rodolphe Agassiz was born May 28, 1807, in the Swiss village of Môtier on the shores of Lake Morat. His parents used his second name and he was known during his youth as "Louis." When he came to the United States at the age of forty, a completely new life began for him, and he was known simply as "Agassiz." Even Elizabeth Cary in her most intimate letters to him never called him by any other name.[1]

Louis Agassiz's father was a Swiss Protestant minister and his mother the daughter of a doctor. The parsonage, besides having a view of the Bernese Alps, had a vineyard, an orchard and a kitchen garden, all of which were much to the point for a family that struggled to make ends meet. Four children had died in infancy and Louis was the oldest to survive, with the result that his parents attempted to plan his life for him even more than was customary in that time and place where a great deal of parental control was expected. A brother, Auguste, two years younger, was a docile child devoted to Louis, and there were two sisters, Cécile and Olympe.

Louis could not be called docile, and yet he had such winning ways that no one ever thought of him as self-willed — which he certainly was. In the Agassiz home there was great love of learning along with a happy acceptance of a modest way of life. But as to money, Louis was almost pathologically penny wise and pound foolish.

His father was his teacher until Louis was ten years old. By then he could read, write and speak Latin, so no one objected overmuch when he spent part of his time catching fish in the lake and keeping them in a spring-fed pool in the garden. Both Louis and his younger brother could catch lake trout with a line, a net, or in their bare hands. The fish made a welcome addition to the family table, and when Louis insisted on learning not only their common but their Latin names — when he could find anyone who knew them — this was regarded as a harmless obsession. When he taught himself to dissect fish, to mount them, to clean and compare their delicate bone structure, his mother was pleased. Louis might become a doctor like her father and one of her brothers. They were successful men, the doctors Mayor. It would be a better life for Louis than his father had.

But a doctor's education was beyond the means of a Swiss clergyman, his father thought. Louis was sent to Bienne, a nearby town, to study in a boy's boarding school with a view to becoming an apprentice to another of his mother's brothers — François Mayor, connected with a commercial house. It was a four-year course, and by the time Louis Agassiz was fourteen he had chosen his lifework — knowing full well that he must have his father's consent and that this would be hard to come by. "I wish to advance in the sciences," he wrote. And since there would be no getting out of commerce, he proposed an apprenticeship of a year and a half with Uncle François. "Then I should like to pass four years at a university in Germany and finally finish my studies in Paris where I would stay about five years. Then, at the age of twenty-five, I could begin to write."

It was the kind of letter to fill a parent's mind with a mixture of pride and exasperation. If there had been plenty of money it might have produced an indulgent permission along with a few remarks about overconfidence. As it was, the Reverend Mr. Agassiz wrote a sarcastic, "come-down-to-earth" sort of letter; but a compromise was reached. There would be no nonsense about writing books, of course, but the family could manage two years at the College of

Lausanne for Louis instead of the year and a half in a countinghouse. At Lausanne was located the only natural history museum in the canton at that time. Louis was drawn to it as a compass needle seeks the north, and he found there a director who was actually interested in a boy's collection of fish bones! He would become a museum director himself, he decided. And while he was about it, he would be the director of the world's greatest museum — the Jardin des Plantes.

Louis Agassiz never made a secret of his plans. In fact, he was so openly aware of his own potentiality that while some took him at his own appraisal others considered him conceited. His father made fun of him and tried to point out that the boy must prepare himself for some humble walk in life, and the sooner the better. This time, it was Dr. Mathias Mayor who came to the rescue, suggesting medicine as a career for Louis — and helping to arrange a loan. At the age of seventeen, Louis Agassiz went joyfully to medical school in Zürich.

Agassiz was scornful of the Harvard curriculum as he found it, on his arrival in the United States.[2] Harvard was nothing but a glorified high school for immature boys when it could have been a university for men, he thought. In Europe it was up to the student to learn enough to pass his examinations and how he did it was his own affair. No one told the seventeen-year-old Agassiz what courses to take. He had a letter of introduction from the director of the museum at Lausanne to the Professor of Natural History at Zürich; and this man, Professor Schinz, gave Agassiz the key to his private library and instructed him in the use of his specimens. Agassiz began copying books by hand — books he could not afford to buy but must have if he was to be a scientist. He copied them on all sorts of scraps of paper and stitched them together with thread, for even a common notebook would have been too expensive. His brother Auguste had come to Zürich with him, and helped in the copying. But Auguste was a follower, not a leader, and after two years he obediently went into business as Louis was expected to do.

As for Louis — while still at Zürich, he set his heart on Heidelberg and Auguste became a sort of hostage for him. While working hard at his ledgers, Auguste persuaded his father that one son might be allowed to continue his studies since the other was so willing to earn a daily wage. Probably neither of the boys realized how proud their father was of Louis. "Courageous, industrious and discreet, he pursues honorably and vigorously his aim, namely the degree of Dr. of Medicine and surgery," wrote the Reverend Mr. Agassiz to one of his friends — but he rarely if ever wrote to Louis in the same vein.

The elder Agassiz was actually too sanguine about Louis's "aim." Still only nineteen, Louis arrived at Heidelberg in the spring of 1826, and he could not help it if he had the tenacity, one might almost say the one-track mind, essential to genius. He was intelligent enough to succeed in almost any subject except "commerce," and he really wanted to please his father, so he followed Professor Tiedemann's lectures on comparative anatomy — surely good preparation for a future surgeon. He wrote home that he was making "anatomical preparations." But he failed to mention that these were museum specimens he was working with, and that most of his courses were in natural science.

Although it was impossible for Louis to give up his dream of being a museum director, he was not intentionally selfish. Writing to his parents at Christmas, 1826, he said, "My happiness would be perfect were it not for the painful thought which pursues me everywhere — that I live on your privations." He thought he might borrow money of one of his uncles. "I am confident that when I have finished my studies I could easily make enough to repay him," Louis said, and he would always imagine that debts would be easy to pay.

It was at Heidelberg that Agassiz met Alexander Braun. They were both students of natural history, Braun specializing in Botany and Agassiz in Zoology. Agassiz "has appeared like a rare comet on the Heidelberg horizon," Braun wrote to his father, who was an amateur botanist and who was entirely in sympathy with his son's work. "I learn a great deal from Agassiz," Braun said, "for he is more at home in Zoology than I am. He is familiar with almost all the known mammalia, recognizes the birds from far off by their song, and can give a name to every fish in the water." This was the boy who was supposed to be studying to be a doctor. But life was now a little easier for the elder Agassiz. He had taken a new parish at Orbe, once the capital of Burgundy and retaining ruinous evidence of former importance. It was still a good-sized town, able to support a pastor a little more comfortably, and the strain of keeping a boy in school beyond the age of nineteen was not so great.

It was Alexander Braun, whose father was comfortably well off, who proposed that Agassiz go to the University of Munich with him. Of course Agassiz's problem was to persuade his parents to let him make the change and extend his alloted time before he must produce that medical degree and start a practice. By this time his natural gift of persuasion had been well developed. There were those who later marveled at Agassiz's ability to talk hardheaded businessmen into giving him money for science — but they simply did not know about his early training.

Munich was Agassiz's first big city. The University, although claiming ancient lineage, had been transferred to Munich in 1826 and it was in 1827 that Braun and Agassiz arrived, intent on hearing the foremost modernists on "popular astronomy, natural history, botany, mineralogy." These were attractions too utterly impractical, from the elder Agassiz's point of view, to be brought to his attention. It was Auguste who knew and sympathized. To his father, Louis wrote of the "clinical instruction." "In the morning from seven to nine, I am at the hospital," he said.

Agassiz and Braun had a room in Professor Döllinger's house, and Ignaz von Döllinger was a pioneer embryologist. He opened a whole new field to Agassiz — a field the more fascinating because its possibilities were but dimly seen. Agassiz also went often to call on "Monsieur de Martius," who talked "of his journey to Brazil," from which he had returned the previous year "bringing magnificent collections of insects, shells and fish." This encounter was of immediate importance.

Spix, a colleague, had been with Martius in Brazil, but had recently died before the entire collection could be described and findings published. Martius asked Agassiz to do the folio, *Fishes of Brazil.* Agassiz was not to receive any pay, nor did he expect any — but he was overjoyed at the opportunity to write a scientific work, and that was reward enough. His name was to appear on the title page and this seemed to Agassiz the pinnacle of glory. When Martius suggested that the young man's name would look better with a degree after it, Louis Agassiz seems to have been surprised but willing enough.

Applications for examinations at Munich were filled, so Agassiz applied in Latin at the University of Erlangen and received permission to take the written examinations at Munich and go to Erlangen for oral questioning only. However, when his written examination was received and read, Agassiz was granted his degree without "coloquiam." All this he confided to Auguste, but the brothers knew it would be unwise to mention it at home just yet. After all, Louis still had no M.D. His father would never have approved a Ph.D. and Louis had taken the wrong degree!

Agassiz was warmhearted and affectionate by nature and he missed a father's sympathy. He was at this time only twenty-one — legally a man, to be sure, and entitled to be addressed as "Doctor," but boyish at heart. He cast about for someone in whom to confide, to look up to and admire — and fixed upon Cuvier, leading French botanist. Sixty years old at that time (1829), Georges Léopold Chrétien Frédéric Dagobert, Baron de Cuvier, was founder of the science of comparative anatomy. He was Professor of Comparative Anatomy at the Jardin des Plantes, and Agassiz had become completely familiar with his *Lessons in Comparative Anatomy* and his *Animal Kingdom*, in which he arranged every living thing in a higher or lower scale according to its simple or complicated structure.

Arranging and classifying had already become a passion with young Agassiz. Although he had not been paid for his work on *Fishes of Brazil*, he was given a few copies of this very expensive book, and one of these he decided to send to Cuvier with a covering letter.

A draft of this letter remains among the Agassiz papers and reveals his heart:

". . . Allow me to ask some advice from you, whom I revere as a father and whose works have been till now my only guide," Agassiz wrote. "Five years ago I was sent to the medical school at

Zürich. After the first few lectures there, in anatomy and zoology, I could think of nothing but skeletons. In a short time I had learned to dissect and had made for myself a small collection of skulls of animals from different classes. I passed two years in Zürich studying whatever I could find in the Museum and dissecting all the animals I could procure. I even sent to Berlin at this time, for a monkey in spirits of wine, that I might compare the nervous system with that of man. . . . Then I persuaded my father to let me go to Heidelberg, where for a year I followed Tiedemann's courses in human anatomy. I passed almost the whole winter in the anatomical laboratory. The following summer I attended the lectures of Leuckart on Zoology and those of Bronn on fossils. When in Zürich, the longing to travel someday as a naturalist had taken possession of me and at Heidelberg this desire only increased . . ."

Agassiz spoke of the fact that he had come to Munich to study medicine. "Still I could not make up my mind to renounce the natural sciences," he confessed. "I attended some of the pathological lectures but I soon found that I was neglecting them and once more yielding to my inclination . . ." Agassiz referred to his book on Brazilian fishes as evidence that he was capable of hard work. "Ought I to devote myself to the study of medicine?" he asked. "I have no fortune, it is true; but I would gladly sacrifice my life, if by so doing I could serve the cause of science."

Agassiz proceeded to tell what he had done to prepare himself for scientific travels. "I have learned to skin all sorts of animals, even very large ones. . . . I have tested all the various types of alcohol for preserving such animals as should not be skinned and have thought of the means of supplying the lack in countries where such preparations are not to be had. . . . Finally, I have trained as traveling companion a young friend and awakened in him the same love of natural science. He is an excellent hunter and at my instigation has been taking lessons in drawing so that he is now able to sketch from nature such objects as may be desirable. We often pass delightful moments in our imaginary travels through unknown countries. . . ."

This young man was William Schimper, whose brother Karl, Agassiz had met at Heidelberg.

"I have for six months frequented a blacksmith's and carpenter's shop, learning to handle hammer and ax, and I also practice arms, the bayonet and sabre exercise," Agassiz went on. "I am strong and robust, know how to swim and do not fear forced marches. I have, when botanizing and geologizing, walked my twelve or fifteen leagues a day for eight days in succession, carrying on my back a heavy pack loaded with plants or minerals." But here Agassiz knew he was being naïve. He interrupted himself. "Pardon me if I seem puerile . . . my longing is so great that I feel the need of expressing it to someone who will understand me, and your sympathy would make me the happiest of mortals."

Perhaps it was an entirely different letter which Agassiz actually sent to Cuvier. He had dedicated his book on Brazilian fishes — which was written in Latin — to Cuvier, and the reply he received was gracious but contained nothing that could be looked upon as personal advice.

Meanwhile, at the home of one of his professors one evening, Agassiz and Alexander Braun heard that Humboldt was planning a scientific journey to the Ural Mountains. The professor promised to speak a good word for both young men, for it was understood that Humboldt was looking for assistants. On the way home, "late" on a bright moonlight night, Agassiz stopped and "rolled himself in the snow for joy" over the mere possibility of such an adventure. He agreed with Braun that there was little hope that they would be accepted, but this did not diminish his exuberance.

The book on Brazilian fishes was to be a "surprise" for his father — or, in other words, Agassiz had not dared to tell his father about his work. The copy intended for Auguste had been sent at the same time but arrived well in advance of the Reverend Mr. Agassiz's copy, so the surprise fell flat and all the Mayor relatives had seen the book in advance. Nevertheless, it was "a beautiful book," Agassiz's father said. He "had no terms" to express his "pleasure in it."

Sometime during the previous year, Louis had confessed to his father his longing to go on a scientific expedition. His father deplored his son's "mania for rushing full gallop into the future," and of course he was right. "I have often reproved you for this and you would fare better did you pay more attention to my reproof. If it be an incurable malady with you, at all events, do not force your parents to share it," the Reverend Mr. Agassiz wrote. "If it be absolutely essential to your happiness that you should break the ice of two poles in order to find the hairs of a mammoth, or that you should dry your shirt in the sun of the tropics, at least wait until your trunk is packed and your passports are signed before you talk to us about it." And once more, Louis was admonished to get his "physician's and surgeon's diploma."

It was not surprising that Agassiz never mentioned his hope of going with Humboldt — until he learned that all the places were taken. Then, being so naturally open and confiding, he spoke of his disappointment. "Had we known earlier . . . we might have procured" the place "for you," his father wrote! But Agassiz wasted no time either in regretting a lost opportunity or in trying to understand his father. Encouraged by his professors, he embarked upon a book entirely his own — the history of the fresh water fish of Central Europe.

This tremendous project was to give Louis Agassiz his international reputation as a great natural scientist. If he could have foreseen the difficulties lying ahead, even *his* brave, youthful spirit might have faltered. But the dream possessed him, and he could never have given it up.

CHAPTER SIX
Professor Agassiz

IN these days of fine photography, it is hard to visualize the problem of illustrating a scientific work by means of lithography. Agassiz could draw but he would not have time to prepare the hundreds of colored plates necessary to his work and also accomplish the research that must go into the text. He was lucky to be in Munich, however. There was an Academy of Art in Munich which attracted art students just as the University attracted would-be scientists. Joseph Denkel, a German art student, told, years later in careful, stilted English, the story of his meeting with Louis Agassiz.[1]

"It was at the early part of the year 1828" that Denkel and Agassiz "had an interview about the drawings of which he was most pressingly in want and I agreed to make a few drawings of fresh water fishes. I commenced the next day the two colored drawings of two fishes from life with which he was highly pleased."

Agassiz knew just how to handle an artist. After lavishing plenty of praise on the fish portraits, he suggested that he and Denkel "go to a place out of town where the fish were kept" whose picture from life he simply must have. "We walked to the place and I made a colored drawing of a richly colored trout with many fine colored spots," Agassiz "pointing out to me the characteristic features to be well done."

Denkel was now hooked as firmly as any fish. Enthusiasm is a captivating quality in a world where dull indifference is most often to be met with, and Agassiz and Denkel "both became very friendly to each other." Without exactly knowing how it happened, Denkel found himself "almost daily three or four hours with Agassiz . . . painting fresh water fishes," Agassiz "at my side, partly writing his descriptions, partly giving me information about fishes. . . ." Denkel, who had probably never before looked at a fish except on a dinner plate, was becoming an ichthyologist — whether he would or not. He was associated with Agassiz for nearly ten years.

The young man to whom Agassiz referred in his letter to Cuvier, William Schimper, now worked with Agassiz all day. Schimper's brother Karl, the botanist, Alexander Braun and Agassiz hired a workroom which Denkel well remembered. "Botanical specimens littered the couch, the seats and the floor. Books filled the chairs." The walls were white and had "diagrams" drawn on them to which the artists had added "skeletons and caricatures." The students who wandered in and out had such nicknames as "Molluscus" and "Rhubarb."

Work went on at all hours and coffee was served to all comers — provided the pot the students boiled it in was not being used to boil the flesh from bones to "make skeletons." The smell of flesh (sometimes putrid) boiling slowly away from the bones of a small animal or a fish was not exactly appetizing, but the nose of a young natural history student developed peculiar immunities. Coffee with a fishy flavor tasted delicious, taken with congenial friends in an atmosphere of discovery with visions of future fame.

Scientific students met in this room evenings and took turns giving lectures on their own branches of research. Fierce discussion followed, and University professors who sometimes dropped in intervened to settle a point or raise another question. The group came to be called "the little academy," and in his first year Agassiz "was already most prominent among the students at Munich" according to Joseph Denkel.

Now and then Agassiz varied the studious routine of the workroom with swordplay. There was an artist whom Denkel remembered, "a good swordsman" who fought with his left hand "for fear of injuring his right or painting hand." He "perplexed all who fought with the right hand." But Agassiz "made his studio a practice room for fencing till he could use his left hand as well as his right and did not rest till he had defeated this artist."

Beer was wonderfully cheap in Munich, Agassiz remarked with satisfaction. And food of sorts could be cooked over the same fire that was used for preparing specimens — whether in the same dish or not. Still, it was almost unbelievable that the group of friends could live even by pooling their resources. Agassiz received two hundred and fifty dollars a year from his father; Alexander Braun, whose father was Postmaster-General of the Grand Duchy of Baden, received three hundred dollars. Agassiz also received small amounts from the sale of his Brazilian book, with which he bought a microscope and with which he paid Denkel — whenever he could. Agassiz's clothing chest with its compartment for money was never locked, and the German student was free to take what he needed, if there was any money there at all. Years later, and in the United States, Agassiz's appreciation of good food was sometimes commented upon. He had the appetite of a man who has known what it means to be hungry.

In January, 1830, Agassiz made what might have been a New Year's resolution: he determined to get his medical degree at once. Of course, just at that time, the director of the museum at Munich asked him to work on a collection of fossil fish. Immediately, he conceived the idea of a book on fossil fish which was to give him a unique place among European ichthyologists and prepare him for his more spectacular work on glaciers. Nevertheless he wrote his brother "My resolve to study medicine is now confirmed." He would "devote" his whole day to "his own work about fishes" — and read medicine at night.

This actually he did! And for his degree he presented seventy-four theses, the list of which was published. In one of them he proposed the theory that the human female is hardier than the male, sustaining his idea with comparisons in anatomy. Like many of his ideas, this was at the time scoffed at, but modern death-rate statistics bear him out. Agassiz left Munich at the end of 1830, with his degree of Doctor of Medicine, in obedience to his father's and mother's reiterated commands. Louis joined his mother's brother, Dr. Mayor, who took him to observe an operation at the hospital at Lausanne. "Scarcely had the operation commenced and the blood was flowing" when Dr. Agassiz "fainted away."

This was Denkel's account of what happened, and he knew how Agassiz felt. "The study of natural history delighted him but to practice the medical profession and to move about the beds of the sick, or to undertake operations and the cutting off of limbs — he had the greatest dislike of it. He liked to see people happy and not suffering pains."

Agassiz was by no means the only young doctor who ever fainted while observing his first operation. But Dr. Mayor now agreed to help his nephew achieve a career in natural history, and he was the first family ally Louis had among the older generation.

Agassiz's parents at this time were living at Concise — another Swiss village, another parish where vineyard, orchard and kitchen garden were essential. But they were a little more prosperous: a daughter was married, Auguste self-supporting as usual. Louis bided his time and actually did some doctoring in the neighborhood. But he spent most of his days enlarging his already large collections of fish, flora and fauna — everything so unlucky as to cross his path — and working on his fish researches, fossil and otherwise.

At last, in September, 1831, Agassiz set out for Paris. His uncle had given him some money and so had Mr. Christinat, a Swiss clergyman and friend of the senior Agassiz who had known Louis all his life and loved him dearly. Agassiz's intention was to work on specimens at the Jardin des Plantes, which he could not have found elsewhere, and to complete his work on fossil fish. This foundation, with its collections, laboratories, libraries and lecture rooms, was also called the "Museum of Natural History" and it was more like a college than a museum or a garden.

Although the Jardin des Plantes was a sort of shrine, in Agassiz's estimation, the people connected with it were of still more importance to him. At last he was to meet Cuvier. His feelings were mixed, however, for there was now the grave possibility that an interview with Cuvier would put an end to one of Agassiz's cherished dreams. He had been working on fossil sea creatures, of which there were great quantities in the vicinity of Concise, where he had been living, on the Lake of Neuchâtel. The Baron de Cuvier had recently become interested in palaeontology and it was said that he "intended to write a book." What if Cuvier should refuse the use of specimens Agassiz had come to Paris to study? Suppose the "first naturalist in Europe would not tolerate a rival in the twenty-four-year-old Agassiz?"

"I half thought he might, on seeing my work so far advanced, propose to me to finish it jointly with him," Agassiz said. Cuvier received Agassiz "with a certain reserve," looked at Agassiz's material — drawings and texts which the young man had brought with him for their first interview — but "never said a word" about his own "plan of publication." Full of foreboding, Agassiz went back to the modest quarters he had found for himself. A book on fossil fish by Cuvier would "have destroyed all chance for the sale" of one by Agassiz.

A few days went by, and then Agassiz was invited to spend a Saturday evening at the Baron de Cuvier's house. Cuvier "sent his secretary to bring a certain portfolio of drawings." They were records from the fossil collections in the British Museum and elsewhere. And the sixty-three-year-old scientist gave to young Agassiz the greatest gift that one scholar can give another — the gift of his own work. Agassiz "had indeed anticipated him," Cuvier said, and had gone so far that "the field was his." He not only gave Agassiz "all the preliminary notes he had taken" but turned over to him his own fine collection of fossil specimens.

Agassiz worked "at least fifteen hours a day" at Cuvier's house. "Be careful — work kills," Cuvier warned the ardent young man. But Agassiz was strong, proud of his endurance; and he was short of money, which made him desperately pressed for time.

The gift of his notes, the use of his specimens, and his praise of Agassiz's work were a final bequest from Cuvier to a young man who had loved and admired him almost beyond reason. Cuvier died on May 13, 1832 — about a year after he and Agassiz met. It was typical of Agassiz's good luck that he had arrived in Paris in time to become Cuvier's protégé. But Cuvier had promised to help find a publisher for Agassiz, and his death before this could be accomplished was an irreparable loss.

Récherches sur les Poissons fossiles was to come out in installments, a folio at a time, with subscribers committeed in advance to cover the cost of the entire set of volumes. Cuvier stood in well with the French government and would have been able to negotiate a fair number of subscriptions from libraries and universities. Not that Agassiz ever thought of his loss in financial terms — he mourned the loss of a great scientist who had been wonderfully kind and generous to him.

Affairs were now at a low ebb for Louis Agassiz. He wrote his brother, sending a book Auguste had asked for, costing eighteen francs — and confessing that he could not send it sooner "without being left actually penniless." Unfortunately, Auguste passed this letter around among the family and it drew a long lecture from his mother. She ordered Louis to come home at once and "stop living on brilliant dreams." He was to get rid of his artist — still the faithful Denkel, to whom he gave more money than he kept for himself; to sell or throw away his collections, which, in his mother's opinion, were "a capital yielding no interest, requiring care and to be enjoyed only at the cost of endless outlay in glass jars, alcohol and transportation."

Agassiz patiently replied. If it had not been for Denkel's drawings, Cuvier would never have given Agassiz his notes and his blessing. The collections were an important tool of his trade. But it was of no use — Madame Agassiz could never understand, and she told her son to "come home and give lessons."

Agassiz lived at the Hôtel du Jardin, Number 4 rue Copeau, just about two hundred steps from the Jardin des Plantes — and the cheapest possible lodging. Every morning he crossed a paved square to an old building so rickety that one end of it was propped up by timbers. There were stairs on the left, a brown door, and a sign which said in French PULL HARD — referring to the bell rope that hung down beside it. Agassiz was always the first to arrive and the last to leave the museum of the Jardin des Plantes. *Ce cher Agassiz,* "this dear Agassiz," they called him, years later, pointing out to visitors a pine table in the second room from the door where he had worked, describing specimens. There were labels, written in his small, neat handwriting.[2] Everyone had liked him — and everyone noticed when his usually cheerful countenance grew sad. He willingly explained. He was going to have to leave with his work unfinished because of lack of funds.

But once more Agassiz's wonderful luck held . . . except that it would be more accurate to say that his genius for making friends had not deserted him. He had attended all of Cuvier's lectures in the circular lecture hall at the Jardin, where next to him sat another of his heroes in science, Friedrich Heinrich Alexander, Baron von Humboldt. This was the man whose expedition to Russia Agassiz had so hoped to join. Agassiz had sent a copy of his book on Brazilian fishes to Humboldt as well as to Cuvier, had exchanged a few letters with Humboldt and now made himself known to another object of his admiration. There was no straighter path to a great man's heart than this honest admiration.

Baron von Humboldt was sixty-three, born in 1769, the same year as Cuvier, and seemed immensely old and distinguished to the young Agassiz. The Baron's father had been Chamberlain to Frederick the Great, and people were puzzled by what they considered the dual personality of the son who led the life of a diplomat in his apartments at the Hôtel des Princes in Paris but who became the scientist in his rooms in the rue de la Harpe. The Baron was a mineralogist, astronomer, botanist, mapmaker — and the "intimate friend of Goethe and Schiller." He had been a mining engineer, inventing new methods for the smelting of ore, and he experimented in electricity and galvanic processes. Yet it was as a scientific explorer that Humboldt became famous, with an ocean current off the coast of South America to make his name familiar. He made maps, using astronomic observations (then a new idea), and corrected an error of three hundred miles in the position of Mexico on the maps of his time. South America was his special interest, but he visited for six weeks with Jefferson at Monticello during his only visit to the United States. He spoke with regret to young Agassiz of never having seen the Rockies or the Great Lakes; and Agassiz, undaunted by his present penniless condition, privately resolved to see for himself some day the sights Humboldt had missed.

Humboldt called at Agassiz's extremely modest lodgings and looked at his bookshelf. There were books by Humboldt, fortunately, but by no means many, for a complete collection of all his works would have cost two thousand dollars.[3] There were the books Agassiz had copied out with his brother's help — all sewed together from scraps of paper and showing signs of use. And there was a new encyclopedia. "Where did you get this ass's bridge?" exclaimed Humboldt contemptuously. And Agassiz had to explain that he had not bought a work aimed at giving a smattering of information but that a publisher had given it to him (perhaps in return for an article he had written, hoping for cash).

After looking over Agassiz's quarters, it very naturally occurred to Humboldt to ask the young man to dinner. They went to the Galerie Vitrée, one of the most fashionable restaurants in Paris, close to the Palais Royal. Agassiz had never expected to go there, although he had looked through its windows many a time. He and Humboldt talked for three hours. "How he examined me," Agassiz said. "And how much I learned in that short time. How to work, what to do and what to avoid. How to live, how to distribute my time, what method of study to pursue." [4]

Agassiz listened but he also talked. He told of an agreement he had made for the publication of Fresh Water Fish of Central Europe with a publisher named Cotta of Stuttgart. Cotta had promised Agassiz a thousand louis d'or, or about five thousand dollars, with approximately one half due on publication of the first volume and the remainder as the work continued. Each folio, or volume, was to contain twelve colored plates, and six pages of letterpress describing the plates. Agassiz paid his own artists for the original drawings, but Cotta was to pay the lithographers; and, as they were artists with a trade and not art students, their cost ran high. Material for one or more folios was in Cotta's hands and Agassiz felt that money was due him, but for a long time now he had heard nothing from his publisher. Humboldt promised to write in Agassiz's behalf.

Agassiz was sitting in the courtyard in front of his shabby hotel when "a servant of Baron Humboldt's," in the Baron's livery, handed him a letter saying there was no reply required. The letter was dated March 27, 1832.

I am very uneasy, my dearest M. Agassiz, at being still without any letter from Cotta [the Baron began]. Has he been prevented from writing by business or illness perhaps? Yesterday I wrote him earnestly again concerning your affair (an undertaking of such moment for science) and urged upon him the issuing of the fossil and fresh water fishes in alternate numbers. In the meantime, I fear that the protracted delay may weigh heavily on you and your friends. A man so laborious, so gifted, and so deserving of affection as you are should not be left in a position where lack of serenity disturbs his power of work. You will then surely pardon my friendly good will toward you, my dear M. Agassiz, if I entreat you to make use of the accompanying small credit. You would do more for me, I am sure. Consider it an advance which need not be paid for years, and which I will gladly increase. . . . It would pain me deeply should the urgency of my request, made in the closest confidence — in short, a transaction between two friends of unequal age — be disagreeable to you. I should wish to be pleasantly remembered by a man of your character.

The enclosure was a credit of a thousand francs. To Agassiz, who with Denkel had been living on about fifty dollars a month, this sum of about two hundred and fifty dollars was not only reprieve — it was riches.

Work on the collections in Paris took four or five months longer, but Agassiz allowed himself a brief vacation. Alexander Braun had come to Paris to study and the three friends, Agassiz, Braun and Denkel, went to the coast of Normandy on a walking tour. For the first time in his life, Agassiz saw the ocean, and that "radiant" look his friends so often mentioned never left his face. What an immense number of fish there must be in all that water! "At last I have looked upon the sea and all its riches," Agassiz wrote. "I had almost despaired of ever seeing it."

The problem of a paid occupation for Agassiz remained unsolved but his brother Auguste had a suggestion to offer. The little city of Neuchâtel,[5] on Lake Neuchâtel in Switzerland, had a sort of junior college all its own. There was also a municipal Museum of Natural History with partially empty shelves and without a curator. A wealthy citizen, Monsieur Coulon, was an amateur of the sciences who might be prevailed upon to donate money for a professorship in the college, which had no chair of Natural History, and for a curator's salary. It all sounded ideal to Louis Agassiz, especially in view of the fact that there were fossils to be found near the lake of Neuchâtel. Auguste spread the word among the family, and for once Madame Agassiz approved of something her son Louis wanted to do. As it turned out, Monsieur Coulon was either less generous or less wealthy than Auguste supposed. An effort to collect public funds to create a chair of Natural History failed, and Monsieur Coulon managed to get only a small grant, to which private individuals contributed, so that Agassiz was offered about four hundred dollars a year for three years, to give a few lectures and to look after the museum.

It seems never to have occurred to Agassiz to turn down the Neuchâtel offer. How could he refuse to go there when such fine fossils awaited him! Humboldt was disappointed, however. He wanted to see Agassiz established in a large German university, and when, very shortly, Agassiz refused an offer from Heidelberg, Humboldt begged him at least to tell everyone about the honor. And Agassiz must get on with his books for his "classification of fossils" followed the "succession of geological strata," and he must publish lest his "discovery be stolen." Humboldt was beginning to see that his young friend lacked worldly wisdom.

But perhaps Agassiz was happier in little Neuchâtel than he would have been at Heidelberg. He had only a hundred students. His lectures were given in the city hall, and his collections were stored in the Orphan's Home because they would have inundated the museum. And now Agassiz's great gift for communicating his enthusiasm began to be discovered. From the students, word spread that the new professor was fascinating, and soon townspeople began attending his lectures. An adult science club was started, and on school holidays children followed Agassiz as though he were a Pied Piper while he showed them a new world of wonders on the shores of their own lake. Of course everyone began bringing him specimens.

Neuchâtel was a beautiful little city, with its esplanade overlooking the lake, and beyond the lake a glorious view of the Alps to make men lift their eyes. Behind the city was a seventeenth-century castle which was not merely an antique ornament but the residence of the royal governor, for Neuchâtel belonged by inheritance to the Prussian crown. And Humboldt, with his connections among the German nobility, wrote letters introducing Agassiz which went not only to the King's appointed governor but to Friedrich Wilhelm III, King of Prussia. A subscription was circulated, and Agassiz's collection of all sorts of specimens, which he had been gathering for years, was bought for the City of Neuchâtel for three thousand dollars. This must have astonished Madame Agassiz, who had so long been the foe of her son's messy fishbones, dried plants and smelly glass jars full of the unspeakable results of dissection. Now she assumed, quite wrongly, that Agassiz's mania for collecting was over.

As soon as Agassiz was certain of his appointment to the professorship at Neuchâtel, he went to Carlsruhe in the Grand Duchy of Baden to the home of his friend Alexander Braun. Alexander had been with Agassiz in Paris and doubtless the two friends arrived together in Carlsruhe, Agassiz to be greeted like a member of the family, as he had been ever since 1826. This was a very different occasion, however: Louis Agassiz had come to claim a bride.

When Agassiz had spent the Christmas holidays with the Brauns in 1826 he met for the first time Alexander's sister Cécile, who was seventeen — and Agassiz not quite twenty. Agassiz had been taken ill with what was said to be typhoid, and the Brauns had cared for him like a son. He and Cécile fell in love. With careful pencil strokes, and high lights in chalk, she drew a profile portrait of an unusually handsome young man with a small mustache and thick wavy hair cut almost "page-boy" length — Louis Agassiz, aged nineteen.[6]

Cécile's home in Carlsruhe was a large one in which a good deal of luxury was taken for granted; where music was studied seriously and where books were plentiful. Cécile and her sisters sang part-songs and played various instruments. Cécile's own talent lay in art, however, and she was given the best drawing teachers. She was an enthusiast of the "Nazarene School," a German group not unlike the English Pre-Raphaelites. They set the mental conception above color and form — and form above color, attempting to return to an early Christian simplicity. Cécile could draw delicately and accurately with pencil or pen, using very little shadow, within which, however, she rendered reflected light which she perceived and expressed with great subtlety. For some artists, the return to early Christian simplicity and purity was a pose. But for Cécile, the style expressed her shy personality, her delicacy of approach.

For her father and her brother, Cécile drew botanical specimens with all the accuracy such work required. A room in the Braun's home was fitted with large work tables and microscopes. There were books of reference and shelves for specimens, and here the Brauns, father and son, worked on botany together — a contrast to the attitude in Agassiz's home, as he could not help remembering.

Cécile's parents were modern. While they still preferred the arranged marriage for their girls, they would permit a "marriage of inclination" provided the young man had some means of support. Cécile and Louis Agassiz had probably been engaged for some time. Emmy, Cécile's older sister, was engaged to Karl Schimper, close friend of their brother Alexander and Agassiz, a student of great promise in the field of botany. But when, after twelve years, Karl failed to find a good position, Emmy's parents married her to a wealthy middle-aged gentleman of their choice. Agassiz did not delay. He had his professorship, and in October, 1833, he brought Cécile, his wife, to her new home in Neuchâtel, Switzerland.

CHAPTER SEVEN
The "Great Master"

AGASSIZ was happy during most of his fifteen years in Neuchâtel. He was happy wherever he found himself, provided he had the means for getting on with his work; but he was never a man to add up the odds against him before plunging into new projects. In January, 1833, Agassiz wrote to Humboldt concerning the death of Cotta, his former publisher. Since their relations had been somewhat strained, he expressed no regret but said that he had decided not to wait to deal with Cotta's successor. He was going to publish his own book on fossil fish. There were "two good lithographers and two printing establishments" already in Neuchâtel and Agassiz had sent for an engraver to work "either on copper or stone."

Production would begin in May and he was writing a prospectus, Agassiz told Humboldt. There would be twenty plates and ten pages of text in each of twelve numbers or folios, with the price per folio a "louis d'or." Agassiz figured that 70 advance subscriptions would pay for printing 150 copies of the first volume. He was perfectly confident that he could continue original research, hire artists and direct their efforts, write the text, publish, advertise and sell his book. But the author-publisher would like from Humboldt a list of possible subscribers to approach, along with the name of a house in Germany or Leipsic which would "distribute copies and collect the money" on commission. And he needed "for dissection" a certain eel-like fish of the upper Amazon and a similar one from the Nile. With that disarming boyish enthusiasm of his, Agassiz apologized at the end of his letter for troubling the Baron about so many things.

Humboldt did his best. He got "the Prince Royal" as a subscriber, "whose name seemed to me important for you," he said; and the Department of Mines would take "three or four copies," he thought. But he said that he was "the least apt of all men in collecting subscriptions," a confession which showed the real depth of his affection for Agassiz. Presumably these "subscriptions" were for the whole set of twelve volumes, or a matter of about sixty dollars — not a large sum in proportion to the spending habits of princes but sufficiently hard to come by from the scholars who would be most interested in Agassiz's work. Humboldt corrected Agassiz's draft of a letter of thanks to the King of Prussia for contributions to the purchase of the Agassiz collections and instructed the young professor in addressing royalty. Here was a young man who was going to need to know how to approach a throne — or other sources of largess.

Agassiz's three thousand dollars received for his collections went into his publishing project. He and his bride, Cécile, lived in "a small apartment" in Neuchâtel — the phrase making it seem like a small attractive home in the modern sense. It was in fact the least expensive furnished lodging they could find, and from a woman's point of view it was distinctly dreary.

But during the first years of her married life, Cécile was not unhappy. Every day and all day she worked on drawings for her husband's books — his fossil fish and his fresh water fish researches being carried on together. Her work was finer than Denkel's, her husband's scientific friends said, and Cécile was pleased with the praise. Long years later, after the original drawings were sold to the British Museum, it was noted that those with the initials C.A. (Cécile Agassiz) were the best.[1]

The "colossal monograph" on the fossil fish, when it was finally completed, contained twelve hundred and ninety "splendid plates." The first volume "made a great sensation among geologists and zoologists" and was "the work of a great master." So said Jules Marcou, a young French geologist associated with Agassiz.

It was in February, 1834, that Agassiz received a letter from Charles Lyell, eminent British scientist, which not only contained good news but marked the beginning of a long friendship. Agassiz had won the Wollaston Prize, Lyell announced, awarded by the Geological Society of London — a sum of thirty guineas, for his work on fossil fish. Agassiz replied with frankness. . . . "In the presence of a savant, I need not be ashamed of my penury, since I have spent the little I had wholly in scientific researches. I do not therefore hesitate to confess to you that at no time could your gift have given me greater pleasure. Generous friends have helped me to bring out the first number of my *Fossil Fishes;* the plates of the second are finished, but I was greatly embarrassed to know how to print a sufficient number of copies before the returns from the first should be paid in. . . . " He was sure that his one hundred and fifty dollars, more or less, would finance his second folio, prevent him from falling behind in successive numbers — and pay for a trip to England.

Agassiz managed to make his first visit to England early in 1835. He could already speak a little English, as his friend Alexander Braun remarked back in Heidelberg days. He was received with enthusiasm and given workrooms at the headquarters of the London Geological Society at Somerset House. Scientists were eager to meet him, for he was a mystery — young, only twenty-eight, unknown till now and suddenly a "great master." With his capacity for drama, his strong French accent and his completely uninhibited ways, Agassiz was soon the talk of London scientists, as he would always be in whatever circle he shone upon. Stories began to circulate about his eccentricities.

There was the matter of the "bundle," for example. Agassiz was invited to the College of Surgeons, where they were going to dissect a crocodile. He very much enjoyed looking on, and when the dissection was finished, they gave him "a part" of the crocodile — something embryonic, doubtless, for in his second folio of *Fossil Fishes* he had taken up embryology. It was something he was delighted to have, in any case, and he promptly tied it up in his handkerchief and set out for luncheon with "an eminent scientist who was waiting" for him. "The gentleman looked dubiously at the package" — a bulging, possibly bloodstained object, and "suggested that his servant carry it." Agassiz said, Oh no, it wasn't heavy. Well then, could they take a coach? Agassiz said he was fond of walking.

He and his British scientist acquaintance were proceeding along the London street when Agassiz suddenly stopped in his tracks. "You are ashamed to walk with me, because I have a bundle!" he exclaimed.

" 'I was ashamed to walk with you and now I am ashamed of myself,' " the "eminent scientist" is supposed to have said. Whether the story is apochryphal or not, a student of Agassiz's heard it many years later in London. They said it indicated Agassiz's "simplicity." [2]

The Londoners put "a wealth of fossils" at Agassiz's disposal for study. Always pressed for time and anxious to get home, he nevertheless compared and classified two thousand specimens. He sent for Denkel, who came to England and lived in London "for several years" drawing these specimens for future numbers of *Poissons fossiles*.

Back to Neuchâtel went Agassiz, to teach his classes, to oversee his publishing project — and to study "echinoderms" found near Neuchâtel and in the Jura Mountains. In layman's language, they were fossil starfish, sea urchins and similar fish having a more or less complete shell, and in Agassiz's loving eye they had "a peculiar beauty." He "described 12 species, 8 of which were new — his own discovery.

In July, 1835, Agassiz took Cécile home to her parents in Carlsruhe and left her there while he returned to England to supervise Denkel's work and to continue on to Ireland to study recent fossil discoveries. Everywhere he went, he collected subscribers for his *Fossil Fishes*. He sold his own work much the way Audubon traveled about selling *Birds of America*, and the pattern of his success was similar. Audubon had good success in Great Britain and almost none in France, where being French-speaking and of French descent, he had hoped for the best support. Englishmen of wealth enjoyed building fine libraries, and with many wealthy gentlemen the study of natural history had advanced from the status of a hobby to a serious pursuit. Agassiz also did well in England, but even with Humboldt's help he sold only fifteen subscriptions in France — although French scientists proudly acclaimed him as their own.

In Dublin, English subscribers to the British Association for the Advancement of Science awarded Agassiz a prize of one hundred guineas. As always, the money was more than welcome and he promised himself that he would put it into the publishing of his works. But, of course, under this heading came the support of Denkel in London, and travels to examine specimens found only in places other than Neuchâtel. It was all in the cause of science, all part of the preparation which made Louis Agassiz the greatest ichthyologist of his time. But he was like a small boy with a Christmas gift of money to spend. He wanted so many things and spent his money in imagination so many times that when it was actually gone he had no idea what had become of it. Except of course that half his dreams were unrealized and he could use another gift.

Agassiz returned to Carlsruhe and brought his wife back to their "small apartment" in Neuchâtel early in December, 1835. On December 17, their first child was born — a son named for Cécile's brother, for his father — and for other friends and relatives, as was the custom. He was called Alexander Emmanuel Rodolphe — or perhaps Alexander Rodolphe Albert, as written on his baptismal certificate.[3] After a while, no one could remember which names were the right ones, but they always called him Alex.

"From this moment Mrs. Agassiz, who showed herself an excellent and most careful mother, entirely abandoned pencil and book and devoted herself to her son." So said Agassiz's associate, Jules Marcou, intending this as a tribute to the perfect wife and mother, nobly fulfilling the role for which she had been created. There was no one to tell Cécile that eventually she would have time to draw again, that skill diminished through lack of practice would return, and that books, put aside for a while, would be waiting for her when her children were older. All she could see was that her drawings had contributed to her husband's career; they were her way of keeping in touch with a man whose genius carried him to extremes of preoccupation with a strange world having nothing to do with a wife and children. And now all this was lost. Cécile had been a help. Now she was a hindrance, because children cost money.

On August 8, 1837, a second child was born — a little girl whose name, Ida, they pronounced "Eeda" even after she came to the United States and became a young American. And in 1841 came Pauline, the Agassiz's third child. She was so beautiful that, as she grew up in Cambridge, Massachusetts, far from her birthplace, it was a wonder to behold her; the thick dark hair, the glorious eyes — she seemed to the many young men who admired her to be a creature from another world. She had Agassiz's handsome features and her mother's delicate grace.

Cécile "did not speak French fluently." She "possessed to a high degree the German placidity which borders on complete indifference; she was not impressed by what she saw [at Neuchâtel], and from the first disliked all Agassiz's friends and acquaintances. Accustomed to the beautiful green fields and forests of the vicinity of Carlsruhe, she found herself enclosed by dusty or muddy roads, by high vineyard walls and the inhospitable aspect of the houses. All this, with the rather cold manners of the inhabitants, disposed to copy the formality of the Prussian Court, displeased her so much that she soon greatly disliked the Neuchâtelois, Neuchâtel, and even Switzerland. For her, Carlsruhe was a paradise on earth and her only wish was to return and live there." [4] This is the way that Jules Marcou, years later, passed judgment on a woman he could have known only slightly!

Jules Marcou met Cécile Agassiz not later than 1845, but probably not much earlier. He could not possibly have known how she felt "from the first" about Neuchâtel, although it was reasonable to suppose that she might have been homesick from time to time. The "indifference" noted by Marcou could just as easily have been shyness. As for Cécile's unhappiness, her withdrawal and her tears, this form of melancholia afflicted her daughters years later, and a granddaughter as well. It was associated with pregnancy according to modern interpretation. But Louis Agassiz's reluctantly won medical degree could not have given him the answer in his time. He was also undoubtedly too preoccupied with his fish to be anything but surprised and exasperated by Cécile's unhappy moods.

The picture of Cécile as always cooped up in her narrow apartment at Neuchâtel is not accurate. In the summer of 1836, she and her sister (and presumably the infant Alex) went to the town of Bex, high in the upper valley of the Rhône. It was a delightful outing — although Agassiz had not come to this town entirely for pleasure. The attraction was a huge boulder said by a fellow scientist to have been carried there by a glacier which had long since melted. Agassiz had been skeptical of the idea, but with Charpentier, the scientist, he scouted the valley for more such erratic boulders and found plenty of them. At Bex, Agassiz was swept by an idea which moved through his mind much faster than any ice floe, prehistoric or modern. With mounting excitement, he visualized a whole continent under a sheet of ice — powerful, inexorable, carrying great jagged rocks torn from mountainsides upon its surface, and below grinding rock to pebbles, to sand — almost to dust. It was his friend Karl Schimper who coined a term for such an almost unimaginable world. He called it the "Ice Age."

Now, for the first time, Agassiz met with protest and opposition. Humboldt, who would always love him dearly, begged him to put aside such wild ideas. The boulders he had seen must have been brought by floods, for the Deluge idea, substantiated by the Old Testament, was a theory covering many signs of past erosion. Agassiz's English scientific friends replied to his letters on the subject of an Ice Age with a coldness equal to the ice-floe theory he had propounded. Agassiz was unusually sensitive to criticism but he was also excessively stubborn. The thing to do was to study the glaciers in the Alps, their action upon stone, their carrying of silt and depositing of moraines — and then look for similar signs where ice no longer covered the ground.

In 1838, Agassiz made a short trip to Paris where he encountered a boyhood friend, Arnold Guyot. He was Professor Guyot now, a geologist who became infected with Agassiz's wild idea of an Ice Age and agreed to help with the research to prove the new theory. They divided the Alps between them, as it were, Guyot taking the northern and southern slopes to the plains of central Europe and northern Italy, Agassiz taking the Bernese Oberland, the Valley of Chamonix — and the Matterhorn. He was quite literally covering the high spots. With Édouard Desor, a young assistant recently come upon the scene, the three men were to write a three-volume work on glaciers. Agassiz was to write the first volume, and this, with Desor's assistance, he did, his being the only volume actually completed.

Guyot came to the United States with Agassiz, however. He brought with him his collection of "five thousand specimens of erratic rocks of Switzerland" which went to Princeton when he became Professor of Geology there.

But meanwhile Agassiz began to spend his summers high in the Alps. Again Cécile and the children shared this pleasant change of scene but with little or no companionship with Agassiz. A stone hut on the terminal moraine of the Aar glacier was no place for a woman and three babies.

One side of Agassiz's hut was formed by a huge erratic boulder. The rock was schist, thin layers of which had split apart, and an overhanging upper stratum formed a roof while flat slabs broken from this and other boulders were collected and laid to make a floor and side walls. A blanket was slung across the front and here in the "Hôtel de Neuchâtel" Agassiz and five associates slept and took their meals. Now and then came guests, some skeptical geologist or other, prepared to scoff and remaining to become converted to Agassiz's glacial theory. Although hard work went on all day, there were cheerful, not to say raucous evenings when the plain food cooked in the shelter of another nearby boulder tasted like gourmet fare, and when bottles of wine, kept cool without difficulty in glacial ice, raised spirits already high with Alpine adventure.

Until now, it had been assumed that glacial ice was stationary. There were measurements to be taken which showed a slow, inexorable downward flow. Excursions from the hut on the moraine could be justified by the necessity for determining just how a glacier looked from top to bottom. This required, among other things, the "ascent" of various peaks, including the Jungfrau, "until then reputed unscalable."

Among the skeptics who visited Agassiz on the Aar glacier was Dr. William Buckland, Dean of Westminster and writer on geology. Dr. Buckland, more than twenty years Agassiz's senior, had written a book ascribing certain terraces in Scotland to a prehistoric flood. He hated to give up his flood theory and he returned to England shaken in his beliefs but not converted to the Ice Age idea. Early in the autumn of 1840, Agassiz joined Dr. Buckland in Scotland and together they studied the "famous roads of Glen Roy." And now Dr. Buckland was ready to admit that here were the shores of an ancient glacial lake. When Agassiz read a paper before the Geological Society of London on "Glaciers, and the evidence of their having once existed in Scotland, Ireland and England," Buckland was the only one "among the older scientists that stood by him." It was a stormy meeting, the air thick with refutations and denials when Agassiz finished reading his paper.

Back in Switzerland a month later, Agassiz received word from Buckland. "Lyell has adopted your theory *in toto*." And where Sir Charles Lyell went other British scientists soon followed, with the exception of Charles Darwin. For the time being, he remained as cold to the Ice Age theory as he was to its warm advocate, Louis Agassiz.

Most important of all to Agassiz, however, was Humboldt's capitulation. "I cannot close this letter," wrote Humboldt, "without asking your pardon for some expressions, too sharp perhaps, in my former letters, about your vast geological conceptions. . . . Taught from my youth to believe that the organization of past times was somewhat tropical, I cried 'Heresy' at first. But we should always listen to a voice as friendly as yours." When a man who had been like a father to Agassiz in his student days wrote a letter like this it must have seemed to Agassiz the final accolade.

Agassiz was back on the Aar glacier in the hut made from the boulder the following summer. This time, little Alex was to remember being carried in a basket on the shoulders of a guide, up the glacier to the place where his father was at work. Burkhardt, the artist who had stayed faithfully with Agassiz since student days in Munich, drew a picture of the party which delighted Alex. To be sure, there was no little boy to be seen but you could see the big basket on the guide's back.

By this time, all the previously "unscalable" nearby peaks had been scaled, but Agassiz managed to contrive dramatic and dangerous adventure. Huge holes in the ice called "wells" were a common sight; but no one, as yet, had attempted to go down inside of one. That a "river flowed into the well" he chose to explore made no difference to Agassiz. He had the stream diverted. Then he "fixed a tripod" over the well, had a rope sling made with a board for a seat and had himself let down, "his friend Escher lying flat on the edge" at the top to "listen for any warning cry." It was a good idea to choose a friend for this duty! In any case, the signals went wrong.

Agassiz had himself lowered eighty feet and then he found that the well divided into two compartments. Signaling by pulling at the ropes, he had himself raised a little and lowered into the larger hole. This side also subdivided. So into the smaller of the two new shafts he swung, delighted to find that he could go on, happily counting and measuring blue bands of ice. Suddenly, at a depth of one hundred and twenty feet, he was plunged into ice water. A torrent was running under the glacier and Agassiz's first signal was misundertood — they kept lowering away. That "warning cry" could not be heard, but finally the signals were read properly and Agassiz's precarious seat — like a child's homemade swing — began to rise. But now he saw that "mammoth icicles were all around him, threatening to cut the ropes." Somehow, he "steered around them." Safely on the surface at last, he admitted that he would never have gone into the well had he realized the danger.

A guest on the Aar glacier was a fellow scientist, James D. Forbes. Agassiz told him about the color of the layers of ice, or "glacial bands," and Forbes promptly published material on glaciers, claiming "bands" as his discovery. It so happened that Agassiz had already described glacial bands in 1838 in his *"Observations sur les Glaciers"*

— printed in the Bulletin of the Geological Society of France — so Forbes's claim was of no consequence. Agassiz was too busy, at this wonderfully productive time in his life, to bother with petty larceny.

Études sur les Glaciers (*Studies on the Glaciers*) was eventually published in 1846 with an Atlas of 32 plates. The introduction was in Agassiz's most exuberant style. He painted a world before history in primary colors and with all the dash and daring of a young muralist splashing pictures on a plaster wall:

"The surface of Europe, adorned before by a tropical vegetation and inhabited by troops of large elephants, enormous hippopotami, and gigantic carnivora, was suddenly buried under a vast mantle of ice, covering alike, plains, lakes, seas and plateaus. Upon the life and movement of a powerful creation fell the silence of death. Springs paused, rivers ceased to flow, and the rays of the sun rising upon this frozen shore (if indeed it was reached by them) were met only by the breath of winter from the north and thunders of the crevasses as they opened across the surface of this icy sea."

It was all news in Agassiz's time. There was no generation which had been led by the hand, as children, through a great museum to stare in fascination at the skeletons of mammoths, mounted and rising almost skyward, it seemed, above their heads. The scholarly world had hailed Agassiz's knowledge of fish, both fossil and extant. But the popular imagination was stirred by his glacial studies.

Agassiz had now been at Neuchâtel for thirteen years, and he had made not only himself but the small town famous. Scholars flocked to hear him whenever he addressed a scientific society, tourists came to Neuchâtel just to look at him in the street. All opposition to his glacial theory seemed to have been swept away — even Darwin agreeing with him. One might say that Agassiz was a complete success — but disaster had actually overtaken him.

It all began when he did a good turn to an unknown young man. The cause of disaster was within Agassiz himself: his complete ignorance of the value of money, his utter absorption in science to the neglect of his private life. But for these factors, Édouard Desor would assume the guise of evil incarnate. As it was, Desor was a malicious opportunist who injured Agassiz through the many chinks in Agassiz's armor. But if it had not been Desor, it would have been another — for a genius such as Louis Agassiz was hopelessly vulnerable.

CHAPTER EIGHT
Defeat and Victory

ÉDOUARD DESOR arrived in Neuchâtel in 1837, "with his traveller's stick in his hand, a cap on his head and a gray blouse on his back and very few pennies in his pocket." [1] He was a German student, aged twenty-five at the time, and he was a fugitive, having joined a students' uprising at Heidelberg. He had been studying law; then had fled to France, where he kept himself alive teaching languages. He was delighted to get a job as Agassiz's secretary in return for food, shelter and no pay — unless Agassiz happened to have money. At first he had board and room nearby, but soon he was living at Agassiz's house and eating at Agassiz's table.

The printing establishments in Neuchâtel, which Agassiz had relied on, proved incapable of turning out the kind of work he required and, by the time Desor came on the scene, Agassiz had a master lithographer, draftsmen and workmen of his own, until finally he had assembled two hundred and eighty-five employees and had set up his own press. Desor's duties were to "write letters, keep accounts, oversee what was going on at the lithography and printing press and put Agassiz's notes in order." It was a large assignment, but the young man was smart. He learned fast and kept Agassiz from being troubled by business affairs.

The press just managed to break even while Agassiz's great monograph on fossil fish was being published. Then Agassiz tried to find something else to keep his men busy while he and his assistants worked on his fresh water fish treatise. He set Desor to translating a book of Dr. Buckland's from English into German, and published this as a German textbook, but the project lost money. For the sake of science primarily, but also in the hope of making his press pay its way, Agassiz ordered translations from other scientists without bothering about permission from the authors or publishers. Considering the casual way in which copyright was regarded, and the practical nonexistence of international copyright law, this was an all too common practice. But Desor, with his smattering of law, answered letters of protest in a manner to infuriate rather than to conciliate; and Agassiz, who had scores of friends because of his personal magnetism, now began to have enemies.

Agassiz's attitude toward money was a serious defect but understandable. It was said of him that he "lived like a rich man," but this was not true, for no man ever remained "rich" for long who lived as he did. Agassiz lived like a poor student, stretching his pennies to pay for humble lodgings and short rations, but he never learned the value of any but the smallest sums. A modest prize, a small grant, would always seem limitless to him, and he was penny wise and pound foolish to a startling degree. And if Agassiz was extravagant with moderately large sums, in behalf of science, then Édouard Desor, keeping Agassiz's accounts, was more than generous with Agassiz's money — often in his own behalf. Of course he was lawyer enough to cover his tracks. Had he not a verbal agreement that he was to take whatever he needed?

Desor was an attractive young man with much of the personal charm characteristic of Agassiz. He was "a devoted and cheerful companion" on an expedition. His "graceful irony" gave his friends a sense of superiority — always provided that his sarcasm was directed toward someone other than themselves. He was "indefatigable at work," which certainly commended him to Agassiz who worked like a demon himself and "gave his assistants so much to do that it was impossible to keep up with his eager desire and ardor for scientific publication."

That this engaging youth deliberately planned the ruin of Agassiz's printing establishment in Neuchâtel; that he meant to set himself up as a scientist supplanting Agassiz — such was the opinion of some observers, notably Jules Marcou, who saw the whole series of events almost from beginning to end. That Desor was a delightful person, just as much enamored of science for its own sake as Agassiz and an even better scientist — such was the opinion of others, Theodore Parker for one.[2]

If Desor deliberately wrecked Agassiz's printing establishment, he killed the goose that was laying golden eggs for him — even if they were small ones. In any case, the establishment failed in 1845, and was sold at auction. This was heartbreaking for Agassiz, especially as he had borrowed money from his brother and other relatives in order to finance the business. In agony of soul he resolved to pay back every cent, and he was sure that the means to do this would come to hand. With equally sublime faith, he refused at this time to listen to a word against Desor.

When, at a later date, Desor claimed to be a better scientist, this was something Agassiz could not agree to. The man had taken no scientific courses in any university, he pointed out. Desor knew nothing except what Agassiz taught him. That the pupil should surpass the master was something Agassiz would always find hard to accept, even with pupils of proven ability and integrity.

The year 1845 held not one but two disasters in store for Agassiz. It seems to have come as a shock and a complete surprise to him when his wife showed him a letter from her brother, Alexander, headed Carlsruhe and dated March 16, in which he told his sister that his home was ready to receive her, not for just a visit but permanently. Cécile and her two little girls were leaving at once, and they had arranged to visit Agassiz's mother on their way. Young Alex could keep on with his school and live with his father.

All too often, "love flies out of the window when poverty walks in at the door" — but it was not entirely poverty that drove Cécile away. It was true that she had a German sense of thrift, and that Agassiz's carelessness with money distressed her. More important was the fact that she was quiet, preferring a few friends, or even solitude, to groups of noisy people. She was not much of a talker, and perhaps it was impossible for her to explain to Agassiz that the presence of two of his assistants at family meals distressed her. What little private family life Cécile might have had was gone when not only Desor but Vogt appeared as nonpaying boarders.

Vogt was a Swiss naturalist, quarrelsome by nature. He was tall and "very corpulent for his age" (which was twenty-six) and his nickname was "Le Moutz," which was the name of the Bernese bear, a folk-tale character. He was fond of practical jokes, the butt of most of them being a small, inoffensive assistant of Agassiz's who had a trick of "cleaning fossils with his tongue" and was otherwise somewhat uncouth but a hard worker. Vogt's laughter would have "startled a Quaker meeting into uproarious merriment," Marcou said, but the "reverse of the medal" was Vogt's cruelty. At Cécile's table, he made "jokes of doubtful politeness . . . and made remarks of a satirical and anti-religious nature" which she thought her children ought not to hear. Desor, with subtle cleverness, tempted Vogt into atheistic arguments which Cécile was powerless to refute. She could only lapse into silence or else give these *savants* the satisfaction of seeing her in tears.

Vogt was indispensable to Agassiz during the production of *The History of Central European Fresh Water Fish*. Telling of his five years at Neuchâtel, Vogt said, "We had a scientific factory with community property; only unhappily neither the number of workmen nor the capital engaged was sufficient in proportion to production." "Community of property" might work among young students, none of them married, and all of them scrupulously honest about equal sharing. When a man acquires dependents, community of property becomes a different matter. To the wife of the only married man in this group it seemed rank injustice.

Obviously, Agassiz should have made arrangements for his two assistants to go elsewhere, since his wife disliked them so intensely. But he was away a great deal — in England, in Scotland or Ireland. These men were clever, and doubtless they behaved decently to Cécile in his presence; Agassiz had come to lean on them both, and on Desor in particular, to whom Cécile must have had to go for her household allowance, since he controlled Agassiz's purse. She may have sensed that the books, if any, were not properly kept; but in any case Agassiz was voluble in his friends' defense, and Cécile was never good at stating her case.

It was "the most painful incident" of Agassiz's life, when his wife returned to Carlsruhe. The word "incident" which Marcou used in telling of it, was unfair, as time would show. But Agassiz's optimism promptly came to his aid. A grant from the King of Prussia to make a study of glacial evidences outside of Europe seemed the happy solution for all difficulties. He would go to America, pay all his debts, return triumphant and make a new start. Meanwhile the King's grant seemed limitless, of course. He placed the fifteen thousand francs in a Paris bank, and Desor had the right to draw on it for a trip of his own to the Scandinavian countries in search of glacial evidence. Agassiz mentioned the King's gift in a letter to the Prince of Canino,[3] dated January, 1845. It was said that Cécile knew nothing of her husband's plans till she saw the King of Prussia's grant mentioned in the papers and, if so, they had indeed drifted far apart. But Agassiz visited her in Carlsurhe in 1846 before he left for England and America. Cécile promised to write to her husband.

Agassiz's son Alexander was now (in 1845) ten years old. It was easy to see why his mother had attracted Agassiz — her delicate physique, her shyness being in such contrast to his own strength and gregariousness. But when his only son strongly resembled his mother, it exasperated him. The boy was small of stature and retiring by nature, at least as a child. Alex resembled his father mentally in many ways, however. He developed an early interest in zoology and had a wonderfully delicate touch in dissecting, so that Agassiz took pleasure in teaching him. These lessons were punctuated by outbursts of temper on Agassiz's part which were received with silent resentment on the part of his son.

Alex had high marks in school, which pleased his father. But in school there was a group of boys who considered themselves young patriots, favoring freedom for Neuchâtel from Prussian rule. Alex became a "red" at the age of ten, ardent for Swiss national freedom. And Alex's father was a protégé of Frederick Wilhelm, King of Prussia, to whom Neuchâtel belonged!

The governor of Neuchâtel was a retired Prussian army officer. He saw young Alex Agassiz in the street and later complained to the boy's father that Alex had failed to salute properly. Alex got caned for this. Next day, Alex saluted the officer so obsequiously that his sarcastic intent was obvious; another complaint followed — and another caning for Alex. At the end of the school year, the governor, who had come to address the students, held up Alexander Agassiz as a shocking example of bad behavior. Alex had won prizes for scholarship, as usual, but when it came time for the governor to award them, Alex walked out of the assembly when his name was read. Surely he had a touch of his father's sense of drama.

The climax came when Louis Agassiz was invited to a state dinner given by the governor at his residence in the castle overlooking Neuchâtel. Some boys scaled the castle hill and threw rocks through the windows of the banquet hall. The governor was the Prussian King's representative, and Agassiz had felt honored by this dinner invitation. But everybody knew by now that Agassiz's only son was a "red" and not a "swell" as the boys belonging to the royal faction were called.

Angry, humiliated — and mortally afraid that his son was in jail — Agassiz hurried home. Young Alex was in bed, apparently asleep. Perhaps he had not been involved in the escapade at all, for he was only ten, and lying there in bed he looked childlike and utterly defenseless. Agassiz's anger, though violent, was always of brief duration. He loved his children with all the strength of a naturally passionate nature although he was capable of forgetting them for days on end in his preoccupation with his work. But although no longer angry, Agassiz was still faced with a dilemma. He felt that it was an honor to have a royal patron and to accept money from a king in the name of science. And here was a boy so brilliant that he might advance far beyond his father — but a boy who hated kings.

Alex remained in the school at Neuchâtel after his father left for England and the United States, but in 1847 he was sent to his mother

in Freiburg, Baden. His uncle, Alexander Braun, had become director of the Botanical Garden in Freiburg, and his mother and the girls
lived in rooms near the gate of this walled city. There was a good
school for Alex and an opportunity for him to work with his uncle
in botany.

At home, Cécile taught her children to draw, using *Schubert's
Natural History* with its many colored plates of animals, which they
copied, enlarging their own pictures with mathematical accuracy
and learning by heart the descriptions in the book. Surely there was
no bitterness in Cécile's heart, for she was teaching her children to
enter their father's world.

It was soon evident that Alex had inherited both his mother's and
his father's gifts, for he drew not only accurately but with a certain
verve that gave his copies a touch of originality all his own. Cécile
gave her two daughters music lessons herself, using her guitar, but
for Alex a violin was somehow acquired and there were music lessons for him at the cathedral, to which he trudged through the winter's snow, arriving with fingers blue and stiff with cold.

Alex was soon head of the family. His mother's cough could no
longer be called "the result of a cold." She had tuberculosis, and the
bracing air of Freiburg which was supposed to help her only seemed
to cut through her lungs like a knife. Increasing weakness kept her
in bed more and more often, with her two little girls to take care of
her. Alex went forth to market, entrusted with the family funds,
learning early the value of the coins held tightly in his hand. He
was always a little hungry as he wandered from stall to stall, looking
at the piles of produce and choosing carefully only what he could
afford. . . . In later years, Alexander Agassiz's gourmet dinners
were to be the talk of Newport, Rhode Island.

Since no letters have been published and perhaps none have survived, it might seem that Agassiz — by now much lionized in America — had forgotten his wife and children. That such was not the case
is proved by reports of certain American travelers. Mrs. Bruen, wife
of a wealthy New Yorker, came to Freiburg to see the Agassiz family and with her was her daughter, who had been a school friend of

Julia Ward Howe's. They would report that Mrs. Agassiz was sweet but frail, the children charming, Freiburg quaint. Next came Charlie Perkins, cousin of Elizabeth Cary and sent by Agassiz with gifts and messages for his family.[4] Young Alex, silent, reserved but observant, could not fail to note that these Americans were not exactly pinching pennies as they traveled around Europe in private carriages with couriers and servants. There would be people in America, evidently, who though not royal could still become patrons of science. And from these visits may possibly have come the germ of an idea which Alex expressed later. In the United States, all the wealth was not in the hands of kings. Even a scientist might earn enough money to support his own work without accepting largess.

Alexander Agassiz at the Age of Twelve, as drawn by his mother, was a solemn little boy with plump babyish cheeks. His eyes were reflective and his mouth unsmiling but gentle. This portrait and portraits of the two little girls went to their father in the United States as a gift from Cécile. With the pencil portraits was a long letter. Agassiz wrote a long affectionate letter in reply, which was the last one Cécile lived to receive.

Cécile dated her portrait of Alexander *Dec. 1847*. On Easter, 1848, she was too ill to go to her brother's house in the country, outside the city walls, but she sent the children. They walked, of course, trudging two miles along the road; twelve-year-old Alex, Ida to be eleven in August, and Pauline, just barely seven.

No sooner had they reached their uncle's house than they "heard the sound of gunfire" and "they were sent back home" — alone.

There was a revolution going on. A young lawyer by the name of Hecker, elected to the Chamber of Deputies of Baden, having failed to establish a Republican "convention," had put himself at the head of a band of men to invade Baden from the south. As the three children hurried down the road, they heard shouts of "Hecker is coming!" There were wounded men on stretchers, squads of soldiers marching, and great confusion everywhere. When they reached the gates of Freiburg, they found them barricaded. The girls began to cry, but Alex talked the "insurgents" into letting them come in. They ran to their mother's house near the gate, bolted their door, closed and bolted the wooden shutters on the windows. Now it was dark in the room, and the little girls lighted a candle and sat by their mother's bed.

Alex watched the street through a crack in the blind. Hecker never arrived — in fact, he was defeated soon after this and escaped to the United States. Government troops drove the insurgents from the city gate, but not before "several cannon balls landed in the attic" of the house where Cécile Agassiz and her children were sheltered. A bullet came through the crack in the wooden shutter, so close to Alex that he felt the heat of it against his cheek.

Cécile Agassiz died during the summer of 1848. The children went to their uncle Alexander Braun, for a while; then the girls were sent to Switzerland to live with their father's mother. Letters traveled slowly by coach and by sailing ship, and Louis Agassiz was on his expedition to the Great Lakes at the time of his wife's death. He did not hear of his loss till autumn, and then he began to make plans to bring his children to America — but negotiations took time. Alex went to school for a year more in Baden and when vacations came he walked from Baden to Neuchâtel or Lausanne — wherever his father's relatives and his sisters were to be found. When night came on, he slept in haystacks along the way, and, as he used to tell the story afterwards, "almost anybody would give such a tiny traveler a piece of bread or a bit of cheese."

When Alex learned, in the spring of 1849, that he was to go to his father, he took his violin, threw it on the floor and jumped on it, smashing it to bits! It was a wild act of vandalism for so controlled a boy, and a boy who had been so mature and responsible for so long. He never studied music again, nor played any instrument, although he went to concerts and one of his sisters caught him absent-mindedly whistling the score of a complicated piece of music he had heard but once. In explanation, the matter of his cold fingers and the damp cathedral of Freiburg was brought up — but not by Alex, who explained nothing. Could the lessons and the violin itself have been in some way a royal gift? Was there a patron involved? No answer to the riddle was ever given.

Alex was going to live with a father whose lucky star seemed once more in the ascendant. In spite of the failure of his printing establishment, Agassiz had left Neuchâtel literally in a blaze of glory, for his students and associates had held a torchlight procession in his honor. In England he had of course talked with his good friend Sir Charles Lyell, who had just returned from a lucrative lecturing tour in the United States and suggested that Agassiz would be just the man for Lowell lectures. With Lyell's help, Agassiz soon had all his arrangements made with John Amory Lowell.

In Boston, Agassiz's first lecture was given at Tremont Temple — just a few blocks beyond the Masonic Temple — that scene in Elizabeth Cary's girlhood of the trial of the pirates. But Agassiz proved even more exciting to Bostonians; there were five thousand in his first-night audience and he repeated the lecture to a full house next day. This meant extra revenue for Agassiz — and in every respect he did better than the pirates!

In 1847 in New York, the College of Physicians and Surgeons paid Agassiz fourteen hundred dollars for lectures and gave him a purse of two hundred and fifty silver dollars and a steamer ticket to Charleston, South Carolina, where he was due to lecture at the Medical College.

Agassiz accepted far more lecture engagements than he had the strength to carry out, and he fell ill more than once. But he was paying back his debts in Europe and preparing a new home for his children. . . . Except of course that Édouard Desor was still handling his accounts!

CHAPTER NINE

Louis Agassiz and Édouard Desor

THE suburb of Boston where I live is built on an island one kilometer and a half long . . ." wrote Louis Agassiz during the summer of 1847. His "island" was "composed entirely of glacial, muddy, deposit, containing scratched pebbles mixed with large boulders or rocks." [1] Native residents might have had difficulty in identifying this island suburb, but Agassiz was describing East Boston.

Very shortly, Agassiz's small wooden house on the mud flat was filled with every sort of crawling or swimming thing, alive or dead. It reeked of fish in various stages of preservation and at the nearby fish market, where Agassiz bought many of his specimens, the fishmonger asked if the genial Frenchman ran a restaurant.

The house was also full of a strange collection of human beings. Many were political refugees, some of them scientists or calling themselves so, and almost all of them spoke languages other than English. They had one thing in common however. Their pockets were empty and they had heard that Agassiz was making large sums of money. Agassiz gave money to anyone who said he needed it and then, when his own purse was somehow mysteriously empty, he might borrow back small sums of his own cash, promising to repay when the next lecture fees came in. By May, 1847, Édouard Desor had arrived in East Boston to expedite the spending.

Agassiz was also the victim of some of his new American friends who nearly killed him with kindness by arranging more lecture engagements for him than any one human being could fill. There was Asa Gray,[2] leading American botanist and Professor of Botany at Harvard, for example. "Agassiz, in his desire to be of service, would just throw himself into your hands and take whatever you chose to give him," Gray wrote to John Torrey, Professor of chemistry at the College of Physicians and Surgeons in New York. But Gray was not going to allow any such thing. Agassiz's course of lectures would be certain to show a handsome profit, so the college must pay at least eight hundred dollars. "Let me add that Agassiz treats his subjects so that ladies may attend, just as they do here," Gray wrote. "Indeed, he likes to have them if you can find room."

Negotiations were going well until someone who had heard Agassiz in Boston came to New York and began "circulating stories calculated to hurt our plans," as Torrey wrote in great distress. It seemed that Agassiz had "broached sentiments that are considered in Boston as hostile to revealed religion." He had been "attacked in one of the pulpits."

"How can this be! Can it be possible!" exclaimed Torrey. He hoped that there was "no foundation to the report" and that Gray would furnish him with "evidence to contradict it and to assure the subscribers to this course that their religious opinions shall not be assailed." He had been thinking that Lent might be just the time for the lectures because ". . . many Episcopalians who are too conscientious to attend balls and the theater . . . would not scruple to spend their evenings listening to Agassiz."

What Agassiz had done was to propose the theory that all human beings might not literally have been descended from Adam and Eve in the Garden of Eden, but that the different races might have originated in different parts of the world. It seems unlikely that Gray made any excuses for Agassiz. He was much younger than Torrey and one of the first of the American natural scientists to accept Darwin's theory of evolution. But in any case, the New York lectures were postponed. "It turns out better for Agassiz to remain here at this time," Gray wrote. He knew of "a society in Boston that has funds and will put a clear $1000 into his pocket."

Agassiz, the son of a Swiss pastor, knew how to talk to people who felt that their own religion was "revealed" while other religions were not. But attacks from the pulpit were something he had probably never encountered in Switzerland, and they distressed him. There was no one to tell him that Boston clergymen were forever attacking someone and that they often quarreled among themselves. The need for money to pay his debts in Europe and to support his army of dependents who had pursued him to the United States made Agassiz overanxious to placate a public he did not entirely understand. He was able to set Dr. Torrey's fears at rest so that the lecture course in New York was given the following October and November, 1847, and Agassiz received a total of sixteen hundred and fifty dollars. Later a society in Brooklyn which had theological restrictions in their charter demanded and received from Agassiz assurances that he would not upset their pre-conceived ideas, derived from the Book of Genesis. He was undoubtedly sincere when he managed to satisfy these people; but the freedom of thought he had enjoyed in Switzerland was lost to him, and his mind was growing less hospitable to new ideas.

Agassiz had rarely been ill. He was so proud of his physical strength that he told how "he could carry one man on his back and at the same time one under each arm; and he could lift an iron anvil which the smiths were unable to raise." But he was taken ill in Boston — the result, he said, of being "brought into such a state of excitement" because of his lectures and because of the wealth of "every species of animal" he collected from the market and from "excursions on the beaches in the vicinity" of East Boston. He felt he must "examine" everything, and it never occured to him to let so much as a starfish get away. He still planned to return to Europe; and when would he ever again have such opportunities both to earn money and to study?

Agassiz was "radiant with the prospect of sailing with Captain Charles Henry Davis" who invited him to go dredging aboard the Coast Survey steamer *Bibb* off Nantucket. He would be able to "barrel up thousands of fish." In July he set out for the White Mountains with John Amory Lowell, Professor Felton and others, including

Desor. Lowell paid the expenses while Desor withdrew "expenses" from Agassiz's account, feeling sure Agassiz would never notice. They hired a buckboard and a man to drive; but every few miles they ordered the horses stopped while all the men jumped out to examine some glacial scratch over which Agassiz exclaimed with as much excitement as though he had found diamonds. The rocks and polished ledges of the White Mountain district were jewels of glacial evidence, as a matter of fact. The name "Agassiz Basin" is still given to a large, deep, green pool with potholes, on the Moosilauke River near Woodstock, New Hampshire, and Agassiz's subsequent lectures with mention of all the wonders he had seen contributed greatly to the romantic attraction of the mountains. Near Bethlehem is "Mt. Agassiz," now a tourist attraction.

But Professor Felton grew tired of climbing around on rocks. He sat in the buckboard and read from a Greek text he had brought along while his friends went rambling off. Observing the specimens, from insects to chunks of granite, which the other men brought back and which now loaded the floor of the wagon, the driver broke a long silence to ask Professor Felton who his friends were. "Oh, they are Naturalists," Felton answered absently. The driver said he had thought so all along. And Felton realized that the man thought the word was "naturals" — a name for natural-born idiots.

In June, 1847, Abbott Lawrence gave fifty thousand dollars to endow the Lawrence Scientific School of Harvard University. A few weeks after the announcement of the gift, Lawrence wrote to Agassiz offering him a professorship. Agassiz was still under obligation to Frederick Wilhelm IV of Prussia, so he wrote asking to be released. There was no answer, and in September the Harvard Corporation formally offered Agassiz the chair of zoology and geology, at a salary of fifteen hundred dollars a year including fees, and with a three-year tenure. Agassiz accepted and sent for his friend Jules Marcou to assist in geology.

Compared to the four hundred dollars a year Professor Agassiz had received in Neuchâtel, this was a princely salary. Compared to the lecture fees he could command, it was something less than generous, but he was assured that fees from students could be depended upon, that his duties would be light, and that he could have the long midwinter vacation and the summer vacations for private lecturing and research. Then there was the honor of being a Harvard professor — which was, of course, beyond price.

Agassiz's classes would not begin until April, 1848. Accordingly, he made an extensive lecture tour, going to New York, Philadelphia, Albany and Charleston with various stopovers along the way. He collected specimens of all sorts and urged everywhere the importance of establishing museums of natural history. He made friends with local naturalists, who promised to send him practically every unfortunate creature they could trap, net or ship to Cambridge alive. Returning to Boston in March, he found a great deal to do with not much time in which to do it. There was the matter of a house. Harvard professors were required to live in Cambridge, and Agassiz hired a house on Oxford Street not far from Harvard Yard. Mr. Lowell, who was attempting to watch over Agassiz's finances, pointed out that the East Boston establishment must be closed. Harvard was persuaded to buy an abandoned bathhouse on the Charles River near Brighton Bridge for a marine laboratory.

Agassiz went out to East Boston to explain matters to Édouard Desor, who had been left there to help with a textbok called *Principles of Zoology* which Agassiz had written with Augustus A. Gould, Boston physician and conchologist, as collaborator. Agassiz was not pleased with what he found on the island of glacial mud. Without permission from his employer, Desor had sent for a cousin from Germany, a gardener, a lithographer and his wife, a librarian, a draftsman, a pressman and two Swiss servants, inviting them all to come to East Boston and live at Agassiz's expense. A protégé of Agassiz's, once a servant but educated by Agassiz, had been dismissed, and Desor's cousin had his place. This proved the last straw. Agassiz not only told Desor to close the East Boston establishment but to reinstate the young scientist at once. It had been a long time since Desor had taken any orders from Agassiz. He now threatened blackmail.[3]

On the morning of the eighth of April, 1848, there was a bit-ter scene between Agassiz and the man he had befriended so long ago. Desor had been a penniless fugitive. He now boasted that he would ruin Agassiz with the American public, discredit him with Harvard — and step into his place. It was plausible, for there was an American prejudice to the effect that foreigners, especially Frenchmen, were immoral. There were the clergymen who had de-nounced Agassiz and would welcome a new avenue of attack. There were the audiences who had so lionized Agassiz during his recent six months or so of lecturing. A popular figure, once shown up in a bad light, would have many hands pulling him down. Agassiz walked the floor and wrestled with his problem all day, but by evening he had reached the only solution.

With no other salutation than "MR. DESOR" he began a letter:

"You have afforded me this morning the measure of what I was hereafter to expect from you, by reminding me of the use it would be in your power to make in this country of the knowledge you have of some acts of levity in my past life.[4] It would be disgraceful, were I to rest under the weight of such a threat. I have taken the whole day to reflect upon what course I ought to adopt under the circum-stances. There can be no further fellowship between us. . . ."

Desor was dismissed at last. Now Agassiz could write to his wife and tell her of his plans; of his appointment as a Harvard Professor; of his intention to visit her and the children as soon as the college term was over. He could give her the one piece of news she wanted most to hear. The man who, in Agassiz's own words, had been "pre-viously the cause" of his "domestic troubles and especially of" his wife's "leaving of her husband's house" had been sent on his way, to trouble them no more.

Agassiz should have known that a man who could threaten blackmail would not be disposed of so easily, but he began his col-lege lectures full of confidence. He was the "first European-trained scientist on any Harvard faculty" — he was in every way something new at Harvard; and he began to enjoy himself in the new situation. He "smashed all traditions of correctness of demeanor and chilly aloofness. The Frenchman's hat, black and broad of brim," always came in for comment and likewise the big cigar which Agassiz smoked not only while striding across Harvard Yard but in his lecture room as well. Following his example, his students also smoked cigars in class.

Agassiz "had a way of leaning over the lecture desk and hurling whole paragraphs of his lecture with great vigor full in the faces of the students in the front row, who were apt to feel that this was a personal appeal and that they must get to their feet and say, 'Quite right, sir, we heartily agree with you.' " Reminiscences of his students are many and colorful, and it seems as though journalizing must have been a habit peculiar to young scientists, since so many first-hand accounts of Agassiz at Harvard have survived.

He was required to teach only one term; before that term was over, he had talked up a plan for a scientific expedition to "Lake Superior, the Mississippi Valley, the Rocky Mountains and the states of Michigan and Wisconsin." Having no real conception of the distances involved and the difficulties of transportation, Agassiz thought that such a trip could be done in a couple of months. Friends disabused him of the idea in its entirety, but enthusiasm for a journey to the Great Lakes was kindled. Members of the party would pay their own way and his. Agassiz wrote to his wife Cécile that he would not come to Europe after all, but that the following summer would surely find him there.

On the fifteenth of July, 1848, Agassiz, with an assistant and eleven Harvard students, "left Boston . . . in the cars for Albany." They were joined there by three scientists, among them Jules Marcou, recently from France. The "narrative of the journey" was being written by James Elliot Cabot — until recently a young man with little beyond scene-painting for the Temple Place Players on his mind.[5]

Packing up his pencils and water colors, J. Elliot said good-by to all his cousins on Temple Place, Elizabeth Cary among them, and set out as though on a camping trip. He soon discovered that he was supposed to work hard, and this he did, turning out a good story of the expedition, as well as some competent sketches of geological formations and general scenery along the way.

There was a geology lesson or a lesson on ichthyology every evening for the whole party. Agassiz would take out "a piece of painted linen on a roller," which was his portable blackboard, and talk about "the region over which we had passed during the day." The young men had been "warm and well powdered with dust" from their train ride, but they found they should have been paying more attention to the freshly cut ground through which the tracks were laid. They had failed to notice that the "exposed rocks were all erratic" and they would become more observant travelers as time went on.

In Buffalo, Cabot recorded for posterity that there were "pigs in the streets the same as in New York City." There was certainly nothing geological about his observation this time, but doubtless the pigs came under the head of zoology.

When the party arrived at Mackinaw it was raining heavily. "On the beach, some Indians were leisurely hauling up their canoes or engaged upon their nets. . . . The Professor was soon in the midst of them." Here was something Agassiz had dreamed of as a boy — a scientific expedition into a wilderness, complete with "aboriginees." He promptly made friends with them in French, English and sign language, and began bargaining for "a white fish and a large pike." He "soon engaged all the inhabitants of this place to supply him with a complete set of all the fishes found here." This decidedly unscientific language of Cabot's described exactly what Agassiz would always want, wherever he went — a "complete set of fishes."

The young Harvard students thought they knew enough to go in when it rains. Those few who were really to become natural scientists now learned to stay out in the rain with Agassiz, "wet and cold . . . soaking in the canoe, enraptured by the variety of the scaly tribe, described and undescribed." Agassiz never insisted that all his students become ichthyologists, however, and young Cabot was encouraged in ornithology, welcome to his opinion that the song of the white-throated sparrow was "something like the opening notes of the European nightingale."

Men of the Hudson's Bay Company's outposts were glad to see Agassiz. A party of geologists making a survey of the "copper region of the south shore of Lake Superior" crossed Agassiz's trail and spirited geological discussions ensued over campfires by the lake. Plenty of hard work was done, but the whole expedition retained its holiday air. Agassiz grew a mustache "such as he had worn in his youth." It was luxuriant — it was *formidable*, his French friends must have said.

The wilderness adventure was over all too soon, the "birch bark canoes" and the "buffalo robes" in which the campers wrapped themselves at night were all part of a past experience, and Agassiz returned to Cambridge with his "four barrels and twelve boxes mostly of a large size" filled with specimens. He went at once to Professor Felton's house, which had been a home to him ever since he arrived in the United States. He was accustomed to run in almost every day when in Cambridge, often staying to supper (or "tea" as they called it), talking out problems and asking advice of both Felton and his wife. This time, when he arrived fresh from the deep woods, he had no time to ask advice. Mary Felton took one look at the new and beautiful mustache and gave a shriek of horror. Meekly, Agassiz departed to get a shave.

There was little time for Agassiz to enjoy the holiday mood in which he returned from his successful field trip, in any case. The news of his wife's death was awaiting him. Cécile had died on the twenty-seventh of August, two days before her thirty-ninth birthday, and they told Agassiz that "a few days before her death" she had received a letter from her husband which gave her "great joy." But he was filled with remorse because he had put off his intended visit to her in order to go to the Great Lakes.

In December, Desor brought suit against Agassiz. He claimed "642 francs . . . for money lent." He wanted one third of the proceeds from *Principles of Zoology* written by Agassiz and Dr. Gould — on the ground that he, Desor, "had written the whole of this work and made many of the drawings." He laid claim to exclusive authorship of fifteen scientific papers written in the United States and to the two works on glaciers plus a monograph on fossils written in Europe. Desor also claimed money from Agassiz because of the "difficult position in which he . . . was placed by parting from" Agassiz. Perhaps the most outrageous of Desor's claims was that Agassiz had "spread calumnies" about him. It was soon proved that Agassiz had not stooped to such a thing. But Desor had been making good his threat of blackmail. He had said nothing about "levities in Europe." Instead, he was using the American scene for a fabrication far more scurrilous, more sordid than any story of youthful indiscretion might have been.

Edward Clarke Cabot, brother of J. Elliot, had known Desor slightly in Europe and had liked him. To Cabot, then, Desor "contrived to make disclosures" about Agassiz "in such a way as to make it seem accidental and almost involuntary." The story Desor told was that Agassiz had had improper relations with a servant girl named Jane, who had been employed first by his lodging-house keeper, a Mrs. Talbot, and later by Agassiz himself in the East Boston establishment.

When Desor brought suit against Agassiz, it was Captain Davis, of the coastal survey, who suggested that three arbitrators be appointed. Agassiz had chosen Felton to represent him, Desor chose Edward Clarke Cabot; and these arbitrators chose Mr. John A. Lowell. On hearing Desor's "accidental disclosures," Edward Clarke Cabot went straight to Agassiz and found out for the first time that Desor had been dismissed because of a threat of blackmail. Angry at having been "kept in the dark" by Desor, Cabot no longer cared to represent him, and a new set of arbitrators was agreed upon who immediately called upon Desor for proof of his calumnies, which were by now "the subject of conversation in Cambridge."

Desor's "proof" was a series of insinuations. He said that Agassiz "had given the girl, Jane, rich presents." But he could think of only one — a gold watch — and he "appealed to the referees whether such a gift could be made to a girl in her station except under improper circumstances."

Dr. Gould, Agassiz's personal physician as well as his collaborator, knew all about the watch, and so did Mrs. Talbot, the landlady. They both testified that during Agassiz's illness the previous year, Jane had been given extra work on his account. Agassiz had asked Mrs.

Talbot "how to make remuneration" and she had "advised that he give her some trinket that she would value more than money." Agassiz sent to his cousin, a watchmaker in New York, for "the showiest watch for the least money," and it was "worn openly by Jane and everybody knew the circumstances under which it was given." Landladies are supposed to be suspicious by nature, but Mrs. Talbot was certain that Jane's watch was not the wages of sin.

Desor next cited his cousin Maurice as a witness against Agassiz. But Maurice had departed for parts unknown, and when called upon to affirm by letter a story he had told to Desor, he told an entirely different one — "not being blessed with an accurate memory," as the arbitrators put it. The Reverend Mr. Christinat, the friend of Agassiz's father who had helped Agassiz as a student, was now a political refugee and an inmate of the East Boston house. The referees asked him his opinion of Maurice. The boy was "lazy and gluttonous," said the elderly clergyman. It was already obvious that Maurice was a liar.

Jane was "in the habit of going into Professor Agassiz's room and staying till a late hour," Desor then claimed. She "went to see to the fire," agreed Mr. Christinat — but only when Agassiz was away in Boston. And there must have been at least a faint gleam of malicious amusement in the elderly Swiss clergyman's eyes as he added that Jane "had often been known to go into the chamber of Mr. Desor of an evening. But no unfavorable inference had been drawn."

That was the sum of Desor's "proof." Jane had "a familiar manner toward Agassiz." But she was just as "free and bold toward other men," Desor's housemates testified; Agassiz was "never familiar towards her." Desor seemed not to realize that he had no case, and even while the investigation was going on he called Agassiz "cowardly and mean," saying: "I do not longer hate him. I only despise him." On February 9, 1849, the arbitrators came to a unanimous decision.

They found that Desor's charges of "an improper connection with an Irish girl, a servant in his own family in East Boston" were "totally destitute of foundation." They wished "to declare that nothing has been established in the course of this inquiry of a nature to derrogate from the high personal and professional character of Mr. Agassiz."

Among those to whom Desor had just happened to let fall some of his scurrilous remarks was Captain Davis. "It appears from the award of the arbitrators . . . that in every point in dispute, you have done injustice to Mr. Agassiz and have misled those of your friends who were influenced by your representations," Captain Davis wrote.

Three of Elizabeth Cary's Cabot cousins living on Temple Place had been associated with Agassiz and Desor, and two of them had sided with Desor. But Edward Clarke Cabot had found that Desor "concealed the truth" about his dismissal from Agassiz's services, and Dr. Samuel Cabot had but to read a letter of Desor's to discover out-and-out lies. J. Elliot had come back from the Great Lakes full of admiration for Agassiz, and his brothers now agreed with him. All were particularly impressed because Agassiz only defended himself when he might easily have won a countersuit for defamation of character — not to mention misappropriation of funds and plagiarism.

There is a peculiar kind of loneliness that lies in wait for a person living in a foreign land — committed to the use of a language not his own day after day. Few people realized what the loss of a friend meant to Agassiz, and Desor had been a close friend for about twelve years. In times of loneliness and depression Agassiz always sought out the Felton's home; but during the spring of 1849 it was not Mollie but Elizabeth Cary whom he saw in Mollie Felton's parlor. Mollie was expecting her first child and her sister Lizzie had come to help take care of the two little stepchildren. Lizzie spoke French, using a prim textbook vocabulary which amused Agassiz, and in front of his French friends she was shy about her accent and would speak only English. This touch of diffidence in an otherwise remarkably poised young woman also had its charm.

On March 16, 1849, Louisa Conway Felton was born and, until the whole family left for Nahant in June, Elizabeth Cary lived with her sister. Agassiz had many opportunities of observing her "uniformly calm manner and temperament" as she managed her sister's house and coped with two little girls, aged ten and seven. When the children were finally put to bed, there was still time in the evening for Lizzie to sit down at her sister's piano, play her own accompaniment and sing for Agassiz. Soon there was his "favorite song."

Only Elizabeth Cary knew the real Agassiz, the man of moods with quick and violent anger soon over and with the generous impulse to forgive and forget quickly returning. Did he confide all his troubles to "Leezie"? That can only be a matter of speculation, but that she knew a good deal about the Desor affair was inevitable. Her sister's husband Professor Felton had been Agassiz's representative in the first attempt at arbitration and he was by no means a taciturn man. Then the matter must have been talked over at length on Temple Place while the Cabot cousins were taking sides. Agassiz continued to be a frequent dinner guest at the Cary's, showing that they never lost faith in him. Whatever was or was not put into words, Agassiz could depend on Lizzie's friendship. In Mollie Felton's parlor, listening to the tinkling piano, watching the glowing coals in the iron grate, Agassiz began to hope that Lizzie loved him.

There was one flaw in the otherwise perfect evening hour. Charles Sumner developed a habit of calling on the Feltons at this same time of day. A coolness sprang up between Sumner and Agassiz. (They disagreed about abolition, people might have said, and this of course was true.)

On October 2, 1849, Agassiz wrote to Sumner: "Do you care to learn from myself that I am engaged to be married to Miss Lizzie Cary? I wish you should, and if so, excuse me for not sending you sooner this expression of my particular regard and friendship." It was a somewhat cryptic message and one point was quite understandably left out — the date of the wedding. Agassiz did not as yet have the consent of Lizzie's father to their marriage.

CHAPTER TEN
The Agassizs [1]

WITH the breakup of the East Boston establishment, most of the members of that household came to live with Agassiz on Oxford Street. He had not authorized the journey to America of Sonrel,[2] the Swiss lithographer and his wife, nor of the librarian, the draftsman and the pressman. But they were here, and it never occurred to the large-hearted Agassiz to turn them loose in a foreign land. He tried to find employment for them — and in the meantime he had twenty-two or more guests. The only one of the penniless refugees who was willing to pull his weight was the Reverend Mr. Christinat. He took over the management of Agassiz's household.

"Papa Christinat," as everyone called him, spoke only about half a dozen words of English. Every day, he walked from Cambridge to Faneuil Hall Market in Boston with a basket on his arm. He started at daybreak, because at that time he could go through the toll booth at the Cambridge end of the long bridge over the Charles before the toll collector got there. If the man at the other end of the bridge assumed that a fee had been paid, Papa Christinat did not consider it his duty to enlighten him.

At the market, also, Papa Christinat had his own system for saving money for Agassiz. He would ask the price of a cut of meat, cry out that such a price was robbery and put the meat in his basket, paying what he considered fair. Then he would proceed to stalls selling other produce and repeat the process. At dinner, he would ask Agassiz to guess the cost of the ragout of lamb and then joyfully announce the small sum he had paid. Agassiz would praise the old man — and sigh. All the market men knew Louis Agassiz, the Frenchman who bought fish, and it did not take them long to discover who Papa Christinat was and to send Agassiz a bill for the difference in price of all the bargains.

It rejoiced Pape Christinat's thrifty soul when edible duplicate specimens arrived for Agassiz. It was wonderful what could be done with spare turtles, and on one occasion Agassiz, his guests, and his student assistants all ate "a female caribou from Maine which arrived frozen, entire." With his few words of English, Papa Christinat made a wonderful French cook out of Ellen, Agassiz's Irish servant. He planted a kitchen garden in the back yard of Agassiz's house, for how could he teach Ellen to cook properly without tarragon and scallions and a pinch of sage? There was a hutch for hares — why pay the butcher even a quarter of what he asked, when such delicious meat could be so easily raised?

Constant encroachment on the space for a kitchen garden was opposed by Papa Christinat, in French and in German. But Agassiz's students nevertheless built a tank for "a small alligator" in one corner of the yard and against the fence was "a cage for eagles, a tame bear and a family of opossums." Stories about Agassiz's Oxford Street house began to go the rounds in Cambridge and to gather embellishments, like folk tales. Agassiz gave an open-house supper party every Saturday night, and they said that one night his bear got loose, helped himself to a barrel of beer in the cellar, and then — into the midst of visiting scientists, students, Harvard professors and regular pensioners — here came the drunken bear. He climbed onto the supper table to sample Irish Ellen's French cooking, while the invited guests scattered in haste.[3]

Smaller specimens were forever getting away. Miss Caroline Cary, Lizzie's sister, complained that she met two snakes on the stairs. The eagle, although his wings were clipped, escaped, and had to be chased across Cambridge backyards for several blocks. When some of

Agassiz's students finally cornered it, the eagle gave a good account of itself with talons and beak.

But Louis Agassiz now had a home for his son to come to, even if it were a slightly strange one. After a passage of forty-five days by sailing vessel, Alexander reached New York during the summer of 1849. He was thirteen years old and trying very hard to appear a man. His father was at the wharf to meet him and it was a pity Alex could not have seen the letter his father wrote. ". . . Now I am happy," Agassiz said. "It is the exact truth and has nothing to do with paternal pride, when I tell you that he [Alex] is a charming boy."

When Alex arrived in Cambridge he was taken to a party at the Feltons'. He spoke not a word of English, but he took refuge in the correct German schoolboy manners his Uncle Alexander Braun had taught him, plus an added touch of formality from his matriarchal Swiss grandmother. He hoped no one would know how scared he was. And then, across the parlor, he saw Miss Elizabeth Cary. "From the time that I first saw her . . . ," he said later, "she belonged to me and I to her."

The entire Cary family had already moved to Nahant for the summer and Elizabeth must have come to Cambridge especially to greet Alex. Agassiz soon brought his boy to the stone house on the promontory overlooking the sea. It must have seemed like a horde of Cary and Perkins relatives whom Alex met that day — the boys his age speaking no French. But they solved their language problem. Like Alex, all the Perkins great-grandsons had been firmly grounded in Latin, so they all spoke Latin together.

Elizabeth Cary and Louis Agassiz went out on the rocks, along the cliff path, and then beyond to the little crescent-shaped beach. For once, Agassiz paid little attention to sea worms or jelly fish. Elizabeth had always loved the sight and sound of breakers. But recalling this day, a few months later, she said that she could not remember if Agassiz told her whether he "thought the sea beautiful or not."

"We strolled on the beach and our thoughts were more of each other than of the ocean," she said.

In America the "marriage of inclination" was the rule and the European "marriage by arrangement" the exception, but Agassiz knew that he must ask Thomas Graves Cary's consent before he could hope to marry Miss Cary. He was not too surprised to receive only a tentative permission to pay his addresses to her, pending investigation by her father. Concerning the Desor affair, Mr. Cary was satisfied with the findings of the referees. But there was the matter of financial difficulties in Europe — the failure of the Neuchâtel publishing business, which in turn had contributed to the failure of a bank in Switzerland directed by a cousin of Agassiz's who had subsequently lost his reason. It was a painful subject to go into, but Agassiz could show that although he had no judgment in financial affairs, he had never been dishonorable.

In his journal, Longfellow was apt to jot down a word or two about his friends' love affairs. He had complained because Felton's engagement to Mollie Cary had been such a poorly kept secret. Now Elizabeth's engagement, lacking final permission, was not announced, and Longfellow could not resist the temptation to ask questions. On a "rainy, cold, bleak, cheerless day" in December, 1849, he met "Madame Cholet, in the mud" on a street crossing, and asked her "if Agassiz is really engaged." Madame Cholet was the wife of one of Agassiz's immigrant scientists and she answered promptly: "*Oui, Monsieur. Il a eu beaucoup de piene à se decider: mais il a bien fait. Il a besoin de quelqu'une pour soigner sa maison.*"

This was about as accurate as most onlookers' statements. It was Elizabeth, not Agassiz, who "had a lot of trouble deciding" — at least at first. But it was true that Agassiz had "done well," and that he "needed someone to look after his house."

Jules Marcou, Agassiz's future biographer, had much to say about Agassiz's courtship of Miss Cary — some of it true, perhaps; some of it certainly false. He said that Papa Christinat had written to Agassiz's mother, now in her eighties, that Agassiz planned to marry a well-bred young American lady with a rich grandfather but with no money of her own, and that Madame Agassiz wrote sternly, forbidding the match and reminding Agassiz that he must marry an

heiress. Perhaps Madame Agassiz wrote such a letter. But when matters were settled, she wrote warmly to Elizabeth Cary, welcoming
her as a daughter.

Marcou said that Papa Christinat did not approve of the coming
marriage and left Agassiz without a word of farewell. This was un-
true. Agassiz was in Charleston giving his annual lectures at the
Charleston College of Surgeons during Harvard's long winter vacation, and Christinat had a chance to go to New Orleans to become
pastor of a French Protestant church. He discussed the matter of his
leaving with Miss Cary and gave her a letter to send to Agassiz. "I
gave to Mr. Christinat your portrait and my own," Elizabeth told
Agassiz. "It was hard for me to part with yours, for it has been a
great pleasure to me, but he was very much delighted with it and it
would have been selfish to keep it when I hope to have the original
so soon."

December, 1849, was a fortunate month for Agassiz. Mr. Cary,
dating his letter December 30, wrote, "By British steamer today,
I have received some information of a very agreeable nature . . .":

> *When you expressed a wish that I should sanction your pro-
> posal of marriage to my daughter, you referred me, for information
> of yourself, to the gentlemen who investigated your relations with
> Mr. Desor, and proposed that I should make such inquiries as I might
> think proper of the character you had sustained in the various places
> where you had resided in Europe.*
>
> *I was so well satisfied with what I learned from the arbitra-
> tors, in confirmation of my own judgment in your favor, that I was
> not disposed, for my own gratification, to inquire further.*
>
> *Still, it seemed best in a matter of such deep importance to
> my child, to omit no precaution, and I wrote accordingly not only
> to our Minister, Mr. Lawrence, whose professions in your favor are
> so well known that he might be supposed to act under the bias of
> friendly prejudice, but also to those who would inquire and report
> with the impartial accuracy of men of the business world.*
>
> *I wrote therefore, among others, to a banker in London,*

who is connected by marriage with the Belgian minister and had therefore means of more extensive inquiry.

The first letter that I received brought me general impressions that everything was as I could desire, but with promise of inquiry.

The next letter came with the intelligence that there were points which required investigation, and recommended to suspend opinion.

I have learned today that inquiries made through three several channels result in entire confirmation of the favorable impressions that I received of your character.

I have therefore the great pleasure in now saying to you that I cordially consent to your union with my daughter; and assuring you that I am, my dear Agassiz, very truly and affectionately yours . . .

Elizabeth Cary now had permission to step out of the small world into which she had been born, with its comfort and security, its narrow circle of friends. Agassiz's departure for Charleston gave her the opportunity of putting in writing how much she loved him — and also how unsure she was of herself.

"You have already seen how ignorant I am of the life that lies before me," Elizabeth confessed. She and Agassiz held "opposite views on some essential points," she said, but she did not mention what these were. Her own home had been a happy one and her ideals for marriage were high. She wrote her "Dearest Agassiz":

"You will see from the day of our marriage (if I know myself, at least, you will) that I am capable of following the course I now choose, and you will find I have not spoken lightly when I told you how earnestly I longed to find complete support from someone, and give up, as far as it is possible to do so, the responsibility of all important decisions. You find it difficult to believe this, because through my engagement, I have often been so unwilling to yield to your judgment; but this is because I cannot feel, until the marriage vow makes me your wife, that I have the right to give up this responsibility.

"Don't consider this a foolish feeling, dear Agassiz — it is so natural, and it will not be long before the day, which I now anticipate with as much eagerness as you feel."

Lizzie, though still anxious about differences of opinion, was sure that Agassiz "had too much tenderness" for her to "urge anything not absolutely important." She was twenty-seven years old, a thoughtful, mature young woman, and she felt sure she had found a way to insure future happiness. "Let us only, so far as we understand it, bring our lives into accordance with God's will, and pray always for his light and blessing on our way."

While many of her friends longed only for independence in married life, Elizabeth looked forward to giving up responsibility. As fate would have it, this was something she could never do. Already, she was in charge of putting her future husband's home in order while he was away. She superintended the efforts of paperers and painters, taking a hand at painting, herself. This refurnishing had a good effect on Agassiz's crowd of hangers-on and, as their rooms were required for doing over, all but one of them found lodgings elsewhere at their own expense. This one exception was Jacques Burkhardt.

Agassiz had met Burkhardt back at Munich in student days and had hired him to help draw fossils. He was the one who had made the sketch of Agassiz's party in the Alps — including the basket containing little Alex. Burkhardt had left Agassiz soon after that, confident that he was ready to become a great artist. He worked diligently, but nobody bought his pictures and he finally joined a somewhat military group of men being organized by the Belgian government to "establish a colony in the district of St. Thomas" in Guatemala.[4] The adventurers were on board ship when the President of the Republic of Guatemala made a strong protest to the Belgian government because of the military character of the would-be colonists. The ship was sent to the United States instead, and the men were disembarked in New York; they were marched to the Belgian consulate, where they were given two months' pay and told they were now on their own. Poor Burkhardt earned a little money painting landscapes on window shades, but comparatively few people cared for this form of art. He saw in the papers that Louis Agassiz was in New York lecturing, and to Agassiz's hotel came the tall, still powerfully strong, but very hungry Burkhardt, his bushy beard beginning to show streaks of gray. Agassiz's generous heart was touched, of course, and Elizabeth was generous too, so that Burkhardt became a fixture in the Agassiz family for the rest of his long life.[5]

Agassiz's secretary, successor to Desor, went on vacation when Miss Cary began cleaning up Agassiz's Oxford Street house, and he made it known that he would not return unless he were paid a higher salary. Elizabeth wrote anxiously to her fiancé. This man was getting six hundred dollars a year, or nearly half of his employer's salary, and Lizzie thought it was already too much, although she hated to say so. But Agassiz was delighted to have someone firm with his employees regarding money and his secretary was told to look elsewhere for more pay. After her marriage, Elizabeth for a long time handled all her husband's correspondence in English, edited his papers and publications when they were in English and took notes on all his lectures.

Caroline Cary heard of her sister's engagement about a month before their father's consent made it official. From this time on, she went more and more often to Cambridge, getting acquainted with the friends of her future brother-in-law. She and Lizzie read French together to improve their vocabulary, because it seemed that wives and daughters of foreign scientists would never learn English. Carrie was somewhat conventional-minded but she did her best to understand these strange people. She spent a day with the Guyots "and greatly enjoyed it, all but the constant embracing. Everybody kissed everybody else every two minutes." And later at the house of this future Princeton professor there was "a party of grown-ups playing children's games, — a thoroughly French evening." Caroline was the dignified member of the family. She was receiving calls from a young man she called "Mr. Curtis" until ten days after her engagement to him, when she went so far as to call him "Charles" but never "Charlie." She would always be a trifle envious of her sister's exciting life — and also a little shocked by the friends she sometimes encountered at her sister's house.

Lizzie, as the time for her marriage drew nearer, had made many adjustments — more, perhaps, than Agassiz would ever realize. "Every day, my desire becomes stronger that our life together should begin," she wrote to her lover on Sunday, March 24, 1850. She was "learning how impossible it" was for her "to be happy without" him. And Agassiz, enthralled though he was by the dredgings from a South Carolina ricefield, found time to tell her that her letters made him "feel happy and confident, too." [6]

There were passages in Lizzie's letters which must have amused Agassiz. She visited a friend in Northampton, Massachusetts, for example, and admired the "mountains," referring to the Mt. Tom and Mt. Holyoke ranges. "To you, I suppose the mountain scenery at Northampton would seem almost tame with your recollection of your own country, but for me, it is sublime and I never went out for a walk without wishing you were with me." Mt. Holyoke, which Lizzie found sublime, had an elevation of 995 feet, while the Jungfrau, scaled by Agassiz only a few years previously, was 13,670. It was one of Agassiz's characteristics, however, that he never laughed at other people's ignorance or at their enthusiasms. When he finally visited the vicinity of Mt. Tom and Mt. Holyoke, the dinosaur tracks by the Connecticut River made him just as happy as though the mountains had been alps, and he engaged to buy rocks showing tracks, from a quarry nearby. Meanwhile, however, he must have looked forward to the day when he would show his "Leezie" some mountains that she would surely also call "sublime." He wrote asking her to set their marriage date.

April was to be the month, and if Agassiz had sometimes feared he might never win the whole heart of his Lizzie, her letters to him drove away all doubt. "I think the happiest day of my life will be when we meet in Mary's little parlor — for the last time as *lovers*," she wrote. "When you first left me, I had much to think of by myself — much that I felt it important to consider fairly, before we should meet again, and these engrossing thoughts left me less time for regret. But now I long only to give and receive the fullest expression of affection, and were it not for the constant hope of reunion, life without you would have been desolate. . . ."

Elizabeth had "already arranged the furniture in our room," she said. She "rested on the sofa in our dressing room and fancied the days when" she should "sit there for the first time by your side, and you would call me in very truth your wife." She "played" Agassiz's "favorite airs on the new piano in our parlor . . ." which her parents had given her. Caring nothing for being the center of any stage, "Oh, I wish so much that it were all over, that the ceremony which I dread more and more were performed and we were on our road to the home where, by God's blessing, we may be so happy." In her final letter before marriage, but before she knew exactly when he would return, "Ah, Agassiz," Elizabeth said, "if it should be possible that in a fortnight from yesterday, we should go to our home together, would it not be happiness too deep for words." [7]

The wedding date was finally set for April 25, 1850; and it was Caroline Cary, in her brief line-a-day diary, who gave the first-hand account of all that happened. Thursday morning was "Lizzie's Wedding Day." Her cousin, Mary Gardiner, and her sister Carrie "sat with her all the morning." Caroline "made a cap" and "Poor Lizzie, looking pale and nervous, tried to calm her nerves by hemming a duster."

A little before five in the afternoon, Agassiz arrived at the Cary's house on Temple Place. He seemed almost as nervous as the bride and Caroline went downstairs and "took a brotherly walk up and down the two parlors till Lizzie was ready. At 5½ we went to the church."

Lizzie "looked lovely, dressed in a green silk, white camel's hair shawl, straw bonnet trimmed with white and feathers on each side." The officiating clergyman was Dr. Ephraim Peabody and King's Chapel must have been filled with late afternoon sunlight, but Caroline made no mention of these things but said only, "After the ceremony, the bride and groom drove directly out of town. I went to walk." That walk was not such an anticlimax as might be supposed, for Mr. Curtis just happened to join her. Caroline would soon be the third Cary bride to walk down the aisle at King's Chapel. She would be the last, for her sisters Sallie and Emma never married.

Marriage customs seem curious, as recorded by Caroline. On April 17, eight days before the wedding, she came home with Mr. Curtis after a "waltzing party" and Mr. Curtis "helped cut up the wedding cake." But it was the day after Lizzie's wedding that the Cary house was "Wedding cake and distraction all morning" as callers came by, although apparently the bride and groom were not there. In the afternoon, Caroline and Sallie made their "first visit to Lizzie," on Oxford Street in Cambridge. They "found her hemming a crash towel, and Agassiz smoking a cigar. Their home looked charming and they as happy as possible."

Wedding calls continued with a vengeance. It seems improbable that Elizabeth Agassiz could have finished hemming her dish towel — whether this time to quiet her nerves or to express domestic contentment. Carrie went over to "help receive" and she "found all the world running in and out of Agassiz's front door." There was the "funny little Polish exile" with the "blue spectacles" whom Carrie had noticed on the omnibus. And Dr. St. Julien Ravenel, of Charleston — not as romantic-looking as his name, Caroline thought. She met Monsieur Ampère, son of the electrical pioneer, and observed that he had "an enormous bushy beard." He had the reputation of having been "Madame Recamier's last lover" but this was not the sort of thing the maidenly Caroline wrote about.

People watching young Mrs. Agassiz receiving her guests with the poise and dignity for which she was afterwards famous probably never dreamed how anxious and unsure she often felt. Her first test of courage was the impending arrival of her husband's two little girls. In a panic, Lizzie sent for her sister Sallie, who was so gay and pretty and had such a way with children. "Eeda" would be thirteen in August and Pauline was nine. It was feared that neither of them had been particularly happy about leaving their grandmother in Switzerland and coming to a strange land where a foreign woman would be their stepmother. With dictionary and grammar at hand Elizabeth had written them in French, telling how much she wanted them. At best, it must have been a foreign-sounding letter. The new Mrs. Agassiz and her sister now waited at home while Alex went to the station to meet the girls and bring them out to Cambridge.

In due course, the horse-drawn omnibus rumbled over the toll bridge and down the long dusty road to Harvard Square. And shortly, along Oxford Street came two little girls who spoke only French or German — all alone! A few minutes later a red-faced and breathless Alex arrived. He had watched his sisters get off the train. They had not recognized him and he thought it would be funny to watch and see what they would do. Their competence in finding the right omnibus and in asking their way (surely not the first travelers to ask the way to Agassiz's house in a foreign language) had upset Alex's plans. His sisters were in no plight from which he could rescue them. They just went off without him. In the excitement of the arrival of all three of the children, strangeness was forgotten, however. The girls liked their new Aunt Sallie. And their brother was already calling their stepmother "Ma."

Elizabeth Cary came of a long line of adventurous people, familiar with Europe, the Indies and the Orient. She herself, however, had traveled no farther than New York, Northampton or Nahant, and at first Agassiz seemed to take it for granted that she would never want to go anywhere. In January, 1851, when he set out for a survey of the Florida reefs, he went alone.

All was well at home, Elizabeth wrote her husband. Ida and Alex had gone "to a large party at Mrs. David Sears," Ida looking "lovely in a white dress" which her stepmother had a dressmaker make for her for the occasion. Pauline and little Mary Felton, who now considered themselves cousins, were "in rapturous anticipation" of a party. "All the children are well," Mrs. Agassiz wrote, as though she were actually their mother — and so it would always be. The idea of Alex, Ida and Pauline being stepchildren completely left her mind and no one ever dreamed of calling them so.

But Elizabeth Agassiz was also still a bride. "It seems to me incredible that you are truly mine; that you have chosen me for your wife," she wrote her husband. "You say you are homesick — so am

I, as much here as you are there, for though this has the name of home, no place is so for me on earth but where you are." But Elizabeth could not possibly have imagined what adventures lay in store for her when she wrote the words, "I think you must not go away again without me if we can do otherwise without doing wrong." Henceforward, they would find it "right" to be together on almost all of Agassiz's scientific expeditions.

CHAPTER ELEVEN
Wife of a Naturalist

ELIZABETH AGASSIZ received an early initiation into the kind of life that lay before her. The story was often repeated, the scene laid in various places, but she herself said that it was in the house "in dusty Oxford street" where she was "watching the sunset" and writing to her sister Sallie.[1]

"By the way, I must tell you something that happened to me to-day — in solemn warning to any woman who thinks of becoming the wife of a naturalist. In a hurry this morning to prepare for church, I ran to my shoe cupboard for my boots and was just going to put my hand on them, when I caught sight of a good-sized snake which was squirming among the shoes.

"I screamed in horror to Agassiz who was still asleep, that there was a serpent in my shoe closet. 'Oh yes,' he said sleepily, 'I brought in several in my handkerchief last night — probably (yawning) they have escaped. I wonder where the others are.'"

When all the snakes were finally rounded up, Agassiz "had the audacity to call upon me to admire their beauty," Lizzie said.

"All the Agassiz family started for the South" on December 14, 1851. It was Elizabeth's first expedition as the wife of a naturalist and their first destination was Charleston, where Agassiz was to deliver

a series of lectures at the Medical College. A most congenial circle
of friends awaited them. There was Dr. Edmund Ravenel, physician,
planter and conchologist, most of his famous collection of shells having been found on Sullivan's Island in Charleston harbor. He owned
The Grove, on the Cooper River, a 3360-acre rice plantation employ-
ing over a hundred slaves. Then there was his nephew, St. Julien
Ravenel. He, too, was a physician but devoted himself mainly to original research in agricultural chemistry. He was the one whose name
struck Caroline Cary as "romantic." And there was Henry William
Ravenel, who had wanted to study medicine but whose father, a retired doctor, gave him a plantation with slaves and set him up as a
rice planter. Henry William Ravenel published a pioneer work on
the fungi of South Carolina. Another Charleston resident was Dr.
John Edwards Holbrook, who collected reptiles and was preparing a
huge illustrated monograph, *North American Herpetology*. It is
doubtful if Agassiz could have found anywhere else in the United
States a more distinguished group of naturalists.

Alex had been to South Carolina with his father the previous winter. He had learned to ride at The Grove, had gone hunting at Hampton, the Rutledge plantation on the Santee.[2] But it was all new to his
sisters, who had little to look back upon except their restricted lives
in a German walled city and their subsequent experience of being
passed from one relative to another in Switzerland. At first the Agassiz girls were painfully shy. But soon they found there were plenty
of partners for them when dancers stood up to face each other down
the long parlors in the candlelight. The steps were not hard to learn
after all, and the music, though different from anything they knew,
was irresistibly gay. Elizabeth Agassiz, with her Temple Place background, fitted into the scene with ease and grace. She was "proud
of her children" and well they knew it, her reassuring presence giving them courage.

Thirteen-year-old Ida drew sketches of the various houses which
she visited — signing them I. AGASSIZ. The girls went down the rivers
in barges rowed by slaves, to visit neighboring plantations. And
after the Christmas holidays, when they went back to Charleston,

there were still more parties at the town houses of their plantation friends. It was fortunate that Elizabeth Agassiz and her Swiss children had a glimpse of this fairy-tale existence, for soon the whole scene would be one of ruin and desolation. The grim side of slavery was something that they never saw.

Mrs. Rutledge of Hampton lent Agassiz her summer cottage on Sullivan's Island to use as a laboratory. Sullivan's Island was a sandy spot of land having the ruins of a Revolutionary fort on it, and cottages of plantation people who went there in the spring to escape the clouds of mosquitoes rising from their flooded rice paddies. A few Charleston townspeople lived there the year around and there was a regular ferry service. About ten years previously, Edgar Allan Poe had made Sullivan's Island the scene of his mystery, "The Gold Bug," and there were pirate tales connected with the place. Its interest for Agassiz lay in the quantities of shells that centuries of storms had washed ashore and the marine life swarming in its offshore currents.

"We have just returned from Sullivan's Island," Lizzie wrote her mother, three days before Christmas. She and the girls had left Agassiz, Alex and assorted assistants on the island and Agassiz was "very busy and happy with some exceedingly thin, scrawny-looking monsters with no bodies and amazingly long legs. He had intended returning to town with me until these emaciated gentlemen were brought in from the beach, and of course, against such attractions, I had nothing to plead. We passed however a charming day with reading, gathering shells,[3] sketching a monster, hunting, according to the different tastes of the company. . . .

"The unprecedented, unexampled cold that we have had during the three or four days of last week," Lizzie went on, "is the topic of all conversation in street, shop, exchange or drawing room — one hears of nothing else, and if half the city had been destroyed by a conflagration, there could not be more amazement than is caused by the slightest possible coating of snow that has remained in the streets for two days. I was sitting in Mrs. Rutledge's chamber the morning after the first storm, and she told me that in the fifty years that she had passed in that house, she had never before seen the leaves of the

Magnolia tree that looks in her window, tipped with snow. . . . One cannot be warm, even in the best, most comfortable houses in the city and I assure you, in my Cambridge house where I thought myself such a victim to the cold, it was not like a Charleston house in a cold spell." Humorously, she suggested that people thought she had brought the cold from the north in her trunk.

"The town is as empty as Boston in August — everybody gone to the plantations for the Christmas festivities, and we expect to leave tomorrow or next day for 'Belmont' where we shall pass a week." Belmont belonged to the Holbrooks.

Elizabeth's next letter was dated January 2, and the new year was 1852. "I wanted to write from a new home and have been waiting till we should enter upon the honors and responsibilities of housekeeping." The girls wanted to stay in Charleston "for the gay season," but to Agassiz's surprise and pleasure Lizzie elected to go out to Sullivan's Island. . . . This was their first evening; she told "how auspiciously our honeymoon begins":

"You must imagine a small parlor with a large fireplace in which the cheeriest wood fire dances and sparkles. I have been out on the beach gathering driftwood this afternoon and whenever we throw on a bit, it breaks into the brightest flame and lights up our little room."

She had shopped at a secondhand store for a few things to make the cottage comfortable. "For furniture, we have a sofa, rocking chair, dining table, writing table, and a number of common chairs, and what I value most, a little oval, three-legged mahogany stand exactly like the one Grandmother used to use, on which she almost always had her work basket and the last new novel . . ."

"We have just had tea, I have cleared away the tea things, drawn the tables near the fire. . . . Agassiz writes at the other side, beginning his winter work." A "honeymoon" this might be, but Lizzie was perfectly reconciled to the fact that she and Agassiz were never to be entirely alone. "Burkhardt is contentedly smoking his pipe in the chimney corner," she said. "The wind moans mournfully outside and threatens storm." Elizabeth would not mind bad weather except that the ferry might not run and she had hired a piano which was to come out from town next day.

There were upstairs rooms in the Rutledge cottage; Agassiz had installed stoves "so that his people can work there and he has everything going on under his own eye while I am not in the least disturbed by his scientific establishment."

When the weather was good, Elizabeth walked the beaches, "searching for shells." "Angel-wings," orange-colored "tree sponge," and even "worm rock" — all were new to her and there was always the chance of bringing in something that would be new even to Agassiz, who would be as excited as a child with a Christmas toy. On stormy days there was always music — for the piano arrived safely — and books and sewing at the little table so like Grandmother Perkins's three-legged stand. Only one flaw marred Lizzie's happiness on her Sullivan's Island "honeymoon." She had begun to feel anxious about her husband's health.

"If only he is well," she said, "I think he will be able to accomplish a great deal this winter." But she put her finger on the real difficulty when she observed that "it seems impossible he should finish all he has marked out for himself in three months." Agassiz's immense optimism concerning what he could accomplish would always be followed by acute disappointment as he discovered again and again that he was only human after all and that neither he nor his corps of student-assistants could really carry out his plans. Work on the island was interrupted by trips to town for lectures at the college three times a week. Almost immediately, it seemed, it was time to go back to Cambridge by way of Washington, D.C., where Agassiz had lecture engagements.

As usual, everything was new and delightful to Mrs. Agassiz, beginning to see the world for the first time. "I walked to the capitol with Agassiz" and became "gloriously patriotic of course, and felt my soul properly stirred at seeing the Father of my Country sitting out on the grass on such a cold afternoon, with a very slight degree of clothing." Long and intimate acquaintance with the Greenough family led Elizabeth to look especially for this huge marble statue of George Washington by Horatio Greenough. She had followed the controversy concerning the Roman drapery, or lack of it, and the miscalculation by which the statue proved too heavy for the capitol rotunda and was set up outside. "Speaking seriously though," Lizzie added, "I liked Greenough's statue much better than I expected to — the drapery is very stiff, as well as the attitude of the figure but the head and face are noble — full of dignity and intelligence."

Agassiz was intensely interested in the Smithsonian Institution, which was still in its infancy. He was particularly anxious that the great land surveys being planned by the government should take along natural scientists and that collections should be made for the Smithsonian. The Agassiz girls had a "nice time with the Henry children," their father Joseph Henry, pioneer physicist, being the first Smithsonian director. But for the most part, Mrs. Agassiz and her girls did their Washington sightseeing alone. It was a trifle difficult, because they never knew what time it was. Elizabeth had lent her watch to Ida and the poor child had lost it. "She was so heartbroken, poor little soul, that I tried to seem as if I had been wishing all my life to judge of time by watching the shadows. . . ." Ida "grows more interesting every day," her stepmother thought. They were reading Sir Walter Scott's poems together evenings, out of a volume given to Ida in Charleston by the Rutledges. Ida had not been able to understand the poems because of the "Scotch phraseology," but when she was given a little help, her quick mind delighted Mrs. Agassiz. "I have never seen any person of her age enter into them with such delight. So quick and just an appreciation of poetry in her own language would be unusual, and when you consider that she knew nothing of English 18 months ago . . . it certainly shows more than common intelligence."

The children had been such a pleasure both to their father and to Elizabeth that it was with real regret that they set out for Charleston without them, the following Christmas vacation. Ida and Pauline were going to stay with the elder Carys on Temple Place, Swiss children learning to become Bostonians. Lizzie meanwhile would advance her own education in the matter of overland travel in the United States.

During the winter of 1852, Elizabeth had noted how often "Agassiz's face was flushed" and how he "spoke of giddiness in the head," but the modern definition of the word "hypertension" had yet to appear in the dictionary and there was no one who knew enough to make any suggestions that would help him. They settled down on Sullivan's Island and at first all went well. It was good to get back to the sea and the sand and the quiet evenings beside the fire. Agassiz began laying out too much work for himself as usual, but he was always happiest where there was a chance of acquiring that lifetime desire of his — a "full set of fishes." They left Sullivan's Island at Christmas time for Belmont, the Holbrook's place, "thinking to be gone only one" week. Eight weeks later, a very thin and weak Louis Agassiz returned with his wife, whose eyes were still haunted by the fear of losing him.

The doctor called it "liver complaint," although Agassiz's illness sounded very like a bad bout of malaria. They gave him "two hundred grains of calomel" and when they told him of it as he began to recover, Agassiz was horrified. "Europeans never give it except in small quantities," Lizzie said, and Agassiz "looked as if he considered himself as good as dead."

"When I look back at his illness, and those terrible hours of fear — a fear that I would not acknowledge in all its extent even to myself, it all seems like a hideous dream." Agassiz had "never had anybody caring" for him at home so that he used to lock himself in his room "admitting nobody" and now for the first time he had a wife with the physical strength, the courage and the skill to watch over him. Much of the credit was due to Elizabeth, although she did not say so, that Agassiz recovered.

Back on Sullivan's Island, Agassiz began "gaining strength every day." In fact, he seemed "better than before he had this terrible fever." His face was no longer flushed and that "giddiness and fullness of the head" had disappeared. He slept well and was "in such spirits at finding himself able to return" to his work that he seemed "to have grown younger." In March, Agassiz had "finished his course for students" and was in process of giving public lectures. Five of Agassiz's lectures were over when Thackeray appeared in Charleston and began lecturing "three times a week, alternately with Agassiz."

"The Charleston people say they are not lecture-going," Lizzie remarked, but on six evenings a week "the lecture hall was crowded." She "thought Agassiz would lose his audience, or part of it, with the coming of this new star, but the Charleston people" were "very constant and they seemed really fond of Agassiz."

Thackeray's lectures were "very entertaining," said Lizzie, who thought nothing of going out six nights a week in behalf of culture. She thought his "manner of delivery" was "monotonous," but excused him by saying, "How can he help being tired of reading the same thing through all the cities of the United States?" For Thackeray's manners she could find no excuse, however. "It seems to me unworthy of a man of his talents, but he says himself, and repeats it whenever he has an opportunity, rather vulgarly, that he has come to America 'for the tin.' " [4]

Thackeray said he never bothered to read Dickens, and Mrs. Agassiz considered this "not very becoming in a fellow author." He was reading *Villette*, however, a "new novel, just out," which "so enchained him that he could not leave it." Lizzie very evidently had never heard of the Brontë sisters, but she had it from Thackeray that the author of *Villette* lived "in great retirement and indeed is kept almost a prisoner by her father who is extremely jealous of her literary reputation and doesn't like it to be spoken of before him. . . ." She went right around to the bookstore in Charleston and bought a copy of *Villette*. It was just the thing to take on the journey that Agassiz planned, although at the time Lizzie did not know how fortunate she would be to have something to read.

Early in April, the Agassizs started out for Mobile, Alabama and New Orleans, their other stopovers being unintentional. They traveled by coach from Charleston, South Carolina to La Grange, Georgia, where a river boat on the Chattahoochie would take them to West Point, Georgia — beginning of the railroad. Mrs. Agassiz was "the only woman stagecoach passenger," and "in the company was an Alabama Representative just coming home from Washington, as drunk as a lord." A friend who was with him kept giving him "opium and brandy alternately to keep off the delirium tremens." The Representative from Alabama "had the southern gallantry toward women which expressed itself in hiccupping apologies" to Lizzie "for not being in a state appropriate for ladies' society." Spring rains had been playing havoc with the roads. "After going some miles, the road became so intolerable that all the men had to get out, excepting the drunken man, who couldn't walk," and Mrs. Agassiz, "who couldn't swim. The stage every now and then stuck in the bog, out of which, by some miracle, the horses succeeded in dragging it" although up to their knees in mud.

"Farther on, the gentlemen got in again and the driver, finding the regular road impracticable, struck into an old road, never used now, through the woods. The jolting and banging was fearful and we ended by upsetting in a quagmire. . . . We all got out as best we could, the men by pushing and the horses by pulling, at last righted and extricated the stage." This was their "last serious adventure," but when they got to the tiny town of West Point, on the Georgia — Alabama line they found that there would be no train. The railroad bridges had been washed away.

They waited at a country inn which was "clean and the country food excellent." It was "good for Agassiz to have an enforced rest," and he "found some new friends" in the fish of the Chattahoochie River. As for Lizzie, she had *Villette* to read.

Arriving safely in Mobile at last, Elizabeth said she "loved the river boat after the fairly perilous railroad," but she made no complaint about anything — for this was travel, and it was what she wanted.

Where Agassiz collected fishes, Lizzie was apt to collect people. In Mobile she met "a Mrs. LeVert, a bright, talkative little woman who asked with great interest after Grandfather [Perkins]; said she had known him at Saratoga and had eaten grapes with him at his cottage." Her grandfather "had been a terrible flirt," she suspected, "for every now and then" she met "some pretty woman who wants to know" how he is, and "seems to have a very tender affection for

him." Elizabeth met a friend of her father's who was "perfectly bitten" with the "delusion" of "table tippings and spirit rappings" and
she was sorry to "speak with disrespect" but she thought the man
was "a solemn goose."

Although the world of human beings would always mean the most
to her, it was on Mobile Bay that Elizabeth had her first glimpse of
Agassiz's world beneath the sea. The magic never faded for her and
later after Florida coasts became familiar she would write, "we
floated for hours in our row-boat over the coral reefs, lying fathoms
below us, and with the help of our water glass, watched the floor of
the transparent sea as we might have watched a vast aquarium. I
first became aware that a life full of physical enjoyment and the
mere joy of living was provided for the tenants of the sea as well as
for those of the forest. Among the purple and green flexible coral
fans, as they stirred gently with the movement of the water, were
swimming bright colored fishes, sometimes singly, sometimes following each other in zig-zags as if they played a game of hide and
seek. . . . Lovely sea-anemones, crimson or pale green, opened
themselves to the waves, or perhaps to the light." It seemed to Elizabeth a pity that she had never known about all this under-water
beauty when she was a child, and she began to think of writing a
book about sea creatures for children.[5]

She had enjoyed every adventure, including the rough roads, yet
to Lizzie it was good news that she was to "go home by sea" from
New Orleans. This coastwise journey was her "first ocean voyage"
and she was proud to be able to say that she was not seasick "except
when a squall struck." The month of May was more than half over
when she and Agassiz returned to Cambridge, and by the end of
June it was time to gather the family together and go to Nahant.

Being at Nahant was almost like sailing the Atlantic in a miracu-
lously steady ship. When fog closed in, there was nothing to be seen
except the sullen rise and fall of the ground swell a few yards from
the cliff. On stormy days, the surf lashed the headland, making the
safety even of the rocky point seem precarious. And on clear days
the Salem and Lynn shores across the wide expanse of blue water

were spread out like a picture with perhaps "a British steamer in sight, smoking away toward Boston." [6] No wonder Colonel Perkins, after many voyages, bought the eastern promontory of Nahant for a summer home and built houses for as many of his children as wanted them. No wonder his granddaughter Elizabeth Agassiz loved the place!

With his retirement, Colonel Perkins became more and more interested in his Brookline gardens and greenhouses. He specialized in foreign plants, and his gardens were said to cost him ten thousand dollars a year — but he could always be sure of prizes at the horticultural shows, especially for his grapes. He gave up Nahant entirely, and turned over the cut-stone house with the wonderful Chinese landscape wallpaper to Mrs. Agassiz's father. Married daughters with families soon filled it.[7] There was Mollie Felton with her two stepdaughters, her own "Lisa" and after 1852 her boy, named for his father and called "Con." She would add one more boy to the list of Cary grandchildren, named Thomas for her father. Elizabeth Agassiz brought not only her husband and three stepchildren but all sorts of foreigners. The little Polish exile with the blue glasses came to Nahant, the Count de Pourtalès was a frequent visitor and he was joined in 1850 by his wife, newly arrived from Germany. She shocked poor Caroline Cary by asking her "how often" her fiancé Charles Curtis kissed her, and insisted on showing Carrie "the pattern of her chemise."

The reactions of Thomas Graves Cary to all this are not a matter of record, but he came up with a good idea. There was plenty of seafront property that went with the stone house, and he found a sturdy little cottage for sale down in the village of Nahant. He bought it and had it hauled up to the headland, where its genteel doorway with side lights faced seaward. Seen from the cliff path, it had an air of faint surprise as though it had just awakened from sleepwalking to find itself far from Main Street. An ell was added and porches, so that from the land side the house looked like a rather shapeless nineteenth-century seaside cottage, with nothing to indicate its earlier village origin. "The Butter Box," they named it, and Mr. Cary gave it to his two daughters, Lizzie and Mollie, share and share alike. They and their husbands and their children occupied it together for years, a tribute to the good temper of all of them. By degrees, the cottage became more the Agassizs' than the Feltons'. Professor Agassiz loved fog better than clear weather and he found Nahant stimulating — because of the jellyfish! Fog depressed Felton and sea air made him sleepy. He had little or no use for jellyfish.

Elizabeth herself described the excitement of catching jellyfish, impossible as it seems that any such thing could be so considered:

"On a warm, still morning at Nahant, in the last week of August, with a breath of Autumn haze in the air that softens the outlines of the opposite shore and makes the horizons a little dim" — that was the time to begin this sport. The proper time to start was "about eleven o'clock, for few of the jellyfish are early risers." The "sea should be white and glassy with a slight swell but no ripple." Three or four people usually "shoved off in the dory" with Agassiz and it was a constant source of surprise and pleasure to him that his wife would want to be one of them. They brought several buckets — a big pail for the "Twinfinger" which was "phosphorescent and of a pale lavendar," and one for the "Aurelia," which was "bluish-white and sometimes over a foot in diameter." There must be separate buckets, too, for the "small fry"; and nets and glass bowls. The proper place for jellyfishing was in the "shallows . . . between the inner and outer rocks of Saunders Ledge."

A rising tide was no longer mere sea water to Elizabeth Agassiz. It was "laden with treasures. . . . A sudden cry from the oarsman at the bow, not of rocks or of breakers ahead, but of 'A new jelly-fish astern' " — this was the hoped-for climax.

"Now what excitement!" Mrs. Agassiz wrote. "Out with the net! We have passed him! He has gone down! No, there he is again! 'Back up a bit.' Here he is floating close by us; now he is within the circle of the net, but he is too delicate to be caught safely in that way, so while one of us moves the net gently about him — another slips the glass bowl under him, lifts it quickly — and we have him. And now we look more closely; yes, decidedly, he is a novelty as well as a beauty" — something "unknown to zoologists, undescribed by any scientific pen. . . . We float about here for some time, hoping to find more of the same kind, but no others make their appearance and we keep on our way to East Point. . . ."

When the buckets were "nearly full" the boatload of enthusiasts turned homeward. Mrs. Agassiz, looking down at the catch, described it and practiced over the scientific names she was intent on learning. "The Idyia glitters and sparkles . . . the golden Melicarta are kept in constant motion by their quick, sudden contractions, and the delicate, transparent Tima floats among them all, not the less beautiful because colorless. There is an unfortunate Idyia, who by some mistake, has got into the wrong bucket with the larger jellyfish where a Zygodactyla has entangled it among its tentacles and is quietly breakfasting upon it."

Night jellyfishing was even more satisfactory. During the full moon, Agassiz and his wife with Alex and a helper or two rowed over the same course. "Pale streamers of the Aurora quivered in the north . . . and cast their faint reflection" on the sea. "Our dirty, torn old net is suddenly a web of gold as we lift it from the water . . . molten metal seems to flow down its sides and collect in a glowing mass in the bottom of the boat. . . . Jellyfish, so sparkling and brilliant in the sunshine, have a still lovelier light of their own at night; they give out a greenish golden light as brilliant as that of the brightest glow-worm. Notwithstanding the beauty of a moonlight row, if you would see the phosphorescence to greatest advantage, you must choose a dark night, when the motion of your boat sets the sea on fire around you. . . ."

On the porches of the little house at Nahant, glass tanks were alive with jellyfish. They were a pretty sight, but the casual caller might be startled, on looking through the glass, to see a somewhat distorted human face with a microscope fitted to one eye. It would be Mr. Sonrel, the lithographer from Neuchâtel, on the other side of the tank; or Mr. Burkhardt, industriously drawing tentacles, the probosis, or a mouth with "fringes" — as the case might be. "Ruffles or fringes," these were words used by Lizzie, as though describing a dress.

The sea anemone was Lizzie's favorite, however. She did not mind "wet feet and a slippery scramble" to see the actiniae in their "grotto" on the East Point rocks at Nahant. It could "only be reached at low tide," and then only by creeping "on hands and knees to its entrance, in order to see through its entire length." But the "whole interior is studded with these animals, and as they are of various hues, pink, brown, orange, purple or pure white, the effect is like that of brightly colored mosaics on the roof and walls. When the sun strikes through from the opposite extremity of this grotto, which is open at both ends," it lights the "living mosaic work, showing the play of the soft fringes wherever animals are open."

It was inevitable that a laboratory must be built for Agassiz at Nahant. And so another wing was added to the little house, and there Louis Agassiz made his sea world alive, not only for his wife but for every visitor who showed the slightest interest. Reactions were varied, of course. Longfellow, who spent many summers at Nahant and who was genuinely fond of Agassiz, could not bear to stay long in the laboratory because it smelled so strong of fish. George Templeton Strong, the New York diarist, went to Nahant one summer — disliked the place, but considered "Agassiz and his wife charming people." He went out on the rocks at low tide with Agassiz and spent two hours being "presented to marine notabilia," sea anemones among them, "beautifully flower-like under water."

Elizabeth Agassiz never claimed to be a natural scientist. When people discovered that she could identify glacial scratches on White Mountain ledges and could tell one jellyfish from another, calling it by name, she always said she just "happened to know" because Agassiz was such a good teacher. But she noticed that the Felton children liked to hear about the sea creatures found at Nahant, and she wrote down some of the things their uncle told them. *Seaside Studies*, she called her collection of chapters in simple, layman's language. At this time, women authors came in for a great deal of criticism — as though they were a freak of nature. Hawthorne forbade his daughter Rose ever to write another story, having caught her in the act of attempting one. And Dr. Samuel Gridley Howe had been deeply mortified when his wife published a volume of poetry — anonymously. Undoubtedly, Lizzie Agassiz first asked her husband's permission, and found that he was pleased with the whole idea. Taking no chances, however, she signed her book "Actinea."

To Elizabeth's surprise, her little book did well. Money, in the Agassiz family, would always be in short supply until Alex fulfilled a certain secret determination. Meanwhile, Elizabeth found that her small earnings from writing supplied many a need — pretty dresses for the girls — a horse-and-wagon trip for herself and Agassiz. Lizzie was an author now, for better or worse. But she would always claim that all she ever did was to put down what her husband or her son told her.

CHAPTER TWELVE

The "Agassiz" Museum

A GASSIZ arrived in Cambridge at a time when Harvard was un-
dergoing one of its periods of turmoil. President Quincy had
recently retired, going to live in Boston, where he said the "un-
earthly quiet" kept him awake at night, after the noise made by
drunken and rowdy students in Harvard Yard. President Edward
Everett was attempting to institute a regime not merely law-abiding
but positively pious. Longfellow, who was certainly no roisterer,
complained of the new rules as childish. Everett wrote "a long letter"
to faculty members, "touching attendance at morning and evening
prayers," Longfellow said. It was going to take time to go and come
from Craigie House on Brattle Street, and Longfellow could not help
being amused when some students "nailed up Everett's gate, so that
he might not get out to morning prayers."

There were worse offenses. Students wore "blue swallow-tailed
coats to chapel," this gala attire being strictly forbidden. They went
to a cockfight in Jerome Napoleon Bonaparte's room on a fast day.
President Everett sent for Longfellow, who "found him alone and
desponding. Some scenes of revelry" had just come to his knowledge
"and quite overwhelm him." [1] Whether on this occasion or some
other, President Everett had to face the discovery that students had
"entertained two females in a college room at midnight." A nice girl
never walked alone across Harvard Yard — she went around it.

Agassiz paid no attention to faculty dismay or student disorder. He simply remarked scathingly that Harvard was no better than a preparatory school in Europe and that the students acted like spoiled children. What the United States needed was a university, and he thought that Harvard could grow up to become exactly that. For all he was so harsh in his criticism, Agassiz loved Harvard, and with that uncanny gift he had for being in the right place at the right time Agassiz's first full year in the United States, 1847, was the year the Lawrence Scientific School was opened. In 1848, with Abbott Lawrence paying his salary in the Scientific School, Agassiz was able to disregard President Everett's ideas. Felton must "hold recitations for at least twelve hours a week" for the three upper classes in Greek. Longfellow was obliged to report "how many hours" he was "occupied in his lecture room each week" and so were all the rest of the Harvard faculty, much to their indignation. But students never *recited* to Agassiz in the grade-school sense of the word. Using his own original method, he gave them a tremendous opportunity to learn to think for themselves and to work out their own problems. He had nothing but scorn for the indolent student and most of the lazy ones quit his courses after a few weeks. The rest became so fascinated that they listened not only to lectures but to monologues which their professor indulged in wherever he went — to the "pudding-stone" quarries at Roxbury or at night during the long walks which Agassiz enjoyed after a day at his worktable.

Nathaniel Southgate Shaler [2] was one of Agassiz's more remarkable students. He was born in Newport, Kentucky, in 1841 and arrived in Cambridge at the age of seventeen, where he was "placed under a tutor" in order to qualify as a Harvard undergraduate. The tutor's first question was not on a particularly intellectual plane. He wanted to know if the lanky, six-foot Kentuckian could box. Shaler had been to "Sherer's School of Arms" and considered himself a swordsman, but he had also "learned boxing," so he agreed to a round. "At the very first tap" his tutor, a Harvard senior, "tipped over, his head going against a window pane, smashing the glass but happily not hurting him." After that, they took up Latin grammar. But Shaler eventually refused to memorize the rules of scanning. He decided to forget about Harvard, but he had "come across Agassiz's essay on classification" which had just been published. It was designed as an introduction to a volume on *Testudinata*.[3] Shaler had always liked turtles. He called on Agassiz.

Shaler reached the wooden shedlike building which was Agassiz's laboratory just too late to meet all of the turtles in person. But Theodore Lyman, another of Agassiz's outstanding students, described what the laboratory was like when the work on *Testudinata* was in progress. "Turtles were everywhere, some in jars, some dried on shelves; then living ones in all directions. Many little terrapins hid under the stairs and soft shell turtles inhabited tubs. The Professor's own house was not free of them and his little garden was at times quite swarming. . . . The excitement culminated when a strong box with bars, containing two huge Mississippi snappers, perhaps the most ferocious for their size and the strongest of reptiles" arrived "by railroad express." They were "getting clear of turtles" and "dropping down among the jellyfish" in 1858, when Nathaniel Southgate Shaler first graced the Cambridge scene. He met Agassiz the following year.

"When I first met Louis Agassiz he was still in the prime of his admirable manhood," Shaler said. "He was then fifty-two years old and he had still the look of a young man. His face was the most genial and engaging that I had ever seen and his manner captivated me altogether." Shaler had been homesick for Kentuckians, "men who had a free swing," he called them, while New Englanders were "cold and superrational" and he was "hungry . . . for human sympathy. Agassiz's welcome went to my heart — I was at once his captive. It has been my good chance to see many men of engaging presence and ways but never have I known his equal."

There was no entrance examination for the Lawrence Scientific School. A candidate approached the professor of his choice, was asked some questions and told to stay or go away, as the professor saw fit. Agassiz was "pleased" that Shaler could "patter a little Latin and Greek" and that he could read both French and German. Nothing at all was said about the rules of Latin scanning. "He did not probe me in my weakest place, mathematics, for the good reason that, badly off as I was in that subject, he was in worse plight."

Agassiz next asked Shaler about his reading, and Shaler mentioned Agassiz's essay on classification, proved that he had read it carefully and that he had also read some of the references cited in it. Shaler also, it might be noted, was a man of "engaging presence and ways." He was as good as accepted — but there was one more preliminary. Agassiz asked Shaler "to bring his mask and foils" for a fencing bout.

Never one to underestimate his own prowess, Shaler was of the opinion that it was Agassiz who "did not fare well" in this test. Shaler had begun to fence when he was five years old, his teacher a French refugee in Cincinnati. He had won various prizes which afforded him no little satisfaction and he found Agassiz "heavy-handed" and lacking in finesse — "not untrained" but "evidently knowing more of the Schlager than of the rapier." It never occurred to Shaler, even in later life, that Agassiz had never had money for fencing lessons, and that all he knew his fellow students in Germany had taught him, or he had taught himself.

Shaler had a "place assigned" to him in Agassiz's laboratory, a room "about thirty feet long and fifteen feet wide" in a "rather small two-storied building looking much like a square dwelling house." The room was "packed" and Shaler was told "to sit down at a little pine table which had a tin pan on it." Said Shaler, "Agassiz brought me a small fish, placing it before me with the rather stern requirement that I should study it but should on no account talk to anyone concerning it, nor read anything relating to fishes until he gave me permission." All this was baffling. What was he to do with the fish?

"Find out what you can without damaging the specimen," Agassiz said. "When I think you have done the work, I will question you." After about an hour, young Shaler thought he had looked at the fish long enough. It smelled of "old alcohol" which he found "loathsome" but later learned to love, as an artist in oils loves the smell of turpentine. Agassiz was "always within call," but paid no attention to his new pupil as another hour went by and finally the whole day, the next day, and then "a week."

Shaler sat staring at his fish and "at first the neglect was distressing." Then he "discerned rather than saw" that the professor was watching him and that "it was a game." So he "set his wits to work" and in "the course of a hundred hours or so" he thought he had "discovered a hundred times as much about the loathsome little fish as had seemed possible at the start." He got interested in the shape of its scales and the way they were arranged and the structure of its mouth — but all he got from Agassiz was "a cheery 'good morning.'"

"At length, on the seventh day, came the question, 'Well?'" Shaler talked for an hour, Agassiz sitting on the edge of the pine table, puffing his cigar. "At the end of the hour's telling, he swung off and away, saying 'That's not right.'" Shaler had an impulse to throw over Lawrence Scientific School the way he had discarded the idea of going to Harvard — for this was as bad as memorizing Latin rules. But his pride was touched. Obviously, the professor was trying him out, so he discarded his first notes "and in another week of ten hours a day labor" he had results that surprised even himself and satisfied Agassiz. Not that Shaler received any praise. His reward was to have "about half a peck of bones" set down in front of him and to be told to see what he could do with them. They were "skeletons of half a dozen fish of different species" and young Shaler began to try to sort them out — a head here, a tail there, like the pieces of a jig-saw puzzle. He got no help "other than an occasional looking over my groping," he said, "with the stereotyped remark" from Agassiz, " 'That's not right.'"

Finally the fishbones were all sorted and Shaler "was set upon alcoholic specimens representing perhaps twenty species of the side-swimmers . . ." And at last he graduated to animals, and discovered "a sense of power." He had "learned the art of comparing objects, which is the basis of the Naturalist's work" and now he was allowed to read and to discuss his work with other students. He "did both, eagerly."

Agassiz never failed to caution his students when they reached this stage in their development. They were to remember that the books they read were not necessarily accurate. He put personal observation and discovery, original research, first — then text. There would be no slavish copying of this or that authority, collected and quoted, to pass for real work on the part of any student.

Lectures were a minor part of Agassiz's method of instruction.

"Though very interesting from their personal quality, the field they covered was curiously limited. In the first term, he gave about twenty-five lectures on zoology and in the second term about twenty-five on geology." And, summing it up, "Agassiz was the worst instructor I have ever known but in diverse ways the best educator," Shaler said. This verdict would have pleased Agassiz, for it made just the point he was trying to explain to the President and Fellows of Harvard College. A university should be for men, not boys. Students should arrive already well instructed so that they could take advantage of an opportunity for education.

"By far the greater part of the instruction I had from my master," Shaler said, was in what seemed to the young man mere conversation. Agassiz often worked with his students for hours, arranging specimens, "routine work which left his mind free. He was a perfect narrator and on any peg of fact could hang a fascinating discourse. Often, when he was working on wet specimens" and Shaler was at work on fossils, Agassiz would come over to Shaler's table ". . . with a fish in each hand, that I might search his pockets for a cigar, cut the tip, put it between his teeth and light it for him. That would remind him of something and he would puff and talk until the cigar was burned out and he would have to be provided with another."

Like almost everyone else, Shaler was struck with Agassiz's ability to get along with all sorts of people. The incident which impressed him most happened in 1866. Agassiz wanted to compare the skeletons of thoroughbred race horses with those of ordinary work horses. Shaler, who knew Kentucky breeders and racing men, had tried in vain to get the bones of a stallion for him. Then early one morning there was a fire, said to have been incendiary, in the stables at the "Beacon Park track, a mile from the college." Shaler went to the fire and listened to the "mob of irate owners and jockeys who would have lynched anyone they thought to blame for the tragic loss of their horses." As he left the group of angry men, he met Agassiz, "almost running, to seize the chance of specimens."

Shaler begged Agassiz "to stay away until the mob had spent its rage." He thought the professor with the foreign accent "would have his head punched," but Agassiz "trotted on" and Shaler turned and went with him, to "protect him." There was no need of Shaler's various fighting skills. Agassiz "went at once to work with those horses that had been hurt but were savable. His intense sympathy with the creatures, his knowledge of remedies to be applied, his immediate appropriation of the situation of which he was at once master, made those rude folk at once his friends. Nobody asked who he was, for the good reason that he was heart and soul one of them. When the task of helping was done, Agassiz skillfully came to the point of his business — the skeletons — and this so dextrously and sympathetically that the men were, it seemed, ready to turn over the living as well as the dead beasts for his service. I have seen a lot of human doing," Shaler said as he looked back on the scene, "but this was in many ways the greatest."

Theodore Lyman also enjoyed the opportunity of studying under the Swiss professor. Lyman had no colorful difficulties to relate concerning his educational career. He was a studious youth who had graduated from Harvard before entering the Lawrence Scientific School. But, like Shaler, his meeting with Agassiz was a turning point in his career and, like Shaler, he distinguished himself in scientific studies. He also tried to put into words Agassiz's magic touch with people. Agassiz had the "Gallic power of pleasing," Lyman said. "No man was ever more set in his aims . . . but he had not the Anglo-Saxon style of riding rough-shod over people who were in his path. He worked his way through the crowd deftly . . . and when he arrived at the wished-for place, it was with a kindly smile on his face and accompanied by the good will of his opponents."

Agassiz's aim, ever since his own student days, had been to be the director of a great natural history museum. His practical parents had scoffed at his boyish idea that he might someday head the Jardin des Plantes in Paris, and Agassiz certainly learned diplomacy while persuading his parents to let him continue his studies. In 1858, his earliest ambition was realized. He was actually offered the directorship of the Jardin des Plantes.

"What an offer Louis Napoleon has made to Agassiz and what an ass he will be if he accepts it," wrote Charles Russell Lowell to Henry L. Higginson. "Twenty thousand dollars a year and a seat in the Senate — but for how long?"

Agassiz was anything but an "ass," but he had a favorable opinion of royal patronage and he lacked the typical American distrust of any and all Bonapartes. And then, to achieve a lifelong ambition was in itself a temptation. Agassiz's mother was still living and to be able to say "I told you so" would have been a small personal triumph.

Agassiz refused the offer, and some of his French friends said that this was because his American wife refused to live in Paris. Those who knew of Elizabeth Agassiz's love of adventure and her ideas of marriage never believed this for a moment. Others said that Agassiz gave up his proposed trip to Europe "because his relatives will try to make him take the position at the Jardin des Plantes." But the trip was only postponed — and he was no longer worried about his family's efforts to dominate him.

Agassiz had not given up his boyhood ambition. He still wanted to be the director of the world's greatest natural history museum, but his ideas of size had expanded almost in proportion to the size of the United States compared to his native Switzerland. The Jardin des Plantes now seemed a trifling affair compared to the museum with its laboratories, lecture rooms and halls for public display of specimens which he planned to build in Cambridge, Massachusetts.

He wrote to Charles P. Curtis, trustee of Harvard, briefly describing the scope of his plan. "I may say in one sentence what our museum in Cambridge may become. It should in the end be as complete a library of the works of God as it is humanly possible to make it, and so arranged that the meaning of the Animal World may be read even by those who do not make the study of Natural History the special object of their attention." [4]

Everyone who would listen heard about Agassiz's dream of a great museum. Even so, he might not have achieved his goal if he had not been thrown with people able to help him. He "is happily married and his social position is as pleasant as we can make it," observed George Ticknor, referring to the group of Boston merchants of whose inner circle Elizabeth was a birthright member. Agassiz's first

American patron, Abbott Lawrence, had died in 1855 leaving a bequest of fifty thousand dollars as a permanent fund to cover his salary. The Scientific School allowed him six hundred dollars for upkeep and purchase of specimens, while his friend and first American sponsor, John Amory Lowell, gave him four hundred dollars a year more.

Francis Calley Gray became Agassiz's next benefactor. Mr. Gray was descended from a pioneer maker of shoes in Lynn, and subsequent forebears "prospered exceedingly in shipping." He was a bachelor in middle life when Agassiz came to Harvard, a lawyer and Fellow of Harvard whose gifts had already pulled the college out of a financial hole. It may well have been Agassiz's influence that led Mr. Gray to visualize Harvard as developing into a university. In any case, it was not difficult to persuade him that a "library of the works of God" would be essential. Together they discussed a name for the future museum. "Physicians would at once claim as belonging to the Medical school any appropriation made for a 'Museum of Comparative Physiology,'" Agassiz warned. Personally, he liked "Museum of Comparative Zoology, Embryology and Paleontology," but admitted that some people might think it a little too long! One thing both men agreed upon — it was to be neither the "Gray" nor the "Agassiz" museum. They felt that the study of natural science transcended the name of any man.

Francis Calley Gray died in 1858, leaving fifty thousand dollars for the establishment of a museum. The money could not be used for buildings or for salaries, Agassiz having impressed Mr. Gray with the importance of having the world's most complete collections. The bequest filled Agassiz with jubilation. Now all he had to do was to find money for brick and mortar and for salaries for more and more assistants. "Each sum [of money] obtained was merely the lever by which additional and usually larger sums were secured," and now Agassiz looked the field over for the American equivalent of the King of Prussia. The King had represented government, so how about the Massachusetts Legislature? He applied for funds and, "contrary to the expectations of his friends and advisors," he got an ap-

propriation of one hundred thousand dollars. There was no use neglecting private sources, of course. A subscription amounted to
seventy-one thousand dollars more.[5]

The name finally decided upon was "Museum of Comparative
Zoology." It was meaningful only to those who followed what might
be called Agassiz's system of cataloguing God's library. He assumed
that his own name would be forgotten while his systems and theories
lived after him, but this was not to be the case. A new generation of
natural scientists, numbers of them Agassiz-trained, tossed aside his
system and many of his theories, while his personality, "joyous, debonair," [6] was not forgotten. No one ever dreamed of calling the red
brick buildings that rose on Oxford Street anything but the "Agassiz
Museum" — or just "The Agassiz." [7]

CHAPTER THIRTEEN
The Agassiz School

"F ATHER says the title to the land is all right," Elizabeth told her husband in 1851, the year after they were married. They were building a new house [1] on the corner of Quincy Street and Broadway, in Cambridge, and the location was ideal. Broadway was just an unpaved road crossing open farmland at that time, and Quincy Street was a private way with houses on one side only, Harvard Yard on the other.

Neighbors were congenial. There were the Feltons, the Henry Jameses at a later date, and the Greenoughs whose move to Cambridge had drawn the Cary girls in their wake. Henry Greenough had realized his dream and had been studying art in Italy along with his brothers, Horatio and Richard. He had now returned to set himself up as an architect and he agreed to draw the plans for the Agassizs. "I am afraid we shall find him very dilatory," Lizzie commented. She had been trying to get him to give her an estimate of costs, "but to no purpose."

Greenough earned his fee, for he had to draw those house plans three times over before "Lizzie was completely satisfied." The house, when it was done, had a peculiarly Cambridge quality of originality and distinction and yet it could not by any means be called beautiful. Set on a high brick foundation, it was a sturdy wooden building of generous proportions. Heavy moldings over the windows and a

Mansard roof seemed to indicate that Mr. Greenough had appropriated everything ugly in European contemporary style, but the
clapboards were in the New England manner. A fence of wooden
rails set in granite posts, a large garden at the side and good trees
helped to soften the effect — the garden being Lizzie's own special
province.

Within, the house showed the results of a woman's careful supervision. A large stone fireplace built to accommodate four-foot logs
made Agassiz's study the gathering place and his friends loved to recall long evenings spent around the fire, listening to talk that seemed
to settle the problems of the universe. Mrs. Agassiz had been cold in
the house on Oxford Street and she did not intend to be cold again.
There was a fireplace in the dining room, one in the parlor, and one
in her little sitting room upstairs. There were doubtless others in bedrooms, most of them burning cannel coal because it was comparatively easy to handle. Two tall chimneys full of flues peered above
the Mansard roof.

In the dining room there was a sunny window full of house plants.
Grandfather Perkins's greenhouses might be famous for exotics but
Lizzie preferred geraniums. Pauline, the younger and more sensitive
of her girls, loved the plants and this made an especial bond between
them for which Elizabeth was grateful. "I do like to give flowers to
anyone who is really fond of them. To me, it is one of the pleasantest
presents to give anyone I care for," wrote "Pauly" when the Quincy
Street house was new and she was about twelve years old. Later,
when she was married, she came regularly "to arrange the flower
window" and to bring flowers to her stepmother.

The new house contained a private laboratory for Agassiz. To
avoid vibration, the pedestal for his microscope was seated in bed
rock, and this and other wonders he was never tired of showing to
his friends. Inevitably, costs ran high and a large mortgage, held by
Harvard, proved necessary.

Agassiz never seemed to worry about his debts, but they "preyed
upon his mind," his wife said. She understood the almost pathological
generosity which led him to take on one student assistant after an-

other, paying them out of his own pocket. These boys would otherwise have had to leave school. Before his wife, Agassiz dropped the mask which led people to call him "genial" and she knew why he slept so badly and why he took on more lecture engagements than he had strength to fulfill. His own work suffered, and Elizabeth knew that this also must prey upon his mind.

At first, Lizzie thought that economy on her part would make ends meet. Her father took her down to Faneuil Hall "to meet his market men" and she found she could get "more variety for less money" in Boston than in Cambridge. But by 1854 she knew that mere penny-pinching was not going to solve the problem — she must think of a way to earn money. Opportunities were limited, but Elizabeth had an idea — except that she was sure Agassiz would never approve of it.

There was a need for a girls' school. Mr. Emerson's school, where the younger Cary girls had gone, had been given up and there was hardly a place in Boston nor in Cambridge where girls could be taught high school subjects. A public high school for girls had met with such opposition in Boston that it was closed and in 1852 a "school for female teachers" had been substituted. Cambridge girls would have to go to boarding school or study with private tutors if they were at all intellectually inclined.

Elizabeth Agassiz consulted her father. She had definite ideas, which pleased him, and an estimate of costs which really impressed him. After her first talk she went home so much encouraged that she told Alex and Ida about her scheme. Joyfully, she wrote her father. "I find that Ida feels exactly as I expected about our plan. It seems the thought is not a new one to any of us — we had it in our minds under different forms. Ida is only too glad to have her desire to assist her father . . . by teaching, put into a tangible shape and one that seems to promise success. She seems to find a genuine delight in the idea of finding full exercise for her superfluous energies." Alex also was "hearty" about the project, and Mrs. Agassiz promised to come in next day to make final arrangements.

"Your approbation and sympathy about the plan have made me really strong and indeed if you had not listened to it so kindly I should never have dared to propose it to anyone else," Lizzie told her father.[2]

The attic in the Quincy Street house contained several small rooms. Mrs. Agassiz's idea was to take out these partitions and substitute a single wall in the middle which would divide the attic into two large rooms. There should be a fireplace in each room and then along one side of the house more windows ought to be cut, to give better light. There must be desks and chairs. All this cost money, and although Mrs. Agassiz had figured everything out, it took great courage to borrow, for she had never done such a thing before. But her father told her she could have two thousand dollars whenever she needed it.

There was one more bridge to cross. Elizabeth and her stepchildren had still to tell Agassiz about the school, and they were sure he would not like the idea. But they should have known that he would surprise them! He was delighted, and declared that he would teach and they must put his name in the prospectus. As soon as Lizzie could bring paper and pen, he began to dictate material for a "brochure." "I, myself superintend the methods of instruction . . . and while maintaining that regularity and precision in studies so important to mental training, I shall endeavor to prevent the necessary discipline from falling into a lifeless routine, alike deadening to the spirit of teacher and pupil. . . ." At least, that was how Lizzie wrote it out from the notes she made in a sort of shorthand of her own invention.

Agassiz said he would "take charge of Physical Geography, Natural History and Botany, giving a lecture daily, on one or other of these subjects, illustrated by specimens, models, maps and drawings." [3] He said that "instruction in Mathematics and Latin will be given by my son and another assistant teacher; French and German as well as some of the English branches will be directed by my daughter." At the end of the booklet he included a favorite idea of his. "Some of the studies may be made elective, as I disapprove of binding every mind to the same kind of training and should prefer to adapt the education, so far as may be consistent with the order of a school, to individual character."

The response to the brochure was almost more than Mrs. Agassiz and her stepchildren bargained for. Eventually so many girls enrolled that the large upstairs rooms proved inadequate and the Agassiz dining room had to be given over to classes, with a small room behind the Professor's library serving as family dining room. A chartered omnibus drawn by four horses gathered in girls from Boston and Brookline and rumbled over the bridge to Cambridge every morning. Most of the Cambridge girls walked to school, but some of them arrived on horseback. Concord girls had to take a very early train.

The Agassiz school opened on September 26, 1855. "Lizzie delighted with her school," wrote her sister Caroline Curtis, after coming over from Winchester to Cambridge to see it. And the school proved such a happy experience that many of the girls themselves wrote down in later years what they could remember of it. Ellen Emerson, daughter of Ralph Waldo Emerson, sat down to write a letter to Mrs. Agassiz because she had been "recalling with joy that beloved day, fifty years ago, when your school began."

"We three Concord girls were in the schoolroom at eight o'clock, and then, and many other mornings we looked over the bannisters to watch the family go down to breakfast." Ellen thought of "Ida, with her wonderful whiteness and the pretty brown of her hair." Pauline was a pupil, but looking forward to the time when she should be old enough to teach. "One beautiful feature" of the school, Ellen said, was "the procession of scholars coming up the stairs, . . . Pauline in a pink calico" leading the line that first day with Martha Parsons. Two by two they came, Mary and Julia Felton, Mrs. Agassiz's nieces, Fanny Greenough — and the beautiful Anna Russell. Ellen Emerson could recall the full names of almost all the girls who had been her classmates.

"And Mr. Agassiz's lectures were to us just what he said he remembered such studies were to him, the opening of unimagined and glorious regions of knowledge and interest," Ellen said.

Soon after Agassiz had flamed with enthusiasm for a girls' school, he conceived another, far grander project of his own. He began

Contributions to the Natural History of the United States, which
was planned as a series of ten volumes to cover practically every living thing on the American continent. He announced this publication
with one of those brochures of his in 1855, the year the Agassiz
school started. Frances Calley Gray, just before his death, arranged
with Little, Brown and Company of Boston to publish the work.
Purchasers were to advance twelve dollars for each volume as it appeared and Mr. Gray figured that five hundred subscriptions would
get the project started. The publicity was something new in publishing annals. The Smithsonian Institution sent announcements free of
postal charges to libraries and colleges in every European country.
On the local scene Jared Sparks and Professor Felton wrote articles
for the papers. A letter describing the proper way to collect, preserve and ship specimens was sent to all the scientists, young and
old, and all the would-be scientists that Agassiz had ever met during
his travels.

Results surpassed even his exuberant hopes. There were "two
thousand one hundred names" on the subscription list "before the
appearance of the first page of a work" which would eventually cost
the buyers "one hundred and twenty dollars." Agassiz began with
turtles, and soon "Geology Hall" and even his own house was crawling with them. In Agassiz's private laboratory, Henry James Clark,
a young man who had graduated *summa cum laude* from the Lawrence Scientific School the previous year, was hard at work dissecting turtle eggs and drawing their different stages of development as
seen through Agassiz's vibration-proof microscope. Upstairs in the
schoolrooms, the girls were reciting "in physical geography to Miss
Bradford and in botany to Miss Clapp."

This is not to say that Agassiz broke all his promises in the brochure for his wife's school. A special session was held on Saturdays
for the girls, and they met in the new museum as soon as the first
section of it was built. Attendance was not compulsory but no one
ever missed a lecture by Agassiz if it were at all possible to get there
— although some of the girls did reproach their beloved professor
for bringing them a live snake and then making fun of them for
squealing with fright.

"The presiding genius of Professor Agassiz's school was Mrs. Agassiz" wrote one of her pupils, Charlotte Whiton, who lived with an aunt in Cambridge in order to attend classes. The language of the school was French, Charlotte said. Many of the girls "had been trained to speak French from childhood," but not Charlotte, who was at first quite unhappy. But "Mrs. Agassiz offered to pronounce French" with her on certain afternoons if she would come over to the house after the school session which lasted from 8:30 till two. And this, said Charlotte "was a marvelous kindness."

Ellen Emerson used almost the same words. She wanted to thank Mrs. Agassiz for her *"great thoughtfulness"* in sending up to the Concord girls "those steaming plates of the best mutton broth we ever tasted." Their train did not leave till late so they brought a cold lunch which they ate in the attic schoolroom with Agassiz mutton broth to cheer them. Ellen too had trouble with her French. "You never taught me, but you let me pronounce French to you," Ellen reminded Mrs. Agassiz. "I wonder if you remember what you usually said after it. 'Surprising — the perfect Yankee sound of it, though you keep all the rules.'"

Alexander Agassiz was twenty when his mother's school was opened. He had graduated from Harvard the year before and was now in Lawrence Scientific School. It was said that he hated his school teaching and it was true that he was shy and that all his mother's schoolgirls fancied themselves more or less in love with him. He was a famous oarsman and the day after his shell lost a race the girls came to school with crêpe mourning bands on their arms. There were the usual pranks — a beetle fell in his cousin Julia Felton's ink bottle and the girls giggled until "Mr. Alex" finally broke down and joined in the laughter. But in the beautiful Anna Russell, Alexander Agassiz had met his fate. She was his mother's pupil from the beginning of the school, as Ellen Emerson bore witness.

Smoothly parted, uncurled hair became the lovely Anna. Not even daguerreotypes and early photographs could spoil her beauty. Alex received a degree in mining engineering in 1857. Two years later he received a degree in Natural History and he could look forward with certainty to a professorship but all his scholastic achievements gave him very little courage where Anna's father was concerned. It was said that Alex walked all the way from Cambridge to Milton, a matter of some twelve miles, to ask Anna's father for her hand in marriage, but when he got to the stone gate-posts outside her house his courage failed him and he turned back. In 1860 however, no longer fainthearted, he won his fair lady.

The Agassiz school continued for nine years. It brought in an estimated total of $19,200.[4] While it seems difficult if not impossible to establish the costs, it would be conservative to say that Mrs. Agassiz contributed about as much as her husband to the family exchequer. Eventually, Professor Felton helped with Latin and Greek; Professor Child was said to have set the girls' compositions; and Professor Pierce gave "mathematical puzzles" to Alex, which he solved and passed on to his pupils. It was this help from Harvard professors which caused people to say later that Mrs. Agassiz's school was the forerunner of Radcliffe.

Although Lizzie loved her school, it was also a heavy burden. But Agassiz was known to call the school his "milk cow" and to refer to it as "my sole dependence for my existence." Early in 1859, Elizabeth and her father went over her accounts together. Agassiz's mother was still living, but growing feeble; she had written that she longed to see her son once more and Lizzie wanted to know if they could possibly go abroad. Her father said yes, for her personal debt to him was paid, "existence" more than paid for and a little profit put by for just such a family project. Ida and Alex would stay with the Cary family but Pauline could go with her father and her stepmother. The Agassiz school would be left in the hands of Mollie Felton.

The Gray bequest for the museum of Agassiz's dreams was announced in December, 1858. The cornerstone for the first section of the building was laid the following June, and on the crest of this wave of success Louis Agassiz returned to Europe for the first time in over twelve years.

It was Lizzie's first trip to Europe, and she wrote about it in terms of a great adventure. "Bravely we sailed out of Boston harbor — rejoicingly, but I must confess in an over-confident spirit," and then a "look of startled and melancholy horror came successively over the faces of our party. Everybody discovered that they wanted a book, or a shawl or something they had left below and descended into the abyss . . . Nothing was seen of me, for one, until we arrived in Halifax." But that was the end of her seasickness while Agassiz was perfectly well the whole time and "radiant all day." The voyage was slow because of icebergs, which Agassiz enjoyed as though they had been personal friends of his.

Ever since her girlhood, Lizzie had listened patiently to the accounts of European travels taken by her friends and relatives. Now she was on her way at last, but all her experiences were different — just as everything else in her life was different from the Boston pattern. Agassiz took her to Ireland "on the nastiest little steamer . . . built especially for the accomodation of pigs and cattle . . ." They were on their way to look at "gigantic fossil elk horns" at the castle of Lord Enniskillen. They lingered in Paris, but not to see the Louvre or for Lizzie to do any shopping: there were "paleontological specimens" to see, to price and perhaps to buy, since Agassiz had a five-thousand-dollar letter of credit issued by Samuel Gray Ward, Treasurer of the Museum. He had promised to "give a full and strict account" to his trustees when he got home — but, as usual, money which seemed limitless to him would soon be overdrawn as he discovered elderly colleagues much in need of cash and with fine collections for sale.

Agassiz had not realized how much he had missed his native Alps, but they said he wept when he saw them again. He might have laughed when he saw Lizzie's face, however. What did she think now of Mt. Tom and Mt. Holyoke, Massachusetts? Her enthusiasm for the Alps was all her husband could wish, and her only personal disappointment was because there was not time for her to climb the glacier of the Aar.

Agassiz spent several weeks with his mother during July and August. They "sat in an old-fashioned garden where a corner shut in by ivy and shaded by trees made a pleasant out-of-door sitting room." Both of them knew it was the last time they were to be together but there was more of peace than of sadness between them. Agassiz told "of his life and home in the United States and of the museum to which he was returning . . ." and no mother could ask more for her son than the life he described.

Madame Agassiz was living with a married daughter and, leaving mother and son alone together, Lizzie walked about the countryside with her sister-in-law. She saw Swiss families working on the parts for music boxes, at home in their small but immaculately clean houses. "They begin their work at four in the morning and never cease till night-fall," she was told. They "found it difficult to earn as much as thirty cents a day." Never, in all her sheltered life in the United States, had Lizzie seen such straitened circumstances. "They look out over the slope of the Jura to Mont Blanc but they cannot raise their eyes . . . they are so afraid of losing time," she said. It was not the stark simpilicty of the mountain châlets nor the dearth of common necessities that roused her pity half so much as this denial of the beauty before them; the lack of time to raise their eyes.

The Agassizs were back in Cambridge by the end of September. They found the first section of the museum building fairly well along, although their old friend Henry Greenough was the architect and this time not only Mrs. Agassiz but her husband thought him "dilatory." The dedication exercises took place November 13, 1860. "The transfer of the collections to their new abode was made as rapidly as possible," said Lizzie — covering in one sentence many scenes of stress and high drama.

CHAPTER FOURTEEN
Creative Chaos

A GASSIZ'S collections, smelly and revolting as they might seem to the uninitiated, were the apple of his eye. While they were housed in the wooden building Harvard had first provided, Agassiz would rush out of his own house if he heard the clang and clamor of the Cambridge fire department and stare anxiously in the direction of his laboratory building looking for a cloud of smoke. He demanded a fireproof building and this plea aroused considerable public support. Greenough pointed out that fireproof materials would cost a great deal, and the usual hassle over money between architect and client ensued. There was money enough to build only one section of the contemplated museum but bricks walls and iron staircases bore mute testimony to the attempt to cut down fire hazard.

Now that the building was ready, Agassiz could not possibly keep calm while his collections were moved into it. It was said that the old wooden laboratory was carted by the college from the site of a future Hemenway gymnasium to the museum property on Oxford Street without Agassiz's foreknowledge. Tradition pictured him as trotting anxiously across town in the wake of his building, sure that all his collections would be hopelessly broken and scattered. Not a glass jar was out of place, however. But suppose an impetuous young assistant dropped a dozen or so of the jars while carrying them up those new iron stairs! "Wet specimens" must be kept in alcohol and never allowed to dry. What if shells were broken, fossils lost or skeletons disjointed!

It was at this time of creative chaos that Agassiz attempted to form a corps of young assistants, soon to be known as the "museum boys." The old wooden laboratory, placed on a new foundation alongside the new museum, was to be their home. They were to be paid out of the museum's newly raised funds, Agassiz assumed — and blithely he promised them small sums. But a very sad thing, from Agassiz's point of view, had happened. The state appropriation, as much of it as was paid in, and also the public subscription money, had been "funded" by the trustees. They had resolved to spend only the income from their investments and again and again Agassiz's requests for money were refused.

Edward Sylvester Morse appeared on the scene just as the collections were being transferred to the new building and he was decidedly a bad influence among the assistants. He was a truculent boy who quarreled with his father and was expelled from every school he attended. But he had a consuming passion for shells. His collection of land snails was unique at the time and on the strength of the fanatical light that burned in his eyes when shells were mentioned, Agassiz hired him at a salary of twenty-five dollars a month. Eventually, there were nine museum boys given a similar salary and room and board, the cost covered mostly by Agassiz. They moved into the old wooden building.

At first, Morse thought well of everything. "We have a space behind the house plowed up for a garden where we are going to raise tomatoes and squashes," he wrote. "Our breakfasts, dinners and suppers are luxuries now; everything is cooked up in the best manner and everything is of the best. Several professors have visited our building and looked at our rooms and say they are not only the best rooms in the university but the best rooms in Cambridge.

"Night before last, Prof was here and spent the evening. He talked of some of the distinguished men of Europe, told us anecdotes of Arago, Humboldt, Muller and others. You can't imagine how interesting it was to hear one talk who has been intimate with those." [1]

The assistants formed a club, "all members belonging to the Museum" and agreed to read papers "of the right stamp, namely original investigation," every Monday evening. This was an American version of Agassiz's "little Academy" in Munich when he was a brilliant but penniless student already showing his gift of leadership. He was much pleased to see a sense of comradeship and pride in original work developing in his American assistants and although he could by no means afford it, he was glad to make life easier for these boys than it had ever been for him. Then, just three months later, the student assistants got into a quarrel with the cook and her husband whom Agassiz had hired to run the house.

The quarrel was about butter — but not, strange to say, about a shortage of butter "at table" but because "it should be brought on in smaller pieces"! One thing led to another. Katie, the cook, cried, and Glenn, her husband, "shook his fist." The boys immediately decided that "Prof" must fire the couple or they themselves would leave. It entirely escaped their minds that bright but penniless young student assistants could be found without the slightest difficulty whereas a good hard-working couple was hard to come by. "Prof" told them that "Glenn was a valuable man" and his wife had been "put in as housekeeper and that we should everyone of us leave if we did not like it. This from Prof," moaned Morse, "who [sic] we have loved and adored as a father!" The boys' wounded pride and dignity cost them their free meals — they continued to sleep at "Zoological Hall" but ate elsewhere.

Morse reported favorably upon a supper party given at the Agassizs' house on Quincy Street for the Museum assistants. "October 5, Friday [1860] Rainy and uncomfortable . . . We all prepared for Prof's supper tonight and around nine o'clock all of us started in a bunch for Prof's house. He welcomed us in genial style. We were shown into the parlor and talked and chatted awhile, when we were summoned to supper. The table looked very fine; Roast Turkey; Roast Duck; scalloped oysters, Tongue and Ham. Four large decanters filled with wine stood at the corners of the table. We pitched in with appetites such as none but zoologists have, sharpened by our omission of our usual supper. After, the ice cream and cake were

separately brought on with Italian wine. The wines were splendid
and I drank a great deal . . . We sat down at nine and did not leave
the table till quarter of one. Prof told us many things which I wish
I had time to note . . ."

No wonder Elizabeth Agassiz needed to keep school in order to
pay her household expenses! This was only one of the lavish spreads
for men only which she became adept at serving — as unseen hostess.
She and the Agassiz girls had their supper upstairs on a tray. Perhaps
their absence made the family and the Agassiz schoolgirls as well
especially interesting to the museum boys.

"Met a lady, one of Prof's students who I have met before at our
snake cage," wrote Morse, his grammar shaky as usual. He "con-
versed" with this "lady" for some time, he said and when "Prof's
girl students were in the Museum" he observed "some very pretty
girls among them."

Morse's amiable moods never lasted very long and about two weeks
after he had been fed handsomely at the Quincy Street house he
took offense at a scolding Agassiz gave his assistants concerning
sundry goings-on which had come to his attention:

"*October 22, Monday*. This morning Prof gave us a rather strong
lecture on behavior etc. Told us we must not emulate the rich; we
must give up all our social ties and in fact not care for dress or anything; be real diggers. At the same time seek refined and cultivated
society. With ragged breeches for instance! Told us, poor as he was,
he would not change his position for mere living. I thought of the
income he is receiving from his book and school; his 1500 a year as
Professor; his wealthy wife; the house in which he lives for nothing;
his children already engaged to the wealthiest. O consistency, thou
art a jewel!" Morse's own inconsistencies were obvious, his misstatements many.

Edward Sylvester Morse left Agassiz in December, 1861, without
notice. Alex Agassiz commented that Morse "was the laziest and
most troublesome of the lot," although "he did know a good deal
about shells." Morse's own account differed, of course.

"Prof appeared blue enough and when I asked him for money he
said he had not $10 dollars in his pocket or in the world." Next day,

Agassiz brought a "month's wages in New York bills" and it never occurred to Morse that Agassiz must have had to borrow this money. Instead, this charming youth thought his Professor had "lied" the previous day. Morse was bitter because his collection of shells had not been bought by the museum nor yet returned to him but in Agassiz's opinion the shells had been a consideration in hiring him in the first place. In any case, he received training from Agassiz which gave him his start in a brilliant career. Eventually he became professor of zoology and comparative anatomy at Bowdoin; he taught at the Imperial University in Tokyo and was for many years Director of the Peabody Museum in Salem.

Addison Emery Verrill was another of Agassiz's museum boys who kept a diary. The student who did not must have been the exception. Verrill told of the arrival of barrels of specimens, two from Acapulco, Mexico, and one from San Francisco.[2] Alexander Agassiz, hoping to make enough money to marry, had taken a job with the United States Survey of Washington Territory. He was soon convinced that the Survey held no future for him, and he returned to take his degree in Natural History at the Lawrence Scientific School and to work for his father at the museum. But meanwhile he had used his spare time on the West Coast and Mexico to collect fish. The two barrels from Acapulco were from him.

Mrs. Agassiz's brother, Tom Cary, had gone to California. He had done rather well, had fallen in love with San Francisco and may have had a fairly gay time, judging by the fact that he was a great friend of Sam Ward. His sister Lizzie wrote him and he declared that the tone of her letter was such that he dared not refuse to get to work and collect fish for Agassiz. The barrel from San Francisco was his.

All three barrels "were full of magnificent specimens of all kinds and Prof was exceedingly happy," Verrill wrote. Agassiz "whistled and sung and called 'Putty, Putty' instead of his usual 'Mr. Put*nám*.'" And Verrill tried to indicate, by accents, a strong French pronunciation. As Agassiz "pulled a brown, unpleasant-looking specimen from one of the barrels," he told his students that he "had once studied a long time on an old pair of leather pantaloons, . . . mistaking it for a specimen."

When the Civil War broke out, Agassiz said that he hoped to prove that even wartime conditions could not "cripple the advance of science in the new world." He had remarkable success with his fund raising, but by 1863 he had overspent both the museum's income and his own. He could not pay his assistants and asked them to wait while he went on a lecture tour. Verrill lost his temper and said he considered himself dismissed but was talked into staying until 1864 when he became professor of zoology at Yale. His career was as distinguished as that of Morse. In fact, no serious pupil of Agassiz's ever failed to make his mark in the scientific world.

The Civil War period was difficult for Louis Agassiz. In Europe he had seen the effects of civil strife. Students flung aside their books to rise in hot rebellion and as far as Agassiz could see it all came out the same in the end. Injustice reared its head, again and again, and young men lay dead behind the barricades who should have lived to be leaders — in Natural Science for example. When American students came to Agassiz, flushed and joyous with the news that they had just enlisted in the Massachusetts Volunteers, he flew into a rage. Or so it seemed to the bewildered boys who had been expecting praise and could not understand that Agassiz's anger was really an expression of grief.

When "Bertie Ordway" got a commission the students chipped in to buy him a sword which they showed to Agassiz. "He promptly threw himself into an attitude of a fencer and became absorbed in thrust and parry, utterly unconscious of our amazement at his earnestness and skill." The scene however was more like a sardonic comment on the game of war than anything "unconscious" on Agassiz's part.

If he came into his laboratory and found his assistants reading war news he scolded them severely. He said they "must work and show people that amid such exciting times they should not go wild." But his childish young men thought that it was "perfectly outrageous on Prof's part" to tell them to bring no more newspapers into the laboratory and they "expressed themselves freely on the subject." In the course of altercations such as this, Agassiz grew angry far more often than formerly. It was noted that his face grew flushed and once or twice his speech thickened and fluency deserted him. At such times, he would walk out of the laboratory and head for home.[3]

In the house on Quincy Street, calm awaited him. Nothing ever went wrong that Lizzie could not seem to set right. During the long, grueling Western lecture tour in the winter of 1863–1864, she had been with him, seeing that he got complete rest both before and after he spoke — keeping people from him who might literally have killed him with kindness. She had become alarmed by his state of nervous tension and now she was always on the watch for him, ready to see that he rested on the couch near his desk. His anger would subside as quickly as it came and he would go back again, smiling and genial as usual, to talk things over with the boys. To the insensitive Morse, it seemed undignified in "Prof" to forgive so quickly, but Shaler understood.

"In my room, my master became divinely young again." Shaler had "brought with him," from Kentucky, "the Southern habit of offering wine to guests," and Agassiz would take a glass, a pipe, and return in mind to his student days, or to his plans for work in the museum.

Acrimonious arguments were not with students alone. Agassiz quarreled with fellow professors — not more than many professors have been known to do, before and since, but with French verve. broad gestures and extravagant statements. Professor Benjamin Pierce, mathematical genius of the Scientific School, was alternately Agassiz's best friend and his favorite enemy. Pierce had just attacked Agassiz's teaching methods as lacking in thoroughness when Shaler asked to be examined for his degree.

"In the four years I was with Agassiz I had no kind of examination except what he gave when he questioned and in some manner tested my training," Shaler said. "For the rest, there was nothing but criticism of my work and discussions — endless discussions."

"I was placed in a seat upon the platform which I had to occupy when not at the blackboard, for nearly five hours with an intermission for refreshments," Shaler said, describing his examination. The performance began with "questions by Agassiz. He very dextrously drew out samples of my little learning and engaged me in disputations which would be likely to make a good impression." This good impression had to be made on Professors Wyman, Gray, Pierce, Cook, Lovering, Horsford and Felton who, in 1862, was President of Harvard. It was "an august bench of judges," Shaler said, but Agassiz put him at his ease.

Agassiz "pressed me hard on some rather recondite matter but he probably knew my reading made it pretty safe to do so. I have never ceased to admire the way in which, while seeming to put me under the harrow, he was really exhibiting my paces. . . ."

The questioning by Agassiz lasted two hours and then the other professors took over. "Wyman was most kindly. . . . Gray, too, was fair, Lovering tried to find out" if Shaler knew something of subjects other than biology and Cook took him "on a hard road in mineralogy." Then came Pierce "at the end of the second sitting." He asked about "mountain building" and Shaler had just been reading up on this phase of geology. "At the end came a question" which Shaler thought was "unfair." He said he couldn't answer it and asked what Professor Pierce's answer would be. "We had a sharp colloquy which ended in his good-natured acknowledgment that he had put the question in just to see what I would do with it.

"I shall never forget the look of pleasure on my master's face," Shaler remarked. He seemed to realize that his *summa cum laude* had been won not only by himself but by his "master." Agassiz's joy was brief, however. Shaler promptly enlisted in the Union Army.

Word went around that Agassiz favored the South in the Civil War. This was not true. He had students on both sides of the lines and he felt grave anxiety for them all. To an English scientist he wrote in 1862: "It has been agonizing, week after week, to receive the English papers and to see there the noble devotion of the men of the North to their country branded as the service of mercenaries. . . . In the last six months nearly 30,000 men have volunteered

. . . and believe me, it is not for the sake of the bounty." He hoped an emancipation proclamation would stop hostilities and at the same time realized that no early end to the slaughter was in sight. "Our best young men are the first to enlist," he said; ". . . it takes away the best material in the land."

And there were those who said that Mrs. Agassiz, if not pro-slavery, was at least a "cotton Whig." When the first ominous stirrings of conflict began and the fugitive Anthony Burns was ordered returned to his master, Mrs. Agassiz's grandfather, Colonel Perkins was said to favor the return of lost property, whether human or otherwise. Her father had long been associated with the Lowell mills where profits depended upon low-cost cotton produced by slave labor. But Elizabeth's younger brother Richard enlisted in the Union Army. He was killed at the Battle of Cedar Mountain, in 1863.[4]

Elizabeth's father died in 1859. It was a great loss to her, for they were very close. But she was delighted when her mother decided to sell the Boston property and come to Cambridge to live. A good-sized plot was bought on Ware Street, just beyond Quincy Street, where houses were few and gardens large. Lizzie could come "across lots" to see her mother whenever she pleased. Mrs. Cary built a house [5] for herself, her two unmarried daughters, Sallie and Emma — and for Tom if he should ever care to come home from California. And here in 1863 came Helen Cary, the young widow of Richard Cary, with her baby Georgiana. In this closely knit family Richard Carys' death was the first grave loss. It was the family custom, however, to "bear things well" — to smile for the sake of each other. They made much of the baby, little "Georgie."

Before Elizabeth was married she often mentioned how much she loved children. She was proud of her ability to quiet a crying infant and small children "took to her," people said. Agassiz was equally fond of children, as Joseph LeConte, a doctor and briefly Agassiz's student, testified. Dr. LeConte, his wife and three-year-old daughter were guests in Agassiz's home, and Agassiz "took a great fancy to my little Sallie," LeConte said. "Agassiz taught her the names of all his dearest specimens . . . he called her 'little Echinoderm' [starfish

or sea urchin]. A child in the home! It seemed to bring back the joy
of his early married life. He was continually playing with the child,
even taking her on his back and getting down on his hands and
knees and 'playing horse' all around the dining table." There is no
question but what Elizabeth Agassiz wanted children — but this was
not to be. She loved little Georgie, therefore, and all her various
nices and nephews, with more than ordinary devotion. But her husband's children came first, and she could soon look forward to becoming a grandmother — a very young one, to be sure.

They said that Elizabeth Agassiz's school was given up because of
the Civil War. This was probably partly true, but it was also given
up because the teaching force, Elizabeth's stepchildren, were too
busy falling in love and getting married. In the autumn of 1860, Alex
married Anna Russell. Her parents were abroad, but her sister Elizabeth — who had married Agassiz's pupil Theodore Lyman — gave
Anna a wedding in Brookline. Anna and Alex promptly moved into
the Quincy Street house, and no one could have been happier than
Elizabeth. A large family was pure delight to Lizzie — and now she
had another daughter, and such a pretty one.

On November 30, 1860, Pauline Agassiz, aged nineteen, married
Quincy Adams Shaw. "Quin," as they called him, graduated from
Harvard in 1845 and went with his cousin, Francis Parkman, to the
Rockies. Parkman dedicated *The Oregon Trail* "To the comrade of
a summer and the friend of a lifetime, Quincy Adams Shaw." By
the time Pauline met "Mr. Shaw" he was a traveled gentleman. He
had spent a winter in Egypt and Palestine, and seven years in Paris.
No wonder he was attracted to Mrs. Agassiz's stepdaughter, who had
become an American girl but who spoke both French and German
so beautifully. Pauline was also beautiful to look at: "dark and high-
featured," with deep-set dark eyes, and smooth, dark hair. They
were both born in February, but Quin was sixteen years older than
Pauline.

This first Agassiz daughter's wedding was in the parlor on Quincy
Street. No longer was it the fashion for a bride to wear green.

Pauline's dress was white silk, high at the neck and "with tight puffed sleeves." And now the bonnet and shawl era was also over. Pauline wore a "white tulle veil with orange blossoms," and her "look, manner and voice had something very touching in it."⁶ This time, a wedding meant no addition to the Quincy Street household — the bride and groom sailed for Europe.

It would appear that Ida Agassiz, also, had been in love for some time, but the formidable Boston family and circle of friends that she had acquired along with her stepmother did not approve her choice. The choice of Mrs. Agassiz's friends for Ida was none other than Francis Parkman himself! He was a widower, his health was precarious and he was only a year younger than Ida's stepmother.

"A kind note" from Ida Agassiz, telling Parkman of her engagement to another man, took him "wholly by surprise,"⁷ he said. "She is certainly a most exceptional person, for though Mrs. Agassiz and at least one other person had suggested to her that there was more than friendship in my regard for her, she seems not to have believed it, but rather to have believed that the attitude which I had studiously assumed towards her expressed all that I felt. The truth is that for a year or two, my dearest wish has been to make her my wife . . ." The author of *The Conspiracy of Pontiac, La Salle and the Discovery of the Great West* and *The Oregon Trail* felt that his "health was too doubtful and anything like exertion of mind especially under stimulous too dangerous, not to say ruinous" for him to propose to Ida. She was supposed to read his mind and wait for him to feel better. Parkman said that the news of her engagement was such a shock that "it was more than a month" before he had "a tolerable night's sleep."

Ida's choice had fallen upon Henry Lee Higginson, a most charming young man only two years older than herself and, in 1863, just back from the wars as a wounded hero. There were various reasons why Harry Higginson did not suit Mrs. Agassiz's friends as a husband for Ida, whom they referred to as "such a darling." One very black mark against him was the fact that he failed to graduate from Harvard. Poor eyesight was given as the reason but in the opinion of Beacon Hill this was a mere excuse. He went to Europe, took a walking tour, studied German and became passionately fond of music. When he came home he was required to learn clerking under Samuel Eliot. He set no worlds afire. In 1853, Henry L. Higginson inherited thirteen thousand dollars from an uncle, threw up his job and went to Europe to become a concert pianist. In Vienna, he injured his left arm so that the concert stage had to be given up forever. In 1860, Henry Higginson returned to the United States, as a wine merchant this time, and made a little money selling German wines.

Henry L. Higginson's refusal to conform to the Boston pattern was not confined to a lack of aptitude for business. He had been among the vanguard of the abolitionists. He went to antislavery meetings, protested the return of fugitive slaves and wrote pieces for the paper. His family had been closely associated in business with the Perkins family and the Carys, and most of his friends and relatives of a previous generation looked upon Henry Higginson as not very bright. They would have to call him Major Higginson now — and this was no mere honorary title but a rank which he had earned, along with his quite serious wounds, on the field of battle.

Ida Agassiz and Henry Lee Higginson were married on December 5, 1863. They chose this day because it was Mrs. Agassiz's birthday. "We felt that to be married on her birthday was a sure blessing for us," Ida said. This time the wedding was in the Harvard College Chapel — "Ida in white silk and lace veil, and the church filled with friends." For two years, Henry was incapacitated by his wounds, so where would the young couple live except at Quincy Street, of course.

Alex had become his father's assistant at the museum. He was a brilliant scientist, receiving eventually even more honorary awards than his father had — but he also had a sense of the value of money which his father entirely lacked. To say that as "agent for the museum" Alex had his hands full would be to put it mildly. "Father cannot make up his mind to draw in his horns and has laid out all sorts of financial plans which I am doing my best to knock in the head," Alex wrote.

The fact that he was not in the Union Army troubled Alex deeply. "I am ashamed and have been ashamed any longer to stay at home," he confessed to Theodore Lyman. "And yet what is to become of father, if I go? I know the museum (no, not the museum) but father will go to thunder if I don't stay and hold on to his coat tails."

What finally happened was that Alex stayed in Cambridge in full charge of the museum while his father went forth — not to the battlefront, to be sure, but as an unofficial ambassador of good will, in the hope that Brazil would remain friendly to the United States and not side with Great Britain against the Union. Agassiz also realized a lifelong dream of collecting fishes from the Amazon.

On March 22, 1865, Julia Ward Howe jotted down an item in her journal: "Lizzie Agassiz came to take leave of me very kindly, as her time must be fully occupied. She will do much of the work of the Brazilian Expedition."

It was a statement that might have made Agassiz and his assistants indignant, but it was not too far from the truth.

CHAPTER FIFTEEN
Brazilian Journey

ON March 31, 1865, Sam Ward, Julia Ward Howe's ebullient
brother, sat himself down in the New York Hotel to write to
Longfellow — whose opposite qualities made the two men devoted
friends.

"My dear Longo," Ward began: "It may interest you to know
that I took leave of Mr. and Mrs. Agassiz at 11 A.M. yesterday, on the
Colorado which is now doubtless bearing them, as hopeful as a
schoolboy and girl, on their vacation tour to the great empire of the
Tropic of Capricorn . . .

"Your good friends sailed, or rather steamed away in good spirits.
Their only anxiety was about a portable barometer behind time. But
it was at length brought by a wizened-faced Frenchman. . . .
Agassiz's stateroom seemed to me a huge Xmas stocking into which
enthusiastic Santa Clausi-(ae) were perpetually thrusting wines,
cigars, oranges, apples, chocolate drops and books and newspapers.
He had been up all night and some one recommended him to go to
bed as soon as the *Colorado* should have passed the Narrows.

" 'Go to bed indeed,' quoth he. 'I shall at once begin taking my
temperatures for our approach to the Gulf Stream.' . . .

"Agassiz was flying around . . . now drawing a check, now giving an order for storage and distributing *des poignées de main* as
freely as Louis Philippe on his accession." [1]

While Agassiz was distributing handshakes, Sam Ward sat down by "Madame Agassiz" to ask how it was that Longfellow had not come along on the Brazilian expedition. "What a sacrifice to duty and the Lares and Penates you made when you deprived yourself of the wondrous refreshment this voyage could have provided to body and mind," Sam Ward said reproachfully . . .

Longfellow's son Ernest had also been invited. "One of the great regrets of my life is that my father would not let me go with Agassiz on his expedition to Brazil and his exploration of the Amazon," he wrote, years later. "Agassiz had offered me the post of artist to the expedition and I had been wild to go, but I was not yet of age, and my father very much opposed it, fearing I could not stand the climate, so reluctantly I gave it up. It was certainly one of the lost chances of my life. That was very characteristic of my father; he always thought it wisest not to do a thing. He had none of the adventurous spirit. 'To stay at home is best,' " he would say.[2]

Evidently Longfellow never seriously considered his own invitation to go to Brazil. But he wrote, "Agassiz is gone and leaves a gap like that made in a street when a house is pulled down."[3]

Not all of Agassiz's invitations were refused. "My party was enlarged by several volunteers," he wrote, and by that he meant that the peaceful and restful vacation which Lizzie visualized for him had become a major scientific expedition with sufficient personnel to staff a small circus.

Agassiz set out upon this expedition with the wealthiest sponsor he had yet acquired. Nathaniel Thayer, a partner in a firm which eventually became Kidder, Peabody, had "one of the largest fortunes acquired by any New Englander of his day." His father and his grandfather had gone to Harvard, but Nathaniel had entered a countinghouse, and the omission of a Harvard education might be said to have cost him a good deal of money in the end. He was one of Harvard's great benefactors and he was now "the friend who made it possible to give" the Brazilian journey "the character of a scientific expedition."

Oliver Wendell Holmes popped into the office of Ticknor and Fields, publishers, one day, carrying "a book done up in paper under his arm. 'I have here a most wonderful book. It is worth in money value [more than] any other book in Boston.' " And when his listeners were sufficiently intrigued, Holmes said, " 'Oh, I forgot to tell you what book this is. It is Nat Thayer's check-book.' " [4] That check-book was at Agassiz's service, practically without restriction. The student "volunteers" paid their own way, however, and among them was Nathaniel Thayer's son, Stephen van Rensselaer Thayer. "Ren" they called this agreeable young man, for whom Mrs. Agassiz felt a certain quite understandable sense of responsibility.

Another volunteer was Tom Ward, son of Samuel Gray Ward, the Boston banker and museum trustee. Lizzie Agassiz had known Tom's parents when she was Tom's age. During his undergraduate years at Harvard, Tom had dropped in at the Agassizs' for supper many a Sunday night and they were all fond of him. Then there was Walter Hunnewell, blessed with money and an amiable disposition. "Hunney" brought along a new and by no means reliable contraption called a "camera," which he was trying to learn to use. Photographs would be so much better than daguerreotypes — better even than Burkhardt's drawings.

Perhaps the most interesting and certainly the most eloquent among the volunteers was William James.[5] He was twenty-three at this time. His letters to his brother Henry James, the future novelist, and to his parents revealed his variable thoughts and feelings. He was still unable to decide what to do with his life, he blew hot and cold, he tried but failed to be practical, so that his parents' patience with him was remarkable. Yet he was aware of his faults and contrite about them — a human, likable boy who could not yet grow up. William had been studying art in Newport with William Hunt and John LaFarge, doing well, but not well enough for his own satisfaction. His earlier European education had left him unqualified to earn a living and in 1861 he entered the Lawrence Scientific School. He was full of advice when his family contemplated leaving Newport to become neighbors of the Agassizs on Quincy Street. "Cambridge, I confess does seem at first more like a place of transit than a home," he wrote. "The college influence extends all around and makes every house in its immediate neighborhood seem like a boarding house."

The James family evidently discussed all their plans together, and William wanted to help along a decision as to the proper place to live. He favored Cambridge. "I think the society here must be much pleasanter than elsewhere, not so mercantile; the natural beauty of the place, as soon as you recede a little from Harvard Square, is great . . . The chief objection seems to me the bad walking in spring, but that applies to every place but the city. . . . We should not need to keep horses here."

But "all this on the supposition that one or more of us remains here to study. I feel very much the importance of soon making a final choice of my business in life. I stand now at the place where the road forks. One branch leads to material comfort, the flesh pots, but it seems a kind of selling of one's soul. The other to mental dignity and independence, combined however, with penury. If I myself were the only one concerned I should not hesitate in my choice. But it seems hard on Mrs. W. J. . . . 'that not impossible she,' [6] to ask her to share an empty purse and a cold hearth. On the one side is *Science;* on the other *business* (the honorable, honored and productive business of *printing* seems most attractive) with medicine which partakes of the advantages of both, between them, but which has certain drawbacks of its own. . . . I fear there might be some anguish in looking back from the pinnacle of prosperity (*necessarily* reached, if not by eating dirt, at least by renouncing some ambrosia) over the life you might have led in the pure pursuit of truth."

It never occurred to young William James that anyone could conceivably fail in business, either with or without "eating dirt." But he had fallen under Agassiz's powerful spell and he was leading up to this. "I want you to become familiar with the idea that I may stick to Science and drain away at your property a few more years," he said. "If I can get into Agassiz's museum, I think it not improbable I may receive a salary of 400 or 500 in a couple of years. I know some stupider than I who do."

William James went house hunting in his family's behalf and wrote to them (heading his letter "Christmas day" but leaving out the year, as usual): "I enclose another advertisement of a house, which is small for us. I believe it might be looked at though. The *place* to me improves as I go on living here and if I study with Agassiz four or five years I should like to have you all with me, comfortable. I had a long talk with one of his students the other night and saw for the first time how a naturalist could feel about his trade the same way an artist does about his. For instance, Agassiz would rather take wholly uninstructed people 'for he has to unteach them all they have learnt.' He does not let them *look* into a book for a long while, what they learn they must learn for themselves and be masters of it all. The consequence is he makes *Naturalists* of them and this student (he has been here two years) said he felt ready to go anywhere in the world now with nothing but his notebook and study out anything alone."

One of the students "wild to go" on the Brazilian adventure was William James. Most, if not all of the other volunteers had wealthy parents but he hated to ask his family for money. Eventually, an elderly relative gave him what he hoped would be sufficient; but he was always anxious — and more in need of funds than the other boys, as time would show.

Before the *Colorado* had dropped her pilot, William James was writing his first letter to his family. "I have determined to keep a diary and shall begin tonight." "And Mrs. Agassiz is a brick," said William, having come to this conclusion the next day.

Mrs. Agassiz kept a daily record of the expedition. James's diary was kept spasmodically, and afterwards he seems to have destroyed some of it while other sections he sent to his brother Henry. James's comments were often critical; Mrs. Agassiz's pages were decidedly feminine in point of view, and sometimes she was unintentionally funny. Taken together, the two records and Lizzie's letters tell the story of some adventurous Americans, a long way from home.

"Mr. Alan McLane, President of the Pacific Mail Steamship Company" had given "the whole party" free passage on "the magnificent ship the *Colorado*" which was going "almost empty of passengers, being bound by way of Cape Horn for San Francisco." This matter-of-fact statement suggests a reason why the equally "magnificent" Sam Ward graced the scene of departure. He was personally involved in the affairs of the Pacific Mail Steamship Company, in whose interests he often used his powers as "King of the Lobby" in Washington. Just as the scientists were about to sail an official document was handed to Agassiz. It was a general order for officers of the United States Navy to aid the expedition in any way possible and it came from Gideon Welles, Secretary of the Navy. Secretary of State Seward had recommended the expedition to General Webb, United States Minister to Brazil, and Agassiz carried letters to the Emperor.

About ten days before sailing, Agassiz had received a solemn directive from Sumner telling what was expected of the traveling naturalist. "Of course you will see the Emperor of Brazil, whose enlightened character is one of the happy accidents of governments." Agassiz would indeed — he would have Dom Pedro eating out of his hand. "If he gives you an opportunity, I hope you will not fail to let him know that there are good friends of Brazil's here who think a grave mistake was made when this Power, naturally friendly to the United States, consented to follow the lead of Lord Russell in elevating our Rebels to the condition of lawful belligerents on the ocean. It is difficult to see the consequences of this act.

"Of course Lord Russell adopted at once the conclusion that the Rebellion must triumph and thereupon made the concession which he did. The effect of this concession has been infinitely mischievous. Without it, the Rebellion would have been crushed long ago." After a few more similar paragraphs in which Agassiz was told what to think, he was finally told to make "the Brazilian government see the mistake that has been made. . . ." Sumner "assumed" that Agassiz was "a Naturalist but . . . a patriot also." Agassiz had become a naturalized American citizen the previous year, but he might have wished that he need not listen to so much advice — as he deciphered page after page of Sumner's letter.

On the second of April, their "first Sunday at sea," they walked the decks "watching a singular cloud, which the captain says is a cloud of smoke in the direction of Petersburg," Mrs. Agassiz wrote.

"We think it may be the smoke of a great, decisive engagement going on, while we sail peacefully along." Lizzie put her finger on the sensitive spot as she spoke of sailing "peacefully." Alex had been left at home to run the museum and his father would soon speak of him as "sinking under the load of his responsibility arising chiefly from lack of means at hand." He had given up his hope of joining the army but was no less "ashamed . . . to remain at home." The student volunteers had various private reasons for being on board the *Colorado* instead of in either army. They watched the black cloud of smoke but "what it means, or how the battle ends, if battle it be," they would not know "for two months perhaps." Eventually they found out that "it was on this day and the following that the final assaults on Petersburg were made and the cloud which marred an otherwise stainless sky was, no doubt . . . above the opposing lines of the two armies."

On board the *Colorado*, Agassiz gave a lecture every afternoon at two o'clock. It was a "*long*" lecture, William James said. "All the passengers, several officers and the captain came"; Lizzie "feared the lectures were a mistake," because she still clung to her conception of the expedition as a rest for Agassiz. He assured her that "it was a rest for him to systematize his own work and arrange it in his own mind. The recording of these lectures occupies me a good deal but I want to write them out carefully, because I think it will be very interesting, when the work is done, to compare it with the plan . . . ," Lizzie said.

"The Professor has just been explaining over the map of South America and making projects as if he had Sherman's army at his disposal," wrote William James. Agassiz's plan of work would not compare entirely favorably with the ground actually covered and the work actually done — and yet so much would be accomplished that not even the Professor himself could complain, in the end. "*Offering* your services to Agassiz is about as it would be for a S. Carolinian to *invite* Gen. Sherman's soldiers to partake of some refreshment when they called at his home," grumbled young James. But he was as eager as anyone to know what part he would play in the expedition. He found that his especial study would be "sea creatures, other than fish."

It was in Lizzie's mind, all along, that her carefully kept journal, with Agassiz's notes, would become a book when they returned. Into her letters to her family she put details she did not consider proper for print. There was her opinion of the young volunteer assistants, for example. Ren Thayer was "a very amiable boy and always most kind and attentive . . ." but he was "not very fond of study." She managed to get him to join her in "Portuguese lessons every day" and she had a talk with him about his "aims in life" which she reported to his mother. "His thoughts seem to be very seriously turning to entering college or West Point. He has thought, and it seems to me a sound view, that if he did decide upon either of these steps, he should not defer entering any longer than next summer . . ." And as the days went by, Mrs. Agassiz was forced to conclude that Ren, charming though he was, did not "feel particularly drawn" toward "scientific study."

"William James has always been an interesting fellow to me," Mrs. Agassiz said. "Bright, thoughtful, well-informed; his companionship will always be a pleasure. He has been woefully seasick with that kind of seasickness that makes the head giddy and heavy." The "trades" about which Mrs. Agassiz "had heard before leaving and which" she "supposed to be gentle breezes to float us peacefully southward" had been "blowing like fury ever since we were two days out."

And William James gave his own version of how he felt.

"My seasickness did not take an actively nauseous form after the first night and second morning, but for twelve mortal days I was, body and soul, in a more indescribably hopeless, homeless and friendless state than I ever want to be again. . . . The trade winds are hideous moist gales that whiten all the waves with foam. . . . I thought the sky would be of a deep Prussian blue over a sea of the same color, with spice-laden winds, and birds of Paradise; nautilus and flying fish; porpoises and bonitas, phosphorescences at night rivalling the moon, and all that kind of stuff. Neither skies nor sunsets are of any livelier hue than with us. We have seen a few flying fish, but they are not near as interesting as toads are at home."

Mrs. Agassiz continued her appraisal of the students:

"Then I am much more pleased with young Walter Hunnewell than I expected. . . . He is rather heavy, but he is kindly, good-headed and I feel as if we should be quite fond of him though he will not add much scientific weight to the party. The others volunteer is Mr. Dexter. He is a wonderful shot, they say, and when he has brought down his bird, understands how to strip and mount the specimen with rare skill."

William James described Dexter as "a sun-burnt, big-jawed devil . . . from Providence, who is a crack shot and has hunted all over the U. S. He is rich . . ." Tom Ward was "active and tough and a most pleasant companion," James said.

The *Colorado* reached the bay of Rio de Janeiro on April 23, 1865 and came to anchor at eleven in the morning. Customs officers came out to tell Agassiz that, by the Emperor's orders, the whole party could land without inspection; and in the afternoon Agassiz went to pay his respects to the Emperor.

Dom Pedro II of Brazil took the throne when his father, former King of Portugal, abdicated in 1831. Dom Pedro was born in Rio and had no ambitions regarding the throne of Portugal, preferring to assure Brazilian independence. He was forty years old at this time, had fought two wars in order to keep his throne and was becoming embroiled with Paraguay in a boundary dispute, but his personal tastes were scholarly. Agassiz, with his previous experience in gaining the aid of a king, had no trouble at all with Dom Pedro. The Amazon, not officially open to commerce until 1871, was opened to Agassiz with the Emperor furnishing guides and transportation.

The *Colorado* paused in Rio to fill her coal bunkers before going on around the Horn, and the Agassizs were still living on board when the Emperor came to have a look at the ship. He was received with a salute of twenty-one guns and then "dragged his puffing, panting staff from top to bottom" of the steamer. "He poked his royal nose into every crack and corner" to the amusement of the crew who called Dom Pedro and his staff "them kings." At last it was time for luncheon. The Emperor was presented first to Mrs. Agassiz, then to the captain's wife. Mrs. Agassiz was seated on his right, the captain's wife on his left. "I had to get on with royalty the best I could," Lizzie said, "for the captain did not speak a word of French. The Emperor was very gracious — talked with great interest of Agassiz and his expedition."

On the following Sunday, Agassiz took his microscope and some specimens to the palace and spent five hours with the Emperor, at Dom Pedro's special invitation. He "finally had to beg off because he was fairly exhausted though the Emperor seemed as fresh as possible." It was some time before Mrs. Agassiz met the Empress, the former Princess Theresa Maria, sister of Francis I, King of Naples. "At the door of the Palace were only one or two men in uniform" and she and her husband "were shown through long corridors and one or two antechambers where were standing a few groups . . . of gentlemen in waiting and the like." Mrs. Agassiz said it looked to her "like a dreary business — no gaiety and grandeur" such as she had expected to find in an emperor's palace. They finally reached a drawing room where they were told to sit down. "Presently," they heard someone coming down the corridor "walking very fast." Lizzie thought it was another gentleman in waiting come to take them to the Empress, but in walked the Emperor himself, who asked them into still another room, which was "handsome, with dark, heavy furniture." Here they sat down a while longer and the Emperor talked to Agassiz, "enquired after his fishes and was very genial. . . . After about half an hour he asked us to come in and see the Empress and ushered us into a third drawing room . . . where he went to the door and called his wife, just like any other mortal. In rolled a fat little lady with the sweetest expression . . . who invited us at once to take seats. It was just as though she had said 'Make yourselves at home.'"

The Empress of Brazil was "not in the least pretty" but she looked "sympathetic and motherly." They discussed slavery, which the

Emperor said he planned to abolish in Brazil. The discussion, however, was between the Emperor, Agassiz and Mrs. Agassiz, with the Empress listening. This astonished Lizzie, who considered conversation an art and part of a woman's duty.

The Agassizs were invited to the opening of the "Chambers" — the "only occasion of the year when the Emperor wears his robes of state." Lizzie said she felt exactly as if she were "at the Boston theater," except that she thought "Booth would have gotten it up better." The Emperor wore a "tight-fitting suit of white satin, white shoes with rosettes, a long train of green velvet embroidered with gold stars and carried by several small boys, a crown on his head half a foot high and a golden sceptre in his hand some six feet long." She thought the Emperor "did well to preserve his dignity" dressed like that — "I must say, the Emperor is a very royal, noble-looking man, not because of his state robes, but in spite of them."

The Empress and the Brazilian ladies of the court were "magnificently dressed" and "one marvelous emerald glittered across the hall with a green glory quite startling to behold." It was a part of the Empress's "jewelled headdress." The Agassizs sat in the American Minister's box which had a window at the back looking out over the entrance to the building. They watched the departure of the "Imperial procession" and looked down upon the state coach — "Portuguese, some two hundred years old, the sides entirely of glass, the roof of crimson velvet with a gold crown surmounting it." Eight horses drew this coach, and the Empress had a coach of her own. "In the foreground," Mrs. Agassiz observed, "some hundred washer-women working away at a public trough or stream with all the soiled linen of the town."

Lizzie's first impression of Rio de Janeiro was that of "the most rickety, tumble-down specimen of picturesque decay. One good vigorous kick would knock it all down," she thought. The people were a strange mixture of races such as she had never before seen, and she was startled by the misery of the poor. She spoke particularly of "porters who carry enormous weights upon their heads" and she had seen "four of them walking along with a piano" carrying it apparently "as easily as if it were a basket of flowers."

Various delays connected with his plans for an exploration of the Amazon kept Agassiz in Rio. He could easily have used Sherman's army, to go collecting for him, as William James had suggested — but he deployed his students and assistants as if they were an army anyway. Ren Thayer, son of Agassiz's patron, had probably never been on so much as a camping trip before. But Lizzie wrote of his "return from a shooting expedition with Dexter, having been gone ten days. They had cut their way through the woods, swum rivers on horseback, and had all sorts of adventures but Ren seemed to have enjoyed them all, looked strong and hearty and brought back excellent collections."

Ward was in the "first party for the interior," and Tom Ward was a boy who had probably never experienced anything much more wild than Boston Common. He and his comrades were given "hundreds of letters for the whole route, guides and a military escort provided, where one is necessary, and all arranged between Agassiz and the emperor." Nevertheless they were very much on their own, five white men who must stay on good terms with the natives and use their judgment as to the need of military escort. Others set out a week later "to keep nearer the coast and explore the lower reaches of the Rio Doce and Rio San Francisco." Agassiz would reach the Amazon by coastwise steamer, meeting there the cross-country explorers and the second party from the rivers.

The roll call of boys and men going out on independent expeditions lacks the name of William James — and for good reason. His first letters from Rio were full of elation — followed by dismay. He "never saw such physical energy" as had Tom Ward, who "within a day or two of landing knew the country round about." Hunnewell, "big, strong-armed and serious," Tom Ward and James "discovered a delicious little restaurant kept by a French family . . . where the cooking is perfect and everything marvelously cheap."

And "no words of mine . . . can give any idea of the magnificence of this harbor," James wrote. "The boldest, grandest mountains, far and near, the palms and other trees of such a vivid green as I never saw anywhere else. The town realizes my idea of an African town in its architecture and effect. Many of the people are native Africans and tattooed. . . . The Brazilians are of a pale Indian color, without a particle of red, and with a very aged expression. They are very polite and obliging, *all* wear black beaver hats and glossy black frock coats which make them look like *épiciers en dimanche* [grocers in Sunday clothes]."

William climbed Corcovado, that dramatic mountain peak overlooking the harbor of Rio. The excursion was gotten up for Mrs. Agassiz, and she rode a "tall white horse." No one knew that she hated horseback riding and was so terrified that she would write, "It appeared to me a very perilous moment of my existence and that I might as well make my peace with the world and consider this the jumping off place." She enjoyed the magnificent view even though "it faintly dawned upon my mind occasionally that we had to get down from this peak, but I did not allow my thoughts to rest on it for a moment. The awful moment came however, like the dentist's and all other inevitable facts, and then I found that the rest of the party . . . intended to walk down the steepest part of the slippery road and take their horses at a lower station. But I said to myself, I shall never have a chance to learn again as now . . . and if I am going to balk at the first bit of dangerous riding how shall I get on when there are nobody knows how many miles of mule-back before me. So as if it were quite my habit to mount horses on top of high mountains and slide down to the bottom, I announced my intention of descending as I had come, whatever other members of the party might do." Lizzie made it to the bottom, and members of the party "really did commend" her and said that for a person "quite unaccustomed to riding it was a pretty good feat." To her sister Sallie she wrote, "You see, my dear, I brag a little because by nature I am such an awful coward."

James hoped the Professor would send him "to Pará." It had taken two weeks to set up a makeshift laboratory in Rio, and James worked hard "trying to be of as much use as I could to the Professor," he said. The "profusion of the lower forms of life here at low tide" amazed him, and he would have enjoyed classifying jellyfish except that he "suffered unlimited itching of the skin, caused by flies and mosquitoes, and worst of all on both cheeks and one side of the neck by a virulent ringworm." He had not been feeling well but thought he was getting "acclimatized" when a fever hit him.

William's next letter home was written four weeks later from the hospital in Rio de Janeiro. He had smallpox! "I have no idea how I caught it," he said. "It is in the air of Rio and the deaths, especially among the negroes are numerous, daily." The young man apologized anxiously to his family because the hospital had "cost nearly two hundred dollars." He tried to reassure his mother. "My face will not be marked at all, I think, although at present it presents the appearance of an immense ripe raspberry — being covered with red tubercles which will not be absorbed, the doctor says, for some weeks to come. My scabs are drying or dry and in four days I expect the last of them will have fallen off." In this condition, he was dismissed from the hospital, where he had been only eighteen days. "Now that I know that I am no longer an object of infection, I am perfectly cynical as to my appearance," James said.

Professor and Mrs. Agassiz had been on an excursion to the Emperor's summer palace when William James was taken ill. They knew nothing of the state of affairs until they returned, and then Mrs. Agassiz spoke of Hunnewell as "one of the best-hearted fellows" she had ever known. "His devotion to James at the time of his smallpox when we were all out of town and he nursed him, sleeping in the room with him and watching him without a thought of his own danger, was worthy of all praise."

Agassiz, who had that medical degree his parents had forced him to acquire, said that James had varioloid, a mild, modified form of smallpox. No one else in the expedition caught it. But poor William did not feel that his illness was in any way mild. His eyes were affected and he was badly frightened lest he should lose his sight. Homesick, weak from illness, William James decided to turn back and forget about natural science and the Amazon.

"I am now certain that my forte is not to go on exploring expeditions," James wrote. "I have no inward spur, goading me forward. . . . I am convinced now, for good, that I am cut out for a spectator rather than an active life. I became convinced some time

ago of the notion that I was one of the very lightest of feather-
weights. Now why not be reconciled with my deficiences. By accepting them, your actions cease to be at cross purposes with your
faculties and you are much nearer peace of mind . . . I had mis-
givings to this effect before starting out but I was pulled with enthusiasm and the romance of the thing seemed so great that I
stifled them . . ."

Agassiz was most understanding. It was a blow to him "to lose a
pair of hands," as James put it, but he told the boy that he could take
the next steamer home if he wanted to. Finding that James was anxious about the money he had spent, given by "dear old Aunt Kate,"
Agassiz said he would find funds to help him out. "Agassiz is an
extraordinary being," said James. He had "with all his foibles, a
greater personal fascination than anyone I know."

By the 28 of July, William James was aboard ship, bound not for
Boston but for the Amazon after all. An occulist had assured him
that the "neuralgia-like pains behind" his eyes would "soon cease,"
his strength had returned and he was not even seasick. "Now that the
real enjoyment of the expedition is beginning and I am tasting the
sweets of these lovely forests here (at the mouth of the Singu River)
I find it impossible to tear myself away and this morning I told Prof
I would see the Amazon trip through at any rate. . . . I see moreover a chance of learning a good deal of zoology and botany . . .
and I am getting a pretty valuable training from the Professor who
pitches into me right and left and wakes me up to a good many im-
perfections. This morning he told me I was 'totally uneducated.' He
has done me much good already and will evidently do me more before I have got through with him."

The collections made in Rio "amounted to upwards of fifty barrels
and cases," which were dispatched direct to Cambridge. It was almost
the end of July when a "dirty, crowded little steamer" took the
Agassizs northward along the coast of Brazil to Pará, to begin their
ascent of the Amazon. By August 9, "Mr. Pimenta Buena, Director
of the Brazilian line of steamers from Pará to Tabatinga," had a boat,
the *Icamiaba*, ready for the expedition. "The steamer is provided

with everything, fuel, services, food (the table is excellent) for our whole company and no other passengers allowed." The dirty little steamer had made Elizabeth the more grateful for this private yacht, as she called it. All expenses were paid by the Brazilian steamship line and Lizzie described her "good-sized state-room, with dressing-room and bath-room adjoining." She particularly luxuriated in the "great deep bath tub set in the floor," but the deck "proved the pleasantest sleeping place" and they slung their hammocks there. Agassiz gave his "Leezie" a grass hammock woven by natives, rose-colored, with white gauze curtains. It was "gorgageous" she said, using a word coined in her girlhood.

"I must say my slumbers were a good deal disturbed by the wonder of my situation," she confessed. "I lay in my hammock looking up at the beautiful constellations, for the sky at night is wonderful here, and I said to myself, 'Can this really be Lizzie Cary floating up the Amazon with a parcel of Naturalists or shall I come to myself and find it all a dream?' "

CHAPTER SIXTEEN

Brazil Is Not Boston

THE natives, when civilized, are dreary and not beautiful as in their native state." Such was Elizabeth Agassiz's verdict after visiting towns along the Amazon and after living in a native village on a lake a day's journey from the river port of Villa Bella. "Anything more dreary and barren than the civilized homes" she could not imagine. They were all alike. "You are shown into a brick-floored parlor where a cane sofa and four cane chairs, two at each end, are placed in exactly the same position in every Brazilian home of whatever class. The slovenly, broken-down senhora and her children come in. The senhora is kind and cordial," but if the guests are unexpected she would be found with uncombed hair, her clothes far from clean. "The first evidence of her hospitality is to ask you if you will change your gown. If you say 'yes' she gets you a gown of her own, usually muslin, to put on." But the dresses hardly came up to Mrs. Agassiz's standards of cleanliness and she "learned always to say 'no.' " [1]

Elizabeth reached Amazonian Indians in their "native state" by dugout canoe along "a very narrow channel leading into the forest." The overland journeys by muleback, for which she had prepared herself by sliding down Corcovado on a tall horse, did not materialize. Boats were the means of transportation. The Agassizs and

Burkhardt traveled in a dugout which had a "tiny cabin at one end, about three feet high and six feet long, roofed in wood." They had aboard "a small sheep, a pig, several chickens and a turkey — a number of kegs and barrels for collecting and in the little cabin" the luggage "compressed to the smallest compass, besides our hammocks, India rubber blankets, etc." A second, smaller canoe carried Ren Thayer and Major Coutinho, a Brazilian engineer sent by the Rio government to be Agassiz's guide.

This "excursion," as Elizabeth called it, was "wonderfully successful." Agassiz collected 112 different kinds of fishes, "about two-thirds of which were absolutely new to science." It was "a week of hard work" for him because they had "as much as they could do to get the specimens cared for and the new ones drawn and colored as they came in. But the more work, the better Agassiz was pleased."

At a lake village, Mrs. Agassiz lived in the home of a native girl called Esperança who met with full approval — for though a converted Christian, she was in her "native state," as to her house and her way of living. Esperança was "always busy at some household task or other — grinding mandioca, drying farinha, packing tobacco, cooking or sweeping." The mud floor of her "cottage," as Lizzie called it, was "swept and tidied and there was an air of decency and respectability about everything." Esperança, "though not pretty, had a delicious voice and a sort of innocent, child-like way of speaking that was very taking. When tidied up for the evening with her dark skirt, her white chemise falling off her tawny shoulders and a rose in her pretty hair, she looked quite attractive." She usually smoked a pipe, however, and Lizzie thought this "injured the general effect."

When the Agassiz party arrived at the village, the Indian women and children "clustered around the white lady." They "touched, though not in a rude way, my dress, the net on my hair, my rings and watch chain," Lizzie said. She could not understand what they said to each other but her clothes must have puzzled them. She wore a traveling dress, made for her in Boston, with a tremendously wide skirt "quite long enough for riding" and which, when "tied up" to a daring inch or so above the ankle, made "a very good walking dress."

While visiting in Esperança's village, Mrs. Agassiz saw a trader arrive and begin to hand out gifts, so she joined the group of native women. The Indian women seemed "impassive," but when she sat down with them they smiled. The crowd increased and "as things were passed rapidly around the circle, I was taken for one of the Indians and received a very gay gown for my share," Lizzie wrote. And now there were not only smiles but "a general shout of laughter."

Elizabeth Agassiz looked like a Bostonian wherever she went, and it was no wonder that the Indians shouted with laughter when she was taken for a squaw. Eventually, she bought some calico and had it made up into dresses more suitable for the steaming Amazon climate. She never went so far as to wear muslin or the modern-sounding off-shoulder chemise, but whatever she did, the Indian women loved her. They brought her flowers and "little vases they make from gourds" and when she tried to pay them they said "No, it is a gift." She thought that they were just naturally generous, unaware of her own great gift of friendliness for all sorts of people.

One evening, Major Coutinho, the Brazilian engineer, persuaded the natives to dance. They were shy at first, but finally Esperança and her neighbor Michelina "stood up with two of the boatmen" who had brought the Agassizs to the lake. "The music was monotonous but plaintive — ringing the changes on a few simple but harmonious chords. The dance was so languid it hardly deserved the name. They glided over the floor like moving statues, hardly stirring their feet from the ground." After the two native couples had finished, they insisted that the Branca — the white lady should "show them a dance of her own land." So Mrs. Agassiz and Ren Thayer "waltzed for them to their infinite delight and amusement . . .

"After we had taken several rounds and sat down, Esperança came and knelt by me and begged me in such a sweet persuasive way to dance again that I could not resist her, though I must say it was rather warm work." Now Lizzie understood why native dances were so "languid." Although Esperança and her friends let themselves go considerably more as the evening progressed, they never approximated anything so strenuous as a waltz. Ren Thayer danced with the native girls, trying to learn their steps and entering "into the spirit of the thing" till they "shouted with laughter and satisfaction."

Lizzie went to her hammock, sharing her room in Esperança's house with "a fat hen, peacefully slumbering with all her brood and the cockerel beside her" and a small dog who had gotten under the mosquito net which covered the pink hammock. Outside, the dance "kept up till quite late," and she "heard the plaintive chords of the guitar mingling with the melancholy notes of a sort of whippoorwill who sings in the woods all night."

Mrs. Agassiz enjoyed this excursion as she did every new experience, but she was glad to get back to the *Icamiaba* with its luxurious sunken bathtub. She could never quite get used to having women and children stand around and gaze at her while she tried to bathe and dress. She understood that the Indians wanted to see if she were really white all over, and she was sympathetic though embarrassed when her suggestions that she be left in peace were not followed.

On up the Amazon steamed the *Icamiaba,* stopping while the crew went ashore to cut wood for the boilers, tying up at night to avoid running on snags and sand bars. There was always a breeze at night but the days were hot and humid. "Mrs. Agassiz is one of the best women I ever met," wrote William James. "Her good temper never changes and she is so curious and wide awake and interested in all we see, and so ever busy and spotless, that she is like an angel in the boat." James himself was still not well and a prey to gloomy moods.

When the boat was tied up for any length of time, Ren Thayer was usually detailed to go with Mrs. Agassiz "for a ramble" on shore. "Walking is a peculiar and seemingly at first a rather alarming process," she wrote, "for the ground is overflowed in a great part, sometimes far up into the forest." Perhaps because of her rather restricted girlhood among the Perkinses of Temple Place with their sumptuous carriages, walking seemed a symbol of independence to Lizzie and she dearly loved it. They were about thirty days' journey up the Amazon and tied at an obscure boat-landing, when she and Ren took one of their "rambles." They "made a friendly call" at an Indian palm-leaf hut, where they were "cordially invited into the great porch which is their receiving room," she said. "After a little visit, we were leaving but an Indian who was standing at the door invited us to go farther to his house. . . . We gladly accepted for the path he pointed out looked fascinating in the extreme, leading into the very depths of the woods."

Elizabeth's faith in human nature was always without reservation. She referred to the great Amazonian Rain Forest as "the woods" as she might have spoken of a picnic spot near Cambridge. Using floating logs as bridges, "We passed over a number of forest pools," she said, "where I felt it extremely likely I should tumble in. However, our guide, seeing that I was rather unsteady, cut a pole and then I went along quite bravely. After a time though, I came to one where the water was so deep I could not touch bottom with my pole and then the log was decidely rocking and unsteady. Here my courage broke down and I told my friendly Indian in my imperfect Portuguese that I could go no farther — I was afraid. 'Nao mia Branca' ('No, my White'), he said reassuringly, 'Nao temmedo' ('Don't be afraid'). Then, as if a thought struck him . . . 'Wait a little. Manteira — canoa.' He went a few steps up the creek, unmoored his boat and put us across to the other side, just beyond his picturesque house."

After "making a little visit and being shown his wife and children" Mrs. Agassiz and Ren Thayer "entered the boat again," thinking to be ferried back across the deep pool. Instead, the Indian "headed his canoe up the creek" which was "a winding water path through the depths of this marvelous forest, closely overhung with gigantic palms, black with shadows, except where a gleam from the glowing sunset outside penetrated the gloom." Still feeling perfect confidence in the Indian, Lizzie had no thought except for the beauty around her. "Through a circuitous route" the Indian paddled "into the broad river and we found ourselves within a few rods of the landing where our steamer lay. Our Indian Waterman left us at the stair with a very cordial farewell. I am sure by his face that he enjoyed our delight at the surprise he had prepared for us."

On August 26, the *Icamiaba* reached the river town of Santarém, about 350 miles from the coast. Here the "black waters of the Rio

Tapajos" joined the "yellow waters of the Amazon, coming in from a southerly direction." Agassiz told Dexter, Talisman and William James that "a collection of fishes from the Tapajos would be exceptionally interesting" and they knew when to take a hint, so they "accordingly left the steamer" in a native canoe with "a barrel of biscuit and some kegs and cans full of alcohol to put the fishes in." William James was morose about leaving the comfortable boat and about the fact that they were to have "only eight days for this excursion and to rejoin the expedition which would be stopping over at Manáos" more than 300 miles farther up the river.

On September 5 the Agassizs arrived at Manáos, found a house that Major Coutinho had provided for them, and settled down to make this town their headquarters until September 12. "There is little to be said for the town of Manáos. It consists of a small collection of houses, half of which seem going to decay," Mrs. Agassiz wrote. She amused herself by translating some of the signs in Portuguese which were nailed over the doors of "tumble-down buildings": " 'Treasury,' 'Post Office,' 'Legislative Hall' and 'President's Mansion.' " Manáos was just beyond the point where the Rio Negro joins the Amazon and where the Amazon itself becomes the Solimões or Upper Amazon. It was a water crossroads but with little traffic.

Dexter, Talisman and James reached Manáos on September 9 "with considerable collections." "They seemed to have enjoyed their excursion greatly," said Mrs. Agassiz, and this way of putting it would have caused William James to hoot with sardonic laughter. He described his own appearance in a letter to his sister. "What would the blessed mother say if she saw me now, with nothing on but shirt and trousers, both in a frightfully dilapidated state, with shaven head and fuzzy chin and hacked-up hands and sunburnt feet and cheeks bloated with the remains of my smallpox."

The steamer *Icamiaba* left the Agassiz party at Manáos and returned down the Amazon. She had too much draught for the Solimões, and the Thayer Expedition would have to take the regular river steamer — slow, stopping at scheduled stops only, instead of putting in wherever Agassiz wanted to cast a net. But the river steamer proved "comfortable, almost empty of other passengers." At

Tabatinga, the border town, this ship's cargo would be transferred
to a Peruvian steamer, and Agassiz's party could all go aboard the
Peruvian boat if they chose. Agassiz longed to reach "at least the first
spur of the Andes" and to "look for vestiges of glaciers" there.
Whether to go on into Peru was discussed for hours.

They were at Tefé,² about four days' journey from the border,
discussing what to do, when "a most unexpected advisor appeared in
the midst of our council of war," Lizzie said. Someone brought in
"a small fish with its mouth full of young ones." It was called the
acará and Agassiz "dedicated it to the Emperor" — a touching tribute,
surely. The chance to observe its strange spawning habits was "good
fortune unheard-of," and they decided to continue this study instead of going into Peru.

The Upper Amazon had proved disappointing when the expedition reached Tabatinga, their turning-point, on September 19. "The
element of human life and habitation was utterly wanting," Mrs.
Agassiz said — and this meant more to her than to any of the naturalists. "Great flocks of birds rose from the shore, turtles pop their
black noses out of the water, alligators show themselves occasionally
and sometimes a troop of brown capivari scuttles up the bank . . ."
but this was all. Tabatinga, "dignified by the name of a military station" had only "two or three small guns mounted on the bank, the
mud house behind them" being a barracks in front of which "half
a dozen soldiers were lounging."

A fish carrying its progeny in its mouth may have been the main
reason for turning back, but there were others. The Brazilian border
conflict was increasing. All up and down the Amazon, the Agassizs
had seen "recruiting." This took the form of raids upon the native
villages, with all the able men being borne away, manacled, to fight
a war which they did not in the least understand. Women were left
alone to fend for themselves and their children and more and more
often only women were to be seen in canoes on the river. The Amazon might not be such a friendly place as time went on and the
steamers and men so generously placed at Agassiz's disposal would
be needed for the conflict.

The dropping of the water in the river was another hazard. Already, a great deal of water had run off and the steamers were in danger of being grounded. Much as Agassiz enjoyed his expedition, he did not care to stay on the Amazon another year, waiting for high water. As usual, he had underestimated the size of the Western Hemisphere while poring over maps. Distances were too great and time too short always, for a man whose longing to explore was insatiable. The age of the airplane would have rejoiced his soul. A third consideration in leaving Peru unexplored was the fact that Elizabeth Agassiz's brother, Tom Cary, would soon be on the La Plata River in Uruguay, waiting for the Expedition.

Agassiz left his French recruit, Mr. Bourget, at Tabatinga "to pass a month in making collections in that region."

As they passed the Ica River, on their return trip down the Amazon, "Mr. James and Mr. Talisman were left to explore." This was William James's second journey. Dropping on down the Amazon, the party made Tefé their headquarters for more than a month, where "the fish that carries its young in its mouth" grew more "marvelous" every day. They left Tefé on October 23 and steamed down to Manáos, which became the base of operations until the end of December. During the long stopover at Manáos, William James made his third expedition — this time entirely on his own.

"The Prof" had been "working himself out and is thin and nervous," James said. "That good woman, Mrs. Agassiz, is perfectly well. The boys, poor fellows, have all had their legs in awful condition from a kind of mite . . . which gets under the skin and makes dreadful sores. You can't walk in the woods without getting them on you and poor Hunney is ulcerated very badly." William himself had been "laid up with sore legs which were just getting well." His miseries were "produced in the first place by pium bites and then aggravated . . . by our almost exclusively oily and animal diet and the heat. Strange to say, with the exception of wheat flour imported from the U. S. and rice, you can hardly get a vegetable out here," he wrote. "The 'tropical fruits' are the greatest humbug you ever dreamt of. The only fruits we get here are plantains, which you get very sick of, and pineapples. The latter to be sure are splendid, juicy as oranges, as big as a beaver hat, and so sweet you would never think of putting sugar on them."

James worried about his prospective journey, but when he went around to ask questions of Agassiz he got a very short answer. Eventually, he was proud of having been entirely on his own; but before he set out he was most melancholy. He went to say good-by to Mrs. Agassiz — and her efforts to cheer him up failed.

"The excellent but infatuated woman *will* look at everything in such an unnatural, romantic light, that she don't [*sic*] seem to walk upon the solid earth," James complained. "She seems to fancy we are figures walking about in strange costumes on a stage with appropriate scenery, *et pas plus difficile que ça*. She said to me (all turbid and angry with the thought of going again to the mosquitoes and piums of the cursed Solimões to whom I flattered myself I had bid an eternal adieu) in the most enthusiastic manner, 'Well James, you will have a *very* nice time, won't you. I envy you.' Oh silly woman!"

James then went "to the photographic establishment and was cautiously admitted by Hunnewell with his black hands." Hunnewell had studied not only photography but developing and printing in Rio. He had rigged up a sort of studio and dark room for himself and was photographing native types. James went into the studio and "found Prof engaged in cajoling 3 mocas [girls] whom he called pure Indian but who I thought, and as afterward appeared, had white blood. They were very nicely dressed in white muslin and jewelry and flowers in their hair and an excellent smell of pripioca. Apparently refined, at all events not sluttish, they consented to the utmost liberties being taken with them and two, without much trouble, were induced to strip and pose naked. While we were there, Senhor Tavanes Bastos (a Brazilian from Manáos) came in and asked me mockingly, if I were attached to the Bureau of Anthropology." [3]

Apparently William James was not able to think of a mocking retort. He had come to see if Agassiz would let Hunnewell go with him on his expedition, but it was plain that the Professor had other work in mind for Hunnewell, and James went sadly away. He spent his last evening talking with Dexter and Hunnewell on the porch of their cottage. The young men were all homesick, and talked "about what we would do on arriving in New York, namely go on a regular bust, and how we should get from New York to Boston, I disliking cars [trains] but preferring to get home towards evening, etc. For one moment, we got to discussing it as if it were really to be done immediately. Blissful illusion!" James slept not at all that night and started off at 2 A.M. next day.

The party consisted of Senhor Urbano, chief guide "with more black than Indian blood, Senhor 'M.'; four Indians" — and James. "One old Indian, of the regular, respectable type, civilized but still a perfect Indian," had the helm; two others "excellent stout fellows and perfect gentlemen, paddled while a fourth lay sleeping on the . . . slatted bottom of the canoe."

When James first encountered Senhor Urbano, he called him "an old darky," said that he seemed to be about sixty years old and was dressed "in a shiny suit of black alpaca." James was in doubt as to whether this was his "host" or "only" his "pilot," but understood that Urbano was to take him three days' journey up the Solimões to his home and that he had a "companion as brown as an Indian but from his features appearing to be a Branco." This was "Senhor M." whose full name seems to have been too long for James to write on the pages of his journal. "The old darky seems stiff and queer" James said, apparently unaware that his own attitude had anything to do with it. But as the party set out alone before dawn James noted a happy change which augured well for the journey.

"Both my companions seemed to have thrown off their constraint of manner with their shoes and coats and we were soon chatting, laughing and joking like old friends. A weight was taken off my mind." James threw off his superior attitude and immediately accepted Senhor Urbano for the delightful traveling companion that he proved to be. "The Senhor U. is a most humorous and intelligent old blade," he said. "He almost immediately proposed to me to go home in January and to return in May to Pará and thence to Manáos with a large cargo of American goods, cloth, knives, etc. There he would await me and we would go together to his 'plantation' . . . In December, I should go home again with a great cargo of India rubber which I could sell at much profit.

"While we were chatting, the solemn sad dawn began to break and to show the woods standing as if in a picture. Surely no such epithet as 'jocund moon' could ever have suggested itself to a dweller in these regions. The mysterious stirring of the fresh, cool, perfumed air, while the sky begins to lighten and redden and all the noises of the night cease as the day birds begin their singing and crying, all make these early hours the most delicious of the day. Down we went swiftly, the men rowing steadily with their big paddles along the left bank of the brown river. About sunrise, we met a large montaria . . . manned entirely by Indian women, seven in all."

Both boats stopped so that the travelers could have a chat. "The patroness" of the women's canoe, "a little old lady," sat at the mouth of the covered cabin, smoking her pipe. They spoke Portuguese, and James could not quite make out whether the men had all been taken for the war or were in hiding. "I marvelled . . . at the quiet, urbane, polite tone of the conversation between my friends and the old lady," he said. "How can a population with such habits and aims care for a war or wish to enter an army?" His European education had not prepared him for the people he met on this journey alone among them on the tributaries of the Amazon. "Is it race or is it circumstances that make these people so refined and well bred," he wondered. "No gentleman of Europe has better manners and yet these are peasants."

Obedient to Agassiz's requirements, William James caught all the different kinds of fish he could find and plopped them into his barrels of preserving alcohol, but not a word of this did he write in his journal. Instead, he described a scene he would have liked to paint, "two enormous silvery trees," driftwood which had caught on a sand bar. "The river, going down, had left them high and dry. No, not exactly dry, for a deep pool had been excavated beneath them by the current which was now filled with green, stagnant water and covered with minute flies. Oh to be a big painter for here was a big subject. Nothing could be more simple, plain beach, the red west, the giant trunks with their crooked crowns and roots. . . ." If James could have painted it, he might have anticipated a whole future generation of modern artists.

But with the comment that the mosquitoes "began to sing like the great organ of Boston" James made no more entries in his diary until he arrived at the home of Senhor Urbano, and then he summed up his whole experience in terms of human relationships. "I now feel perfectly domesticated in this place with these people," he said. "Never were there a more decent, worthy set of gentry. Old Urbano, especially, by his native refinement and purity, is fit to be the friend of any man who ever lived, however elevated his birth or gifts. There is not a bit of our damned Anglo-Saxon brutality and vulgarity either in masters or servants. I am always reminded, when the neighbors come in to visit Urbano, of our family and the Tweedy family in Newport. Urbano and his gossips talk with just as much beauty and harmony, or perhaps a good deal more, than Tweedy and Father did, in an easy, slow tone, as if all eternity were before them." It might be said that William James, the future Professor of Psychology at Harvard, got his real education not only with Agassiz but while on Agassiz's errands on the Upper Amazon.

Back at Manáos, "Agassiz is generally at work at six in the morning and does not stop except for breakfast, until four in the afternoon when we dine," Lizzie was writing. "He is very well" but his "great success brings with it great fatigue because all the new things must be taken care of." And then, while the party was still at Manáos, there came a disaster, from Agassiz's point of view, but a blessing in disguise according to his wife. They ran out of preserving alcohol and Agassiz was forced to stop work. More had been ordered but the river steamer which was supposed to bring it was late. "I don't want Agassiz to see any more alcohol," said Lizzie, as though speaking of an intemperate husband — as indeed he was where work was concerned. Off they went on a few real pleasure trips.

Under Major Coutinho's direction, they set out at six one morning, "up a winding river." Landing at a "rocky causeway," they took a path through "the trees which came out on what I must call woodland bathing rooms, for I know of no other name for them," Lizzie said. "They are deep pools through which the water rushes so fast as to give them a delicious freshness and are separated from each other by the leafy screens made by the trees. I took the upper one which looked the most lovely and romantic and the gentlemen went below.

"I have never felt so much like a goddess in my life," Lizzie declared as she stripped and plunged into the pool. "I think Diana and her nymphs must have bathed in just such places." And Lizzie was not without her own nymphs, for some Brazilian ladies from Manáos were with her. Brazil was not Boston — she had come a long way from home. "While we were bathing, the boatmen were lighting a fire and boiling coffee so when we came out from our respective grottoes we each had a hot cup waiting for us."

Another excursion puzzled the carefully brought-up Lizzie. They went to a Brazilian country place which was different from any other she had ever seen. "The establishment consisted of several little, distinct houses standing around a large open cleared space." The space was for dancing. There was "one large open room with a very prettily finished palm leaf roof and benches all around it. This they called the reception room and the Senhora told me that the brancos (white men) often came from Manáos and the vicinity to dance here and spend the night."

It was an Indian "Senhora" who showed Mrs. Agassiz around, and Lizzie asked politely after the lady's husband and her daughter's husband — just to make conversation. "Oh, I am not married," said the young girl — and she pointed out her two children, "little fair-haired people many shades lighter than their mother." Somewhat shaken, Lizzie nevertheless pursued her questions in her best phrasebook Portuguese: And where then was the father of the young Senhora?

The elder Indian Senhora replied, "She has no father — 'E fillia da fortuna.' " ("She is the daughter of chance.")

The next day, the still bewildered Mrs. Agassiz asked more questions. There had been a "ball" the night before, and gradually it dawned upon her that white men from Manáos met pretty Indian girls at the "reception" house; that they chose one to dance with in the great circular dancing floor; and that each spent the night in one of the little houses around the edge, with the girl of his choice.

Lizzie asked a "half-breed girl" if the little boy she was caressing was hers, and the girl said it was. Still unconvinced as to the exact character of last night's "ball," and having slept through it soundly, Mrs. Agassiz thought the girl might be a fellow guest, and asked if the boy's father "was here."

" 'Who knows!' " the girl replied. " 'He was just a bird of passage.' " She said she had another child by another unknown father.

"This is an apparent ignorance of morality which in its unconsciousness really seems almost like innocence," said Mrs. Agassiz, more puzzled and bewildered than ever before in her life. The Senhora proprietress and her daughter were "well to do in the world, their house neat as could be, they had a number of servants and were in every way prosperous." And the Indian girls, being well paid, eventually found Indian husbands and went off with them, taking their halfbreed children along, to lead their natural forest lives as wealthy and respected village ladies. "I don't pretend to account for these things," said Lizzie. "I only tell you what I see." And in concluding her letter to her mother, she added that the condition of morals in Brazil was "beyond belief." There were things she couldn't even write, she said — she would have to tell her mother when she got home.

Everyone, with the possible exception of Agassiz, was a little homesick by now. "I think I appreciate more than I ever did before the marked passage of the seasons with us," Lizzie said. "In this unchanging green world, which never alters from century to century except by being a little more or less dank, a little or more less hot, I think with gratitude of winter and spring, summer and autumn. In the psalm of praise when all the earth is called to praise the Lord, the verse, 'snow and vapors, stormy winds fulfilling his word,' seems to have special significance here. The rigors of our climate are remembered with affection, in this continual vapor bath; for really you cannot move hand or foot without being drenched with perspiration."

William James was feeling much the same way: "I have often longed for a good black, sour, sleety day in Washington street. O the bliss of standing on such a day, half way between Roxbury and

Boston, having all the horse-cars pass you, full," he said. But James was to go on one more expedition.

A tiger came "within 30 paces" of James's mosquito net and roared. James confessed he felt "some skeert." Tigers kept him awake most of the night "by roaring, far and near," but no man-eater tried to snatch the future Harvard professor.

The "president" of the province now arrived at the "establishment," the nature of which Mrs. Agassiz had begun to understand. He was supervising the recruiting, by force, of Indians in the neighborhood but there was a great feast in his honor to which Indians came, bearing gifts. After the banquet for distinguished guests, including the Agassizs, the "president" suggested a row on the lake and they all set out, "the gentlemen preferring to row themselves." They left their "primitive dining room to the Indian guests," most of whom would find themselves in the army when the feasting ended.

The lake was like glass and "we did not go very far," Lizzie said — the "amateur boatmen found the evening warm." They stopped to shoot at a white heron and a flock of parroquets but, to her relief, they missed. And now, as they turned back, they were met by a "two-masted canoe, dressed with flags" in honor of the "president." There was music on board, and there were two or three men, but the boat was "manned by women, twelve or fifteen in number, like genuine Amazons. . . . As the canoe drew nearer, with music playing and flags flying," the lake, dyed purple in the sunset, gave back the picture like a mirror. "Every tawny figure at the oars, every flutter of the crimson and blue steamers, every fold of the green and yellow national flag at the prow, was as distinct below the surface as above."

The two canoes "joined company," a guitar was passed between them while "Brazilian and Indian songs followed each other."

As Mrs. Agassiz floated into the sunset, she saw young William James setting out alone in a canoe for a final early-morning collecting trip. They waved to each other, the young man going east to meet the morning and the woman carried westward. Years later they would both remember.

CHAPTER SEVENTEEN
The Agassiz Children

THEY were grown up, married and on their own. She was not even their mother, really — but to Elizabeth Agassiz, Alex, Ida and Pauline would always be her children. The only time when she was really unhappy on the Amazon was when three months went by without hearing from them. Elizabeth had no favorite, but naturally enough the one most in need of her occupied her thoughts the most. At first, this was Ida.

For two years Ida and her convalescent husband, Major Henry Lee Higginson, lived on Quincy Street. In January, 1865, Henry took a job which could not have been more unsuitable for him if it had been devised by his worst enemy. He went to the Ohio oil fields to develop wells in the Duck Creek district. With loving confidence, Ida joined him and "was pleased with the shanty" she had to live in, "pleased with her saddle horse and with life in the open, pleased too with her cows and chickens." Ida and "Hal" were much in love.

Higginson got "signs of oil" in "eight out of nine wells" but labor was expensive and Henry was still not good at figures. His company wrote him to send no more drafts on their account but in July he sent another draft and was fired.[1]

During the long evenings in the "shanty" Henry read "Political

Economy" aloud to Ida while she drew pictures. Her landscape, "Ohio Log-Cabin," was excellent. They had "hot claret and water" and talked late about plans for their future. First they must make their fortune in oil of course, and then they would devote themselves to making the world a better place. The oil fortune failed to materialize, but seven months of planning were not to be scrapped for such a mere detail as lack of money.

Henry Higginson wanted to prove that in the War Between the States it was not might but right that won. He was sure he could do it by "demonstrating that Free negro labor could be profitably and pleasantly employed." Back to Quincy Street went the Higginsons, and Hal gathered his old friends together. Two of them decided to join him in a new and wonderful scheme.

Channing Clapp was one of these friends. He had been a classmate of Higginson's at Harvard; he was Captain Clapp, serving with Higginson at Hilton Head, Beaufort, and in the Virginia campaigns of 1862 and 1863. The other young man was Charles F. Morse, who had been Colonel Morse, marching with Sherman's troops through Georgia. As the three young veterans talked of old times, of political economy and the future of their country, Higginson's idea was accepted and expanded. They would go South and show the Southerners how a plantation should be run, with free Negro labor. Both of Higginson's friends were Boston men whose families had money to back them in their venture. Hal persuaded relatives and his reluctant banker father to raise money for his share.

These three young men were the opposite of the typical Yankee carpetbagger with his much-publicized coming to defraud a beaten enemy. And they were the ones who got as thoroughly rooked as any Southerner ever did. An elderly bachelor by the name of Roberts sold them a plantation in Bryan County, Georgia, about thirty miles south of Savannah. "Cottonham," it was called. The house was in bad repair, and the "beds and mattresses" had to be burned to get rid of inhabitants not included in the bill of sale. Pigs squealed and fought under the house all night, coming in through broken lattices and sheltering in the space between the bare earth and the first floor. The house stood in an eight-acre, fenced yard with a few houses for slaves and it was surrounded by handsome live oaks — the only feature to commend it.

There was also a stable in good repair, a cotton gin, grist mill, and barns. There were "one thousand acres under cultivation" and the enthusiastic Higginson wrote home that he "thought there might be seven thousand acres in all." Channing Clapp was considered the best negotiator so he was given the power to "trade" for the property and paid twenty-seven thousand dollars. Too late it was discovered that Mr. Roberts had title to only twenty-five hundred acres out of the "five to seven thousand" that he sold. Lawsuits availed little, and eventually Cottonham, when it was sold again, brought five thousand dollars.

Cottonham was fifteen miles from Ways Station on the railroad — except that there was no railroad, Sherman's army having torn it up. A water route lay through Ossabaw Sound, up the Ogeechee River and then up Red Bud Creek to "about a quarter of a mile from the big house." The cotton on which Higginson and his friends planned to make a profit would have to go to market by water.

Higginson went to Savannah, where he bought a discarded army ambulance and "half a dozen mules." He advertised for workers to plant cotton. Then he went North and chartered a schooner to bring down furniture, "for there was nothing in the house fit to touch." The last resident had "lived like a pig." Henry also let his father know that he would now need ninety-five hundred dollars.

At Christmas, Henry went home; and in February, 1866, he bought Ida to Cottonham. They came to Savannah by boat, and then drove the thirty miles or so by mule wagon; and Ida was thrilled to see "the branches of the Cherokee rose already green." She still had the bleak New England February in her mind's eye, and she admired "pretty little yellow flowers in the swamp" along the road. It was after dark when they arrived at the plantation, and "Mr. Morse and Channing Clapp came out with a light to the gate." Great trees loomed against the sky. The bobbing lanterns shed only a small circle of light as Ida and Hal walked forward into a new adventure.

The house was "much more low and homelike" than Ida had imagined — she longed for no high-pillared mansion. There was a fire
on the hearth and the rooms looked clean but bare. "Old Matilda"
greeted the young mistress, "grinning and curtsying at every turn."
There was a girl, Mary, doing the same and Mrs. Higginson was
pleased. But Ida, endowed with a German household background
and further instructed under Elizabeth Agassiz's New England
standards, had no idea of how to approach her Negro servants. "Failure to manage [her household] well and quietly" nearly broke her
heart.

The men soon had more serious trouble. Their proposition was
that a field hand should sign a contract to work for a year. Each
man was to receive one acre of land to cultivate for himself, plus
"a good house." A man and his wife would get two acres and "sufficient time to cultivate their plot for themselves," to raise corn and
potatoes, keep pigs and chickens." Fuel was free for the cutting. In
wages, each man and wife would earn "about $370 a year." A store
was to be kept on the place, selling "calico, flannel, shoes, etc. As
well as such staples as flour and molasses." Henry Higginson was to
run the store and to help Ida with a school for Negro children, because he was still not strong enough to work in the fields as the other
young men planned to do.

Higginson was a man of imagination and of heart. He visualized
a happy community where Negroes would earn and save money,
soon being able to own a house and land. But he had not enough
imagination to put himself in the place of another human being who
was without schooling and had experience of nothing save the total
dependence of a slave. Choosing an elderly Negro by the name of
January to work beside him, painting the shack that was to be the
store, Henry began to get a glimmering of a former slave's point of
view as January talked with him. The Negroes were afraid to sign
a year's contract, January said. They were afraid that at the end of
the year they would find themselves slaves again.

Major Higginson gained experience but not enough insight while
tending store. The Negroes were dressed in rags and they were
"much pleased" when they saw the goods that lined the shelves.

They "got their wages whenever they asked for them" and went joyfully to the store to spend the money. The conception of debt was beyond them, and the idea of saving money entirely outside their comprehension. "I find that man and wife spend their wages separately, not paying each other's debts at the store nor sharing each other's money or food," he observed. "Pete, him pay for him, one, and me, me pay for me, one," a woman told him. It was "strange and bad," Higginson said, not stopping to think that these people had never before known family life with economic responsibility.

When it came to selling groceries, Major Higginson was really exasperated. A woman would say, "Give me five cents sugar" and Higginson would "change a dollar bill." Then she would say, "Give me five cents hard bread," and then, "ten cents tobacco." So it would go, with each transaction completed separately. In vain the Major tried to "get all the things before making any change" — the customers would not have it that way, and Higginson, though no mathematician, could not quite understand how it would feel not to know the simplest sum in arithmetic.

Things went rather better in the school. Ida and her husband had fifteen scholars, which they thought a very good number. "They have understanding and quickness enough," Ida said. "They learn quickly and comprehend easily." "Morals" was another matter. Ida's cook, Matilda, referred to as "old" and therefore presumably old enough to know better, went on a spree and got herself disgracefully drunk. The following Sunday, while Major Higginson preached in the Negro church, Ida "preached a sermon in the kitchen to Jane, Mary and the old lady." Her text was "the parable of the sower," but poor Ida was not sure they understood half she said. "They know it is wrong to steal and lie but they do it continually," Ida wrote in despair.

Just before cotton planting, the field hands struck for more money. To their great surprise, they were told that they would not be allowed to stay in the houses allotted to them nor buy goods at the store unless they went to work. But they were promised an extra half-acre per family, the right to grow cotton on their own land, and extra pay for extra work. Out of the one thousand acres of cultivated land, the three young men from the North planted "400 acres of cotton," which gave them land to spare for the workers; and they were sure that their own 400 acres would raise a crop worth $32,000. It almost goes without saying that this figure was forecast by Major Higginson. Neither he nor his forebears had ever had anything to do with agriculture; he came from a long line of clergymen with now and then a not too fortunate banker for variety.

By April, the cotton was planted. Wild azaleas, red bud, honeysuckle and Cherokee roses bloomed and Ida and Hal had never before seen such lovely sights. They rode horseback together every afternoon when the heat of the day was over, exploring the trails through the wild, piney-woods acres they thought were theirs. They were as happy as two people ought to be who love each other and feel sure that the work they are doing together is good.

Henry would have been shocked and indignant if anyone had told him he was now one of the world's greatest gamblers. But so is every farmer. The cotton blossomed beautifully, but by July Henry had begun to hope for 25,000 pounds rather than the 32,000-pound yield which he had originally called a "low" estimate. And his forecast price of a dollar a pound must now be revised downward to eighty cents. For the first time, he mentioned the existence of "insects" which might attack a crop. And by early September, Henry discovered that there was no such thing as "normal" weather, for "continual rains" were "injuring the crop considerably. We found quite a lot of cotton beaten out and lying useless in the sand," he said. The "rain has cut off all our profit, I fancy."

Ida's schoolchildren were just getting over smallpox when she arrived. Then they had whooping cough and three children died. Ida sent for a doctor, "a pale, vague man who had been a Confederate Army surgeon at Fort McAllister" and who had nothing much to suggest except to give the children quinine. As spring advanced "intermittent fever" appeared. Loyal to Georgia, the Higginsons declared that there was as much at home. Intermittent fever appears to be a name for malaria, and they were probably right. But when the wells on the plantation proved shallow, the water evil-tasting,

Henry and Ida were forced to go home to Cambridge and Nahant and stay till September.

Major Higginson returned to Cottonham before Ida, and he had to write her some bad news. Instead of clearing "$5633 apiece" they were not going to pay expenses. But Ida was to remember that "the one great reason for coming here was the work of great importance for these blacks. Money is less valuable than time and thought and labor, which you have given freely." In big letters, he printed, "Do not fret about accounts." But Ida could not help it if she had her mother's streak of German common sense, and it was she who always kept the books. Yet in the end it was Ida who wanted to go on with the disastrous experiment at least one more year. "We had better not leave this place till we have been of some trifling use in some way or other," she wrote, in bitterness but with courage.

In 1866, the partners spent $20,155 to raise a crop which "may bring us $10,000." Channing Clapp gave up before Major Higginson was ready to admit failure, but, with his support withdrawn, there was nothing to do but go home. Morse hung on a little longer; but eventually the $65,000 venture was liquidated for $5000.

The idea had been good, but the time was not right nor the means sufficient. It would have pleased Ida and her husband to know that exactly seventy years later Henry Ford was to open a Community House and a school on Ways Station Road. Seventy thousand acres, including "several old plantations" became a "model community," with school, sawmill, electrical plant, agricultural experimental laboratory. There would be a roadside market where children could sell flowers and garden produce and old people could sell handcrafts. Negro students from the school would be helped to go on to college by Mr. Ford.[2]

Major Higginson confessed that he should have gone into his father's office as a clerk years ago, and he was willing to start at the bottom now, if there was still room for him. There was no question about a place for Henry. In 1867, his grandfather Lee died, leaving "an unexpectedly large bequest" to George Higginson, Henry's

father, in trust for the grandchildren. Major Henry Lee Higginson
became a partner in Lee, Higginson and Company. But Henry's
father was never noted for fortunate investments, and it began to
look as though he were running true to form when he put the Lee
money into two copper mines called the "Calumet" and the "Hecla."
This stock sold heavily in Boston, the Shaw family also being interested along with their friends and relatives. Before long it became apparent that the mines had been irresponsibly exploited, and
a good many Boston fortunes, reduced by the Civil War, threatened
to disappear altogether. This was before Alexander Agassiz set out
for Michigan.

Alex was "tied to the museum" and "sinking under the burden"
for as long as his father stayed in Brazil. The Agassizs left for Brazil
on the last day of March in 1865 and by the end of April Alex
found that museum finances were in worse shape than he had supposed. He felt guilty about taking his own small salary and began
to look for a way to make money so that he could afford to be a
scientist. He wanted to work for the museum for nothing and also
to contribute to its support. He confided all this to his friend and
former classmate, Theodore Lyman, who was now married to Mrs.
Alex Agassiz's sister.

"While in Penna, I invested for other people sufficient in land
to have quite a good interest in the oil business without having
paid any more than my time for it," Alex said. "All I want now to
be clear of the museum and stand on my own legs, is to strike oil
on one of the pieces of land, which I hope will be some time before
the year is out. I should like to be independent of the Museum because I could do so much more for it and trust this will be my
chance. By keeping a little look-out, I can perhaps get into the way
of examining land for mineral companies and if the ore fail, make
enough every year by running around a little from time to time, to
enable me to give my own salary there [at the museum] in a couple
of years."

Alexander Agassiz loved natural science with a passion equal to
his father's. His specialty was corals, and he had a plan — a dream,

rather — of visiting coral atolls in the Pacific and of finding out exactly how they had been formed. But Alex could never beg for funds from wealthy benefactors the way his father did. The boy who had hated the King of Prussia's governor in Switzerland, who had gone to market in Freiburg with a few pennies clutched tight in his fist, had grown to be a man who must have money of his own, and was determined to get it.

Alex went to Michigan during the summer of 1866. There was no Hecla copper mine then; only the Calumet, which Hurlbert, the discoverer, had exploited haphazardly, "buying a hundred teams of horses" to haul ore "thirteen miles" — spending stockholders' money without reason or overall plan. Alex took a good, careful geologist's look at the whole terrain and saw that a fabulously rich vein ran deep. He sent word to Boston and his brother-in-law, Quincy Shaw, and "a party of Boston men" bought land south of Calumet and "organized the Hecla Mining Company." Writing the story of these adventures later, Alexander Agassiz's son George said, "It must have been about this time that Agassiz succeeded in borrowing a comparatively small sum of money with which he secured the interest in these properties that formed the basis of his fortune."

After his first inspection trip to Michigan, Alex was made treasurer of the Calumet and Hecla mines. He went West again to look into management, and this time his reports were alarming. "The value of the mines, both Hecla and Calumet, are beyond the wildest dreams of copper men," he wrote to his brother-in-law, Henry Higginson, "but with the kind of management many of the mines have had, then even if the pits were full of gold, it would be of no use."

At Calumet, Alex found pits sunk with "no attempt to support the roof, timbering entirely neglected." A small rolling mill had been bought but never set up, and there was no plan for transporting rock to the mill. "Systematic deception" was the verdict Alex brought in.

Edwin J. Hurlbert [3] went to Boston with the idea of making trouble for Alexander Agassiz. He said he was "not going to have anyone telling him what to do."

"If anybody wants my place and can do better, let them have it," countered Alex. "I am not anxious to stay here and be in perpetual stew about a state of things I did not inaugurate. One thing is perfectly clear: you cannot run either Calumet or Hecla without equipment . . . and if you try any makeshifts to get out copper except by regular mining, you will swamp both mines." Years later, Alex said of his brother-in-law, Quincy Shaw, "If Quin had ever known when he was beaten we would never have pulled it off." As it was, Quincy Shaw was "pressed by creditors and loaded with lawsuits" brought by the disgruntled Hurlbert, but he had faith in Alex. He got hold of enough money somehow and told Alex to go ahead. The stockholders were heavily assessed and Alex was not able to carry his own assessment, but Quin carried it for him.

"I assure you, it is fearfully lonely up here," Alex wrote. "Not a soul to discuss things with. I hate to saddle all on my back for fear of making any mistakes and as time is too valuable to waste, we must jump faster than I like to." Alex hoped that Quin would "bring Annie and the chicks" out to Michigan. It would not cost any more for them to live there than at home and his loneliness for his wife and children was almost more than he could bear. "I shall write Annie about it, so that she may be ready to move at a moment's notice," he said — knowing that his wife was just as lonely and perfectly ready for adventure.

"The Keeweenaw Peninsula," where the mines were located on Lake Michigan, was then "more inaccessible" even in summer "than Alaska is today," wrote George Agassiz in 1913. He was "a very small boy" (five years old) in July, 1867 when his mother brought him and his brother Max, a baby barely a year old, to live at the mines. Their home was the "hotel," a log cabin with the forest rising directly behind it. Cracks between the logs were badly chinked with mud and moss so that the wind blew right through the building and the baby spent most of his time in his crib. Whenever Annie Agassiz took little Georgie walking she wore a revolver strapped to her waist. But the children, who had been considered delicate, grew strong and rosy-cheeked.

The rolling mills ordered by Hurlbert proved too light for the rock, which was unusually hard. Alex was in great distress about it, because he had advocated heavier machinery and had allowed himself to be talked into letting Hurlbert's order stand. The two ball stamps, set up at the Calumet mine in place of the rollers, were a success; but Alex had now to build a railroad to carry the ore to the lake for shipment by barge. "Railroad has not done well since I paid attention to stamp mill," he wrote. Now that the mill was running well he would give the railroad "a good start after fault-finding all around."

"One man is not enough," Alex realized. "I ought to be at mill, on railroad, and at mine, and it is utterly out of the question to drive things at the same speed." He was constantly hounded by two difficulties: lack of money, and the approach of winter, when the lake would freeze and barge transportation of ore come to an end.

They called Alexander Agassiz a hard taskmaster and a driver — and so he was, but he drove himself hardest of all. When a costly disaster happened to the railroad he did not blame the man who unintentionally caused it. "The locomotive and the track are not of one gauge; locomotive is one inch too narrow. . . . We shall have to relay one rail the whole distance from the lake and alter the axles of all our cars (which fit admirably) to the new gauge," for the locomotive was too difficult to change. "This letter is worse written than usual," Alex admitted, "but I am in such a rage that I cannot write better. And yet I don't see that Weston is to blame; there are two ways of ordering, and from the method used here, he had made a mistake in taking as the distance between his flanges the width of the track *inside* instead of outside the flanges, which makes a difference of just one inch."

One story in the development of the mines reads like something out of Western fiction. Hurlbert and his brother, having gotten nowhere with the Boston stockholders and the law courts, had returned to Michigan to see what trouble they could make for Alexander Agassiz. Water power for the mines was furnished by a dammed-up stream and behind the dam a lake had formed, overflowing part of some land not owned by the mines. Although the dam had been built for some time and no one had complained, Hurlbert filed suit against the mines for creating a public nuisance. It was not a good case and he knew it, but he gathered some malcontents around him who planned to cut the dam and then file an injunction against rebuilding it until the case could be settled.

Alex put a guard on the dam day and night but the night of June 12, 1868, was "very dark." The watchman was "either asleep or scared off" for he arrived at the mine about 5 A.M. Sunday morning "seeming out of his head, flung down his revolver and said the Irish had torn down the dam."

"John Hurlbert [4] is out of the way, having left about three days ago and confided the dirty work" to someone else, Alex learned. Meanwhile the problem was to get the dam rebuilt before 12 P.M. Sunday night when the injunction would be served. The miners had often complained because Alexander Agassiz was constantly urging them to work harder and get out more rock. But now they turned to and helped him with a will. They had nothing that could be called equipment, but they shoveled and heaved at stone and after darkness fell they worked by the light of bonfires and pitchpine torches. They built back the dam before midnight.

A great deal of water had been lost, however. "I am afraid it is a case of assessment now for Calumet unless we have rain," Alex wrote. But the supply of water "proved greater than expected" and, in August, Hecla "produced about 185 tons of ingot and Calumet about 142 tons. . . ."

Eventually, it was Quincy A. Shaw and Alexander Agassiz who steered the course which resulted in a fortune for all three Agassiz children. By 1871, the Hecla mine and the Calumet mine, the Portland and the Scott companies, were consolidated into the Calumet and Hecla Company with a capital stock of one hundred thousand shares. Shaw was president, and later, when he stepped aside, Alexander Agassiz was president. Together with their directors, they worked out control of the price of copper and of foreign markets. Lee, Higginson was the company's banker, and the name of Higginson [5] was on 4574 shares of Calumet and Hecla. Under the name of

Shaw were 14,800 shares, and for Alex, 7802. Eight hundred stockholders held among them 80,000 shares, with Elizabeth Agassiz and her family holding small blocks at one time or another.

After 1868, Alex needed to go out to Michigan only for a short time each year, to inspect, plan and to direct the men he had trained or hired from other mining companies. But it was December, 1869, before Hecla paid its first dividend; and it was six months later when Calumet also declared a five dollar dividend. Alex would one day be able to afford a yacht especially designed for scientific exploration. He would see to the completion of the huge natural history museum of his father's dreams. But meanwhile, in 1865, he was still not able to afford "pure science," and he wished his father and his "Ma" would come back from Brazil, take the management of the museum off his shoulders — and let him see what he could do for himself.

CHAPTER EIGHTEEN
Mrs. Agassiz "Holds the Pen"

O N Christmas Day, 1865, the Agassizs were still at Manáos, on
the Amazon River. They watched "two illuminated canoes"
crossing the river at nightfall, filled with Indians bearing an ancient
wooden figure of the Virgin and a statue of "Saint Rosalia." A "figure of the infant Jesus" was surrounded by flowers, and midnight
mass was celebrated with great crowds of Indians attending. The
children, the family and the home in Cambridge seemed infinitely far
away.

And on that same Christmas Day in 1865, Tom Cary, Elizabeth's
brother, was in the small town of Maldonado on the coast of Uruguay, confidently expecting the "Thayer Expedition." By coast and
by river, the Agassizs were four thousand, six hundred miles away;
and as far as anyone could tell they had forgotten Tom completely.
Tom got news of the expedition, however. "The American War
Steamer *Susquehanna*" came into Maldonado harbor, and "quite a
number of the officers" arrived at the tavern where he was staying.
He acted as interpreter for them, dined aboard ship and learned that
"they had seen several of Agassiz's party in Rio and all seemed to
take a great interest in the expedition up the Amazon." Tom found
himself introduced as "Professor Cary." "I took the opportunity to

say that I had no claim whatever to the title, and that the only assistance I had ever given to science was in making a large collection of fishes taken at random from the markets and fishing boats in California, and that Professor Agassiz himself had said that the great advantage I had over professional collectors was that I did not know anything," Tom said.

Tom thought of home on Christmas Day, but not with longing: "A year ago today I was fretting at my imprisonment in Cambridge and the question is, have I bettered my condition by coming to Maldonado? In point of comfort, decidedly not but as for the usefulness of my present life, the odds are decidedly in my favor. I shall have got a great deal of useful information and shall be able to help Agassiz very much if he comes to the River Plate. I shall be able to make a very respectable collection for the museum and if the Telegraph scheme proves a success, I shall accomplish what will be of use not only to me but to all the world."

Tom was on vacation from his business in Buenos Aires. He was a little anxious about the time element — he could not stay in Maldonado indefinitely, but, although he said "if" the professor came to the La Plata, he fully expected to see the whole expedition arrive by steamer any day. "My first essay at collecting was to catch all the spiders in my room and put them in alcohol," he said. It was not a small job.

On the first day of February, Tom was still patiently waiting for Agassiz. He "bagged a bottle full of small frogs," remarking, "I think this will be sufficient for the frog business." He "read over Lizzie's letters" and saw that "she continually refers to the probability of their coming to Buenos Aires so that I think the chances are they will be along next month" — and with what the family called "Perkins drollery" [1] he remarked that Lent "would seem to be a good time for collecting fish." Tom had great difficulty getting any natives to help him, however. There had been wrecks along the coast and "all the boatmen had been able to steal enough to support them for some time and until they became destitute again, they would not work."

Tom got "conch shells . . . 'all alive 'o' with the critturs in them, crabs, caracoles del mar . . . most interesting because they were covered with parasites of different kinds" and "lizards, hornets and spiders." He realized what he said was his life's ambition and got bitten by a snake, but the wound on his thumb soon healed although the natives assured him the snake was poisonous. He was extremely disappointed in the fish: he was told there were twenty-seven varieties and he could get only twelve. "I shall not worry myself about Agassiz and his movements any more," he said on March 19.

It was the end of April when Tom Cary came back to Maldonado for the last time, after a brief trip to Buenos Aires. He had supposed that the men he had hired would have plenty of fish waiting for him, but there was only one, preserved in a pickle bottle. They called it a "salmon," and it was "rather a small one, surely," said Tom.

"Thus ends my grand scientific piscatorial tour, which was to fill the museum and make it positively necessary that a new wing be added, and a new professor appointed at a large salary with assistants to arrange the specimens and an immense amount donated by Congress for the purchase of bottles and alcohol." Tom could be sardonic when he chose, especially at his own expense. "I shall pack my specimens, such as they are, and leave these gay and festive shores with my fervent blessing. If Agassiz should come . . . I hope he will have a pleasant time. I have been left in the dark about his movements so long, that they are no longer any affair of mine; and if he comes to Buenos Aires there will be plenty of enthusiastic countrymen to make much of him without any care of mine."

Tom's gloomy mood was further increased by the fact that the landlord at the tavern where he had lived so long had "purchased a guitar and sings the most mournful comic songs . . . and has about as much idea of playing a guitar as a jackass has of playing a Jew's harp, and his singing is enough to drive anyone with a properly constituted ear raving mad."

He was glad to leave, even on a small steamer with a drunken captain.

Tom need not have blamed Agassiz for failing to turn up in Argentina or Uruguay. Agassiz had been writing to his benefactor, Nathaniel Thayer, suggesting that the expedition be continued another year. He had used up Thayer's letter of credit, to be sure, but reminded Thayer that "You yourself stated to me and to Mrs. Agassiz that if the sum named in the letter of credit were not sufficient, I should not hesitate to ask for more." But Thayer had been firm. Agassiz was forced to write, in January, 1866: "I yield without hesitation to your wishes to close the exploring expedition on my return to Pará." He could not help hoping that a "later letter" of his had "modified" Thayer's "views," but this was not to be.

Although Agassiz agreed to "close the expedition" and come home, he made it clear that it would not be good for his health to hurry. He must not arrive in Cambridge until winter was safely over with "no danger of return."

Strange flowers were just coming into bloom as the Agassizs started down the Amazon. A side trip was made to collect the *Victoria regia*, a giant water lily with leaves four to five feet in diameter, an armor of spines and huge flowers, creamy white at the outside, changing to crimson at the center. "Livestock" increased on board the steamer as the party turned toward home and animals might be safely transported alive all the way. William James had a turtle he was taking as a present to his medical professor, Dr. Wyman. There were "half a dozen monkeys," but Mrs. Agassiz's favorite was the sloth. "I am never tired of watching him, he looks so deliciously lazy," she said. "If you give him a smart tap, to arouse him, he lifts his head which is sunk in his arms and raises his heavy lids and lets his large eyes rest upon your face for a moment with appealing, helpless indolence; then the lids fall softly, the head droops, the arms fold heavily about it and he collapses again into absolute repose."

On February 4, 1866, the Agassiz company reached Pará, their starting point in August of the previous year. A letter from the Emperor of Brazil was waiting for Agassiz. While "in command of the Brazilian army on the Rio Grande," Dom Pedro had "caused collections of fish to be made" as a "present for Agassiz" which pleased him more than anything else that could have been given him. Eventually, "more than eighty thousand specimens" were stored in the museum in Cambridge.

The party lingered in Pará from the first week in February until the last week in March, and then their journey southward to Rio was punctuated with stopovers. Mrs. Agassiz got her experience with horseback travel after all, as they took off inland from Ceará (now Fortaleza) to look for signs of former glaciers in the "serras of this province." The rainy season was upon them and they rode through mud upon roads hardly to be distinguished from the bed of a stream. They slept in huts along the way where leaky thatch had let in rain to turn the dirt floor to mud, and during a meal Mrs. Agassiz, hearing an odd noise beside her, looked down to see a fat black pig waiting for a handout. But Agassiz knew that he had found the track of glaciers as he "followed morainic soil." [2]

Mrs. Agassiz's ideas in the matter of dress had changed more than once. She had had calicoes made for her in Manáos, and now she decided that "a lady's seat on horseback is too insecure for dangerous mountain roads" — even if a sidesaddle could be found. And "for fording streams a long skirt is an inconvenience." Lizzie thought that "a lady who is obliged to make a journey in the interior of Brazil should dress Bloomer-fashion and ride *en cavalier.*"

A decidedly changed, a dashing and daring Lizzie by Boston standards, left Brazil on the second of July. She came home to become a woman author — in collaboration with her husband to be sure, but to sign her own name with his to a *Journey in Brazil.*

The idea had been that Mrs. Agassiz's diary would merely supply dates and details, and that Agassiz would write of the Thayer Expedition. But he immediately plunged into the sort of life he had been leading before he went away, "saddling himself with 16 lectures for which he will get about $3,000," as Alex put it, "instead of giving 6 and making $4,000." His platform personality had never failed him and now he had something new to talk about. He was as popular as ever, but no better able to drive a hard bargain.

The "funding" of the money, which Agassiz had raised personally, rankled deep. "I should be glad to have nothing to do with the money affairs of the museum," he wrote while still in Rio, "but I cannot admit that my scientific aims are to be put under guardianship." If he was to spend no more than the income from invested funds, then he would have to raise more or resign. As he said, on his return to Cambridge, "Nobody can ask me to remain at the head of a stationary concern" and although Alex was horrified, his father turned to Nathaniel Thayer and got scholarships for student assistants. Agassiz's own salary was raised to twenty-five hundred dollars; he promptly returned to the museum all students' fees and announced that "unless I earn $2000 more I cannot make the two ends meet."

While Agassiz was absorbed in the getting and spending of funds, Elizabeth quietly went ahead with the book on Brazil. She began with a transcription of her notes on Agassiz's lectures aboard the *Colorado* and she managed to get him to write footnotes to her efforts as she went along. During the summer of 1866 at Nahant, when Agassiz was so besieged with visitors that he could hardly get any work done in his laboratory, Lizzie, while entertaining grandchildren and assorted nieces and nephews at "The Butterbox," nevertheless got on with her book.

In June, 1867, Agassiz wrote to his old friend Lord Enniskillen, giving a brief summary of his recent years. "As for myself, I have now been six years a grandfather. That little girl you welcomed so kindly at Florence Court [Ulster County, Ireland] in 1859 is now Mrs. Shaw; she is very well married and has three children. My son, the oldest of my family is now 32 and has two children. My oldest daughter is also married but has no children." He and his wife were living alone together for almost the first time since their marriage and Agassiz was so proud of his Lizzie that he could not help boasting about her.

"She made the journey to Brazil with me and was everywhere, camping out and traveling in the bush among Indians as well as the more civilized population. She has shared everything with me and I owe her a great part of my success, as she could hold the pen for me while I was making my observations and piling up my collections. We have lately prepared an account of our Journey which is now in the press to appear sometime in the autumn. I shall not fail to send it to you. . . ."

The book about Brazil was finished in October, 1867. AGASSIZ'S *Journey in Brazil*, it said on the cover, and on the title page: *A Journey in Brazil*, BY PROFESSOR AND MRS. LOUIS AGASSIZ. You could take your choice what to call it. Ticknor and Fields were the publishers, and Mrs. Fields, who entertained constantly, now included the Agassizs at her dinner and supper parties. Annie Fields adroitly drew out Agassiz for the benefit of other guests who would promote the book.

"Agassiz described Brazil," she wrote in one of the little blue paperback notebooks she kept to be used for a book of her own — describing authors. "He spoke of the red passion-flower among the dark green of the forest, so dark that it is almost black." With a satisfaction very proper in a publisher's wife, she added, "His book is eagerly anticipated. MacMillan is exceedingly sorry not to have it."

There was another dinner party during which all the guests had been urging Longfellow to go up the Nile to see "vast statues which still stand, awful and speechless witnesses of the past." Mrs. Fields asked Agassiz if he would like to go up the Nile. He would indeed. And why? "To catch fish," he said.

Agassiz "was merry and kindly, liked the claret and said so, and tossed it off appreciatively between his science and his fun." He was beginning to be a favorite among the members of Mrs. Field's literary salon. But Mrs. Agassiz's letters contained a comment which will have a familiar ring to many an anxious author: "We think that publication has been unreasonably delayed and are inclined to believe that, with the advent of Dickens, it became important to bring out other things at Christmas, in consequence of which our book is held back."

Longfellow got his *Journey in Brazil* in time for Christmas, 1867, at any rate. He wrote next day:

"A thousand thanks for your Chirstmas present, your new book! I am reading it this morning with the greatest interest and pleasure.

"The idea of mingling the two diaries together is very felicitous. It is like the intermingling of the masculine and feminine rhymes in a French poem. In fact the whole expedition is highly poetical and

St. John's or Hudson Square
New York

Tremont Street and Temple Place

1856

Boston to Cambridge omnibus
known to the Cary girls as "The Hourly"

Thomas Graves Cary,
Mrs. Agassiz's father

Thomas Handasyd Perkins,
Mrs. Agassiz's grandfather

Cary family silhouette by August Edouart, 1841–1842
Mollie (at the piano) Lizzie (about to sing) and
their cousin, Thomas H. Perkins 3rd

Cécile Braun, self-portrait, from *Letters and Recollections of Alexander Agassiz* by permission from Houghton Mifflin Company

Jean Louis Rodolphe Agassiz in 1847

Alexander Agassiz as a child Drawing by his mother, Cécile Braun Agassiz (permission as above)

Agassiz at the age of nineteen. Pastel drawing sometimes attributed to Cécile Braun Agassiz

Anna Russell, wife of
Alexander Agassiz
from *Letters and Recollections
of Alexander Agassiz*

Alexander Agassiz at about
the time of his marriage

Mrs. Pauline Agassiz Shaw
Drawing by
Samuel Worcester Rowse

Ida Agassiz Higginson
Drawing by John Singer Sargent

The Agassiz cottage at Nahant
View from the land side

The Agassiz house, corner of Quincy Street and Broadway,
Cambridge, Massachusetts

Elizabeth Agassiz

Louis Agassiz about 1850
Photographed by Sonrel,
Swiss lithographer
who followed Agassiz
to the United States

Agassiz, seated, looking
up at Agassiz, standing
A bit of Sonrel's
experimental photography

Agassiz's assistants on the Brazilian Expedition
Seated, left to right: William James; Monsieur Bourget;
Walter Hunnewell; Jacques Burkhardt; Mr. Dexter
Standing: Stephen Van Rensselaer Thayer; Major Coutinho

Mrs. Agassiz, President Emerita of Radcliffe

honorable to all concerned. There is nothing like it since Hipparchus sent his fifty-oared galley to bring Anacreon to Athens."

Oliver Wendell Holmes wrote to both authors:

"United in your book, in my note you shall not be divided. I have followed you both all the way from Boston to the Amazons and back. . . . It is a new world to most of us. . . . So exquisitely are your labors blended that, as with the mermaiden of the ancient poets, it is hard to say where the woman leaves off and the fish begins. . . ."

William James, who had watched Mrs. Agassiz faithfully keeping her journel, was in Dresden, Germany, when he heard that the book had come out. He borrowed it from "that unauthorized sort of U. S. Ambassador, the American dentist" and was "agreeably disappointed in it." He had feared there would be too many descriptions of sunsets, but "read the whole of it with interest" and found that Mrs. Agassiz had "varied the contents very skillfully . . . to entertain and interest the reader."

Elizabeth herself spoke of "immense relief" when the book was done. And then came a Frenchman, who had been living in Brazil, to make a French translation of *A Journey in Brazil*. Agassiz promised M. Vogele some special material — but no one, not even Lizzie, could get him to sit down at his desk and write anything out. At last Mrs. Agassiz had an idea. She took the French translator over to the museum; Agassiz gathered some students together and lectured to them in French while his wife took notes. Mr. Vogele had his special section — and Elizabeth had once more the pleasure of hearing her husband lecture in French. She had heard him in Rio, an occasion when, at Agassiz's invitation, ladies made their first appearance at such a gathering. Agassiz's lectures in English were fluent but his French was so well chosen and so beautiful that Lizzie felt sorry for anyone who had never heard it.

Agassiz's health, which had been such a cause of concern to his wife, was improved by his trip to Brazil. It was true that he had worked at a feverish pace while on the Amazon. The smallest "new" fish, the ones that native fishmen threw away as of no value, were as exciting to him as the jewels discovered by an entirely different type of adventurer in the Brazilian diamond fields. Agassiz was a field man, above all else. Faced by trials at home, the business of sorting and writing about his specimens being no small part of them, he became ill again. A French doctor, who had attended Charles Sumner in Paris after his injuries in the Senate Chamber, came to the United States and in 1868 attended Agassiz. He was Dr. Brown-Séquard, who became a friend as well as physician. He urged Agassiz to get away again for the kind of rest which brought satisfaction. Another field trip would be the thing. It was arranged that Agassiz should go West with a Congressman to inspect the progress made by the Pacific Railroad in the Rockies.

It was a severe disappointment to Elizabeth that she was not invited on this excursion, but it was for men only.[3] Lizzie thought she could have gone anywhere the men could, and she was probably right. General Sherman met the party "with ambulances to ride in and an escort of cavalry across part of the Kansas, Nebraska prairies." The railroad went only as far as Green River Station in Wyoming, "where laying the rails had brought to view a bed of limestone, full of fossil fishes and insects." But according to one of Agassiz's assistants, Agassiz had a Swiss lack of confidence in horses, preferring a boat or his own two feet, so he turned east when a farther expedition would have revealed still greater wonders. If this was true, then the Agassizs shared their distrust of horses with this difference: Elizabeth rode anyway, from a sense of self-discipline, while Agassiz believed in discretion.

Elizabeth was sure that Agassiz would not be properly taken care of without her, and in this she was wrong. He returned "vigorous" — and would have believed himself young again, if his "white hair did not remind" him that "winter is approaching." This was in a letter to his doctor which he wrote from Cornell University in October 1869. He was a nonresident professor there, having taken a hand in the founding of Cornell, the strong scientific department being due to his influence. He thought Dr. Brown-Séquard might like a professorship in medicine at Cornell. Writing in French, he said that Cornell students were not too countrified but that they were decidedly wild. He considered them poorly prepared, even in their own language, but thought that the University itself had a great future.

People around Ithaca had something to say about Agassiz. Looking over a bridge, a small boy saw a strange man in city clothes, turning over stones — apparently playing in the brook. Here was a grownup plainly gone mad, and the boy could be excused for staring. But when the man looked up and smiled and invited the boy to come down to the water's edge to see some strange new creatures, another future natural scientist joined the ranks. Sooner or later, someone interviewing Agassiz was bound to ask, "What do you consider your greatest achievement?" And he would say, "I have taught my students to observe."

It was on September 13, 1869 that Longfellow, just home from Europe, met Agassiz on the street and found him "full of the discourse he is to make at the Centennial of Humboldt's birthday, tomorrow." Longfellow turned and walked with Agassiz "to the printing office where they are putting it in type" and next day he and his daughter Alice went to Music Hall in Boston to hear the speech.

It was "a great occasion and a great success," said Longfellow. On the platform sat the Governor of Massachusetts, the Mayor of Boston, assorted clergymen and Professor Wyman of Harvard, President of the Boston Society of Natural History. The Germania band and the Orpheus Musical Society opened the program and when Agassiz got up there was "fervent applause."

Agassiz's friends had been a bit anxious about this affair. They were afraid he might not have taken time to prepare it properly and that he might be overdramatic and oratorical. Everyone who loved Agassiz was occasionally anxious lest he appear too foreign. However, Emerson, who had come in from Concord, and hoped to see Agassiz at his best, was as well pleased as Longfellow had been.

"Agassiz never appeared to such advantage," Emerson wrote. "What was unusual for him, he read a written discourse, about two hours long; yet all of it strong, nothing to spare, not a weak point, no rhetoric, no falsetto; — his personal recollections and anecdotes of their intercourse, simple, frank and tender in the tone of voice too, no error of egotism or self-assertion, and far enough from French sentimentalism. He is quite as good a man as his hero and not to be duplicated, I fear."

"There are necessities which only the destitute student knows," Agassiz had told his audience, "there is hunger and thirst" — not only physical but mental. "Let me say that every dollar given for higher education, in whatever department, is likely to have greater influence upon the future character of our nation than even the millions which have been spent to raise the many to material ease and comfort." Agassiz told of Humboldt's loan to him, personally. "What he has done for me, I know he has done for others, in silence, unknown to the world."

Afterwards, his friends said that Agassiz's severe illness was the result of his overexertion for the Humboldt Centenary. It was more probably an accumulation of overexertions. He suffered a cerebral hemorrhage, or a series of shocks, resulting in paralysis. Dr. Brown-Séquard had feared just this, he said, when summoned from New York. He told Agassiz that he must give up the cigars he enjoyed so much, and his wines, such as that case of white sparkling "St. George's" Charles Sumner had sent him from southern France. Worst of all was the order to give up work and not even to think. It was utterly impossible not to think — of the twelve-volume *Natural History of the United States,* for example, of which only four volumes would ever be finished; of the monograph on Brazilian fishes which ought to be coming out, with some of Burkhardt's one hundred and twelve drawings.

Most important of all was the new wing for the museum. Nathaniel Shaler, now Professor of geology, took temporary charge of the museum planning and Mrs. Agassiz wrote to him in her husband's behalf. "If the present subscription goes well, so that the building can be put up, and he can see his scheme taking visible form, I think it will give him such serenity of mind as will be the very best medicine. It seems to me that he is on the whole improving. It is true the attacks are more frequent but they are by no means so violent — they come in the strangest intermittent way. Sometimes he is free and easy in every movement, as fluent and flexible in speech as possible — the next minute he may find it difficult to speak."

As soon as he was able to travel, Agassiz and Elizabeth, Ida Higginson and the Greenoughs, all went to Deerfield, Massachusetts. They found "a delightful place to stay on the village street" where they had "a cheerful well-furnished parlor and most comfortable chambers for a dollar a day." Even though the Berkshires could not be compared with so much as the foothills of his native alps, Agassiz felt better here than at sea level. Greenough was again to be the architect when the new section of the museum was built, and in "this invigorating air" Agassiz gave up the attempt to stop thinking. He began to plan new and more effective ways for displaying his collections. "I am doing so well that prudence alone keeps me from work," he wrote, "but I have made up my mind not to begin any regular work again before next winter, nor then, only in case I should feel no sign of any disturbance in my head." Planning for the world's greatest museum did not come under the heading of "work."

Although he said little about it, Agassiz had begun to feel that he might not live to see the museum completed and so, during the late spring and the summer of 1870, he wrote letters, most of them dictated to Lizzie. He outlined his policy and his hopes. "Nowadays, a museum is no longer a collection of curiosities," he said. "It is an apparatus as indispensable for the progress of modern civilization as a chemical laboratory." A museum "should be open to all and furnish to all the information required."

Agassiz wrote another important principle to which he hoped the Museum of Comparative Zoology would be true:

"If the Museum is ever to become one of the first institutions of the kind and worthy of being considered the first Museum in America, it must be ever progressing and improving. The moment it is allowed to stand upon its own merits, it will go down and soon take irretrievably, a subordinate position."

CHAPTER NINETEEN
The Voyage of the Hassler

WHEN Agassiz first went to Deerfield in 1870, he had recovered his speech and was beginning to use his hand to write, but he could walk only a few steps without dizziness. Within a few weeks he was "walking several miles a day." He was as "keen as an Egyptologist for the hieroglyphics of his science," deciphering the "local inscriptions of the glacial period, tracking the course of ice on slab and dike and river bed" among the Berkshires. It would have been difficult to find a spot where Agassiz could take a vacation without turning his sojourn into a field trip. He was soon writing about dinosaur tracks which he wanted to buy for the museum.

"We have not one specimen of the foot prints from the Connecticut River sandstone," he wrote to Theodore Lyman, now a trustee of the museum and an Overseer of Harvard. Agassiz had seen a fine collection at Turner's Falls, "more carefully gathered even than that of Amherst." The owner, Mr. T. M. Stoughton, was "willing to part with it for about what it cost him," provided his collection went to the Cambridge museum; and Agassiz had "been twice to see it. . . . There are two applicants for it, Yale and Cornell." Mr. Stoughton had "bought all the ledges known as containing such impressions," and guaranteed to the museum "the pick of every new discovery." But Lyman objected to the price and Agassiz, after see-

ing the Amherst collection again, decided it would be "a tough undertaking to do anything better." He agreed to buy only a few
tracks and let Amherst have the prize collection.

"I am sorry we lost the whale," Agassiz wrote a little later. But he
was "very glad it goes to the Natural History Museum [of New
York]. I want them to know that I shall never do anything to frus-
trate their objects. Nothing is really more important than that we
should work together." Here was a new, relaxed attitude that would
have rejoiced Dr. Brown-Séquard.

Benjamin Pierce was still Professor of Astronomy and Mathematics at Harvard, but he had recently been appointed "Director
of Longitude Determinations of the United States Survey" and "superintendent of the Survey." He showed a capacity for raising ap-
propriations for his projects and a large imagination in making a
project inclusive which was very like Agassiz's own talent in that
direction. "A geodetic survey from ocean to ocean" was what he
proposed. In February, 1871, Pierce was in Washington and wrote
to Agassiz: "Now, my dear friend, I have a very serious proposition
for you. I am going to send a new iron steamer round to California
in the course of the summer. . . . Would you go in her, and do
deep-sea dredging all the way around?"

"Of course I will go, unless Brown-Séquard orders me positively
to stay on terra firma," Agassiz replied. The doctor pronounced him
"altogether free of disease" and without delay, Agassiz began to
gather together assistants for as grand an expedition as the Brazilian
journey. This time the United States government would pay the
cost.

Franz Steindachner would go on the new adventure. He was an
Austrian who had been taken on at the museum to prepare specimens
for exhibition, but he had worked so hard that Agassiz was afraid
he would have more specimens ready than there was space provided,
even in the new wing. Agassiz had already instructed Shaler to send
Steindachner on a field trip as soon as possible, "preferably at Government expense" — and here was the chance.

There was also Pourtalès. Arriving in the United States with

Agassiz, the Count de Pourtalès had become an expert oceanographer. Since 1848, he had been with the Coastal Survey, and in 1864 took charge of the tidal division. In 1866 or so he had discovered an area off the southeastern coast of Florida, "teeming with ocean life" and now called the "Pourtalès Plateau." No one would think of going dredging without him.

Poor old Burkhardt was at last too feeble to follow his master, and a young artist referred to as "Mr. Blake" took his place. Dr. Thomas Hill, ex-President of Harvard, would be on board "engaged in special investigations of his own." Captain Philip C. Johnson, in Command of the *Hassler*, was bringing his wife along.

It goes without saying that Lizzie Agassiz would be with her husband. She regarded every expedition as a sort of honeymoon, and looked forward to sailing through the Strait of Magellan with as much enthusiasm as she had felt for the exploration of the Amazon. But, with the suggestion of a sigh, she said that the people also going were "too numerous to mention."

Elizabeth rented the Quincy Street house and had everything packed and ready for departure. And then the sailing date of the *Hassler* was delayed, week after week. It looked as if the Agassizs would have to live at Mrs. Upham's boardinghouse, "the refuge of all homeless wanderers in Cambridge," but Mollie Felton, Mrs. Agassiz's niece, took them in and the *Hassler* finally sailed on December 4th, 1871. It was a "gray afternoon," with the "first snowstorm of the New England winter" just beginning.[1]

Mrs. Agassiz arranged the cabin for herself and her husband as though she were setting up housekeeping in a new home — as in fact she was. There were pictures of the children and grandchildren. Sarah Whitman, whose friendship was soon to mean much, had painted a picture for Lizzie, a lighthouse, with underneath it the words:

> His blessing, like a line of light
> Is on the water, day and night.

Elizabeth was to "take comfort" from this "often," for the "iron steamer *Hassler*" was only 350 tons and the open Atlantic was extraordinarily rough. On the wall of the cabin went a picture of the Nahant house, where one could look out upon rough seas while safe ashore. There were books to be unpacked, "shoe cases" and "comb cases" made by loving lady friends to be tacked to the wall. There was "a big arm chair" and "a portable table" and a couch as well as berths in the cabin. Lizzie knew from past experience that she would lie miserably in her berth at least at first.

By the time they were in the Gulf Stream, Elizabeth had gotten her sea legs and she was as excited as her husband to find, on coming on deck, that they were surrounded by fields of drifting seaweed called Sargassum and that they had discovered a "nest built by a fish." The nest was a "round mass of Sargassum about the size of two fists" and, when "placed in a bowl of water," the Gulf weed seemed to be "held together with elastic threads," which were "beaded" at intervals. The beads were eggs. Lizzie sat patiently beside the fish's nest, watching for the eggs to hatch and writing up her journal — just as she had done on the Brazilian expedition. She was as interested, however, as though this were her first adventure when the "beads" inside the ball of seaweed developed heads and tails and began to swim.

"We dropped our dredges in various ocean depths from the West Indies to the Southernmost limits of the Continent," Elizabeth wrote. "A pause of a few days was made at . . . St. Thomas and Barbadoes. At St. Thomas the dredge brought up, among other things, a number of stemmed crinoids and comatulae."

Agassiz was happy because these were "living representatives" of the "early fossil echinoderms" which he knew so well, and "it was like turning a leaf of the past and finding the subtle thread which connects it with the present." If Darwin's theory were right regarding evolution in every form of life, then these crinoids should look very different from their fossil ancestors, Agassiz argued. He hoped that the fact of their not changing meant that types remained fixed and that sea creatures found in later times evidenced "a special creation." The dredging operations in general were a bitter disappointment to Agassiz, however. Equipment proved too light, and hoisting engines were constantly breaking down. He knew that he had not been able to raise enough specimens from the bottom of the sea to prove any theory, either his own or Darwin's, to be right or wrong.

Back in Cambridge, Alexander Agassiz was in charge of the museum and in receipt of bulletins from the expedition, from which he drew his own picture.

"The *Hassler*, after much groaning, arrived at last at Montevideo, where Pa undertook to run the quarantine," Alex heard. Agassiz and Pourtalès had therefore been marched off to jail, by a Spaniard who "brandished a huge knife." But the two scientists managed to explain that it was all a mistake and that they had not meant to break any laws — so they "were released on proper representations being made and promising to be good hereafter."

Agassiz had so few specimens, owing to the breakdown of the dredges, that he had preserving alcohol to spare. He saw no harm in selling some of this at a profit when he got to Montevideo, and Alex had his own humorous version of this transaction also. "Not satisfied at breaking the laws of South America, [Pa] cheated the U. S. by selling a lot of alcohol at Montevideo which had been sold to us in bond as a special favor. He was quite elated over the fact and talked of buying some new collections." Probably no one was ever able to explain to Agassiz that there was anything wrong with the deal — since everything was in the interest of science.

Alex had his opinion of the *Hassler*. "The fact is the vessel was built by a second class small contractor . . . The engine is large enough for a 100 ton boat. They will burn coal like fury and get no speed out of her . . . Unless they can put in more motor power at Rio . . . the ship will eat up all the appropriation before it gets to Panama." [2]

The *Hassler* did put in for overhauling at Rio. The Emperor was traveling in Europe so the Agassizs did not have the pleasure of seeing their good friend again, although they were much feted by the Brazilian nobility. Then south, along the coast, went the *Hassler* Expedition. As usual, Agassiz was too much engrossed in collecting to do much writing and it was Lizzie who told of the voyage. She was impressed by the vast loneliness of some of the bays they entered.

The "Port of San Antonio" was the name given to a huge bay below the La Plata River and sheltered on the south by Cape San Antonio, on the coast of Argentina. The name would "imply some settlement," Elizabeth said, but "more than thirty years have passed since the bay was partially surveyed and if any vessel has broken the loneliness of its waters since, no record of such an event has been kept. Of the presence of man there is no sign." The *Hassler* anchored here for several days.

There was dredging, there were geological excursions ashore and the sailors built bonfires on the beach. "Returning to the ship after dark, the various parties assembled in the wardroom" to tell of their adventures and to plan the next day's work. These were some of the "pleasantest days of the voyage," and Lizzie grew fond of the place. When they left, it was on a windless evening and "the light of the beach fires could be seen for a long time. It seemed almost tragic to leave them to be overwhelmed by darkness and to leave the bay to an unknown number of years of emptiness."

Moving out of the area of the La Plata River, where poor Tom Cary had looked vainly for Agassiz over six years earlier, the *Hassler* steamed from San Mathias direct to the Strait of Magellan, pausing only a short time in the Gulf of St. George. The high point for everyone would be the Strait; and on March 13, 1872, "a beautiful clear morning like the best October weather in New England" they rounded Cape Virgens.

A glacier, easily seen from the main channel of the Strait and often mentioned in accounts of voyages but never approached, was to be the first important point of exploration. There proved to be no safe anchorage in Glacier Bay, but the *Hassler* anchored nearby in Playa Parda Cove and the party reached the glacier by the steam launch and by a rowboat which could be lowered from the *Hassler's* deck. It was at first assumed that the ladies — the captain's wife and Mrs. Agassiz — would not go ashore. But Elizabeth Agassiz had been disappointed of her hopes of climbing the Aar glacier in Switzerland

and she was not going to be cheated out of this present wonderful opportunity.

Mrs. Agassiz had advocated a "bloomer costume" for travel on the Amazon, but when she climbed down the ladder on the side of the *Hassler* to get into the small boat, she was not wearing bloomers. She was wearing an "overhaul" — a pair of canvas trousers with bib and suspenders — and a pair of her husband's boots. (How she ever managed to keep her husband's boots on, she did not say.) She had persuaded the ship captain's wife to come along, and Mrs. Johnson was dressed the same way.

Although it seemed so from a distance, the glacier did not come down to the water's edge after all. There was a gravel beach and then a band of dense forest about a mile wide. Agassiz, Steindachner, Pourtalès and Blake had gone ahead. With the two ladies was a young student, a Mr. Kennedy, and the ship's carpenter to help Kennedy cut a path for them. The going immediately proved so rough that Agassiz assumed his wife would turn back.

Mrs. Agassiz had been reading Darwin's account of his voyage through the Strait of Magellan. He repeatedly described the forests along the shores of the strait as "dusky." But this was because he had never gone ashore. Lizzie discovered that the forests looked dusky and gray because there were blighted trees all along the edge of the water. "Within," she was "never so surprised as to find . . . as luxuriant a vegetation in its depths as in any forest she had ever seen," including the Amazonian rain forest. "Every trunk, every branch, every fallen log, every stone was cushioned deep in bright green moss." There were spring flowers everywhere, among them "small white clusters of arbutus" to make her feel at home as though in her own New England.

The moss was beautiful, but it was as slippery as mud to walk on. The stones it covered were smooth rounded boulders polished by centuries of grinding under the glacier and they would have made precarious footing even without the moss. "We climbed over and under great fallen trees, fell into holes and clambered out of them," Mrs. Agassiz said. They were following the stream which flowed out of the glacier and from time to time the banks proved impassably steep, and they waded "through the brawling rapids." When, at one point, the water was too deep for them, they crossed and climbed the stream, a moss-covered log providing a bridge. Kennedy and the ship's carpenter cut a sapling, trimmed it, then each held an end to make a hand-rail. Mrs. Agassiz crossed first and then the captain's wife came "crawling cautiously."

"After about an hour" of this kind of travel they "began to catch glimpses of the ice." The river which they were following "became more and more of a cascade." Suddenly they came out in the open — and there was a great wall of ice, stretching across the whole width of the valley. "You should have seen Agassiz when we came out of the wood," said Lizzie. She would never forget "the look of incredulous joy on his face, he was so pleased" to have her with him "at his first sight of one of the greatest glaciers" he had "ever seen in his life."

Elizabeth's enthusiasm more than doubled her husband's pleasure. The Boston girl who had been hardly more than a hundred miles from home when he married her had proved from the first to be born for adventure.

There were "deep caves of blue, transparent ice at the edge of the glacier." Lizzie promptly went into them and saw "between the lower surface of the ice and the ground, the accumulated mass of stones, pebbles and boulders" her husband taught her to call "ground moraine." Unlike the Alpine glaciers, which are covered with rocky debris on the surface at the melting point (as Agassiz explained), this glacier was of clear, glassy ice in which steps had to be cut if they would climb it. It goes without saying that Mrs. Agassiz climbed.

"After we had looked about at the ice till we were tired, young Kennedy built a fire on the moraine at the edge of the strip of forest." The ladies "sat down to warm and dry themselves" and then they heard "a shout from the woods and there was the captain and several of the ship's company and behind them (oh joy!) some men carrying a large basket." The lunch consisted of "sardines and potato salad and pork" and was "topped off with a drop of sherry" out of the flask which Mrs. Agassiz's nephews, the Felton boys, had given them, and "which our boy William had had the good sense to bring."

They returned on board the *Hassler* late in the afternoon — tired but not too tired to enjoy a good dinner. "We dined gayly," Mrs. Agassiz said, "not forgetting to christen the glacier in a glass of Champagne." At "Agassiz's suggestion, and by right of being the first to visit it," they named it "the Hassler Glacier."

Elizabeth would have been much disappointed if she had not come across some natives, and abandoned huts gave the first evidence of them. These huts were made with "a few flexible branches, stuck in the ground in a semicircle and their [upper] ends drawn together so as to form a kind of a hood in the shape of a chaise top." Lizzie thought very little of them and when she finally saw natives in their boats, "which were bark canoes and well made," she thought they could have built good houses if they had tried. She had no better opinion of their clothes, "which were skins hung around their necks without benefit of sewing." The women were naked to the waist and carried their babies strapped to them "in such a way that a woman could paddle lustily with both arms and nurse a child at the same time." Lizzie thought they should "dress better, for warmth if not for decency in a climate where snow and ice are the rule rather than the exception." There were few natives in any case; they were friendly enough, but loud and insistent in their demands for tobacco.

The *Hassler* entered every bay where there seemed to be safe anchorage and most of these were uninhabited. Mrs. Agassiz was impressed by the silence. "Voices and laughter seemed a sort of sacrilege." Mountains and "forest-covered walls" were mirrored in deep water, and during the long twilight, snow-covered slopes turned "pale pink, blue and amethyst" and then, when the sun had set, "ashy pale" as if the "whole range had been cut in marble." Elizabeth saw "narrow, winding ocean pathways" leading out of uncharted bays, which she "would gladly have explored if only for a little distance." But "a change of weather might have trapped" the *Hassler*, and they must reach their next coaling station.

After more than 360 miles of "precarious navigation" the *Hassler*
emerged safely from the Strait of Magellan and turned northward
along the coast of Chile. At Talcahuana, just north of Concepción,
the Agassizs disembarked and traveled by coach to Curico, a distance of somewhat more than a hundred miles. Post horses, driven
five abreast with an outrider, were picked up at intervals; and inns
were primitive. Elizabeth was that rare type of person, the uncom-
plaining traveler, but she definitely did not care for fleas or bedbugs.
She was blissfully unaware of danger from contaminated food, however, and her husband's European preference for wine over water
probably saved both their lives. (Agassiz once said he never thought
of water as a beverage until he came to the United States.) [3] Wherever the coach stopped, Lizzie knocked at doors and called on natives in their primitive huts. She admired their children, asked them
what was cooking in the pot and how they made such tasty food.
Smiling and friendly, she never doubted that she would be welcome.

While they were on this overland part of their journey, the Agassizs had a telegram from the Emperor of Brazil, who was in Paris.
Louis Agassiz had been elected foreign member of the French Academy, the message said. There were only eight such members and
Agassiz was properly gratified, but he remarked that the honor was
usually conferred upon a man who was nearing the end of his life.
Agassiz had taken this journey "for his health," as he had the Brazilian expedition — and the effect had been almost as good. It always
restored him to get away from bickerings over money at his museum
and arguments with students and contemporary scientists — over
Darwin and his theories, for example. But this time, as the coach
rumbled over the stony roads, Agassiz looked longingly at the Andes
and realized that he could not hope to explore them. "I was never
more disposed for work and yet never so fatigued by it," he said.

At Valparaiso, the Agassizs rejoined the *Hassler* with some of their
most interesting adventures still in store. They were bound for the
Galapagos Islands, and perhaps nowhere else could they have found
more startling contrasts to the Strait of Magellan. A tropical sun
blazed down. Here they found surf rather than mirrorlike bays, and

when Elizabeth looked over the ship's rail, "huge lizards and iguanas were swimming by." They arrived at Iguana Cove, Albemarle Island, on June 12, 1872, and Mrs. Agassiz went ashore as soon as they would let her take her chances, landing in rough water.

"Lava bubbles" were everywhere, strange hollow masses of rock blown up when the volcanic island erupted from the sea. Some of the "bubbles" had a side blasted out through which a "verticle shaft 30 or 40 feet deep" could be seen. In other spots on the island huge masses of lava had cooled, formed a crust, and then fresh lava flowing out again had left an arched roof over open ends like a tunnel. Some of these curious cave-like formations were so small a person would have to crawl through on hands and knees while others were large enough to hold a dozen people standing erect. Mrs. Agassiz flitted about, exploring caves, looking into lava bubbles. There was "one in particular where a stray sunbeam had found its way to the very bottom" of the vertical tube and "lighted up the walls and floor with a strange brilliancy as if lighted from within." She could "see the light quiver and tremble in that dark recess" while all about her shone the sun of high noon.

While she stood "in the midst of this field of strange charred ruins, looking around in blank wonder," she heard Agassiz calling to her "in a strange stifled-sounding voice." Elizabeth looked everywhere, and at last saw him at the mouth of one of the caves. "Heated and dusty with his walk, a large club in his hand, he seemed like Vulcan," and when he beckoned to her she expected him to lead her to "a one-eyed Cyclops at his forge." He led her instead to "the lunch basket" inside the cave, where the rest of the scientific adventurers were waiting, all of them hungry. Agassiz's expeditions took on the character of a glorified picnic at times, and his Lizzie was like a delighted child who had been allowed to come along if she would be good and not bother anyone.

Everybody, including the crew of the *Hassler*, joined in the hunt for "red and orange-colored terrestrial iguanas" and the ground was "honeycombed with their holes." These lizards were about two feet long with "large, clumsy bodies but remarkably elusive, just the same," Lizzie said. She had heard that they were "easily attracted by music and could be quieted and caught that way." Accordingly, when she saw an iguana "running very actively around a tree" she began to sing to it.

Lizzie Agassiz did not say what song she sang to the iguana. Was it one of those which had brought tears to the eyes of old gentlemen on Temple Place? Or was it from *Bombastes Furioso*, with words written by her brother Tom? In any case, the iguana "suddenly stood still," and Lizzie "drew gently nearer, delighted by" her "success, and with the susceptibility of the uncouth creature." Still singing, and "not without a certain self-reproach for taking an unfair advantage of his love of music," she signaled to one of the hunters to come and get the iguana.

" 'Why, Mrs. Agassiz,' the young assistant said, as soon as he came close — 'he's tied!' And now the phenomenon was explained," said Elizabeth, telling it in her own words and enjoying the joke.

The iguana's "seemingly breathless appreciation of my music was due to the fact that he had twisted his rope around the tree till he could not move another step. One of the sailors had caught him earlier in the day and tied him up for safekeeping." Of her efforts at "charming iguanas," Mrs. Agassiz said, "I think a more mortified prima donna was never hissed off the stage." She gave up hunting iguanas and went to sit in the shade and watch flamingoes "sweeping by, their pink necks stretched, their red wings tipped with black, glittering in the sunshine."

On James Island, Lizzie watched a mother seal "with two little cubs, perfectly tame." They were like human babies, each trying to get closest to their mother, she said, and she patted them and offered them soda crackers. Tiny lizards were "crawling all over the mother's back, eating flies." Under no obligation to collect or identify a species, or form a theory of creation, Elizabeth Agassiz was a sort of Alice in Wonderland, looking at everything with pleased surprise and making friends with strange animals. It was with a faint twinge of conscience, however, that she remarked that they had baked flamingo for dinner and that it was delicious.

Dutifully Lizzie set down Agassiz's "aims." He was "looking for intermediate transition types to prove the theory of evolution. The flora and fauna" on the Galapagos Islands were "distinct — the islands comparatively new." She thought the "transition types should not elude the patient student." And she also knew that Agassiz still hoped to prove that there were no "transition types," and that man in particular was a "special creation."

After leaving the Galapagos Islands, the *Hassler* crossed directly into the Bay of Panama and came to anchor at Taboga. Here Pourtalès and others left the expedition to cross the Isthmus and go on to Washington, D. C., carrying part of the new collection for the Smithsonian. "The expedition sent home, first and last, over two hundred and fifty barrels and cases of specimens which included "three or four hundred skulls of Aboriginees. . . ." Agassiz did not say how he came by the skulls. The few aborigines he met in the Strait had been left in peaceful possession of theirs, however much he may have wanted to collect them. There must have been empty graveyards here and there all along the coast of South America. He had "30,000 fish and uncounted thousands of cephalopods, gastropods, echinoderm." The entire collection "probably exceeded a hundred thousand items," for Agassiz had always been like a ten-year-old boy with a collecting mania. Of course his excuse was that he could use extra specimens for exchange with other museums for items not owned by the Museum of Comparative Zoology. The handling of exchanges kept his son Alex extremely busy. Then students were allowed to handle specimens when studying with Agassiz, and such not very durable items as pickled sea worms, for example, eventually wore out. This time, specimens were to be shared with the Smithsonian — an added incentive to collect in quantity.

"It does not make a Museum to have fine things in the Laboratories," Agassiz would soon inform his assistants, however. The handsomest specimens must be selected, cleaned, mounted, labeled and then "all the specimens belong to the *exhibition rooms*, after they have been worked up."

In San Francisco Agassiz was taken ill, perhaps suffering another slight shock. They stayed in the city a month, overwhelmed by invitations from cordial Californians, unable to accept any of them.

But Elizabeth was astonished to discover that she could not so much as go shopping without being recognized as the wife of the great naturalist. Her own nature was so friendly that she always spoke to strangers — a custom certainly not invariable among Bostonians. In San Francisco she felt so much among friends that she understood why her brother Tom wanted to make his home there and why he urged the Felton boys and almost everyone he knew to join him.

Agassiz returned to Cambridge to find a magnificent surprise awaiting him. The Calumet mines, under Alexander's management, were beginning to produce more wealth than even Alex had dreamed of. He left his work at the museum and went to Michigan for his annual visit. And while he was gone his brother-in-law Quincy Shaw "came down handsomely" with a gift of Calumet dividends for the museum. Said Alex, "I was in hopes of having him do something for the future, but the unconditional way in which he gave the money to father is as good a scheme as any we could have concocted. Father is in the seventh heaven, of course and imagines this $100,000 will last indefinitely."

CHAPTER TWENTY
On a Winter Afternoon

A GASSIZ was a pioneer — the sort of man who glories in cutting down tall timber for a clearing in the wilderness but who moves on when nothing is left to do but keep the crows away from the corn. He returned home to Cambridge in October, 1872, sincerely believing that all he wanted was a quiet winter of teaching and writing with a peaceful summer at Nahant to follow. But he found the idea of a summer school for teachers of natural history under discussion. It was an idea he himself had proposed some time previously, seemed to have forgotten — and now took up again with all the ardor of a young scientist embarking on a new career. He wrote a prospectus, which was something he loved to do. And then, like a man who has written a play, he looked about for an angel to finance it.

Of course there was the matter of the material acquired aboard the *Hassler*. By the first of August, 1873, Alexander Agassiz could write, "I have finished the *Hassler* Echini which is to come out as one of the Museum Catalogues in conjunction with Pourtalès's corals of the same expedition." Alex was going to pay for the publication. "I shall take this out of the Dividend and never know it," he said, Michigan copper having solved his problem of being able to afford natural science.

What were assistants and a loyal son for, if not to attend to details? Agassiz applied himself to the task of raising still more money. Displays which would appeal to farmers, businessmen or small-town lawyers were set up, for in March the Massachusetts Legislature made its annual visit to see how the funds they had granted were being spent. Mrs. Agassiz was always on hand at these occasions and an observer who watched her at work said she listened to the legislators as they gathered around the cases. If they seemed puzzled by a display she would "glide up to them" and say, "O, I happened to hear my husband tell about this." While intimating that, as a mere woman, the subject was far beyond her, Mrs. Agassiz would make everything so clear that the legislators could go home feeling like natural scientists in their own right. Although she may not have realized it at this point, Elizabeth herself was learning a great deal about the art of raising money.

In March, 1873, with public funds for the museum not yet guaranteed, Agassiz asked the legislators to finance a new project. He wanted his museum money, plus funds for a summer school. Nantucket might be a good place for such a school, he thought, and "he considered it an educational branch of the Museum."

"Never did he plead more eloquently for the cause of education," said Elizabeth, who was taking down her husband's speech as always. "His gift as a speaker cannot easily be described. . . . It was born of conviction and was as simple as it was impassioned. It kept the freshness of youth, because the thing of which he spoke never grew old to him, but moved him to the last hour of his life. . . ." The resulting publicity reached John Anderson, "a rich merchant of New York," who read of Agassiz's scheme for a summer school of seaside studies in the New York papers. "Within a week" he had offered Agassiz his island, Penikese, in Buzzards Bay.[1] There were buildings on the island — a barn, a furnished house. Agassiz accepted the gift with appreciation and the frank request for cash along with the real estate. Mr. Anderson gave fifty thousand dollars.

Agassiz announced the opening of the Anderson School of Natural History for July 8, 1873. Fifty-eight students signed up for the course — public school teachers, most of them, both men and women. All Agassiz had to do to get ready for them was to build a dormitory, a laboratory, buy furnishings and supplies, hire a kitchen staff, laboratory assistants and teachers, and prepare the course of study. Anyone but Agassiz would have said that it would be impossible to do this in the three months or so at his disposal.

The Agassizs set out for New Bedford, Massachusetts on the fourth of July. A boat was to take them out to Penikese next day, but they found the architect of the new dormitory waiting for them in New Bedford. The dormitory had walls and a roof, but it was not as yet shingled, the architect said. There were no floors, no partitions. Agassiz said he "would not believe in failure till he saw it." The eighth "was his date," and he was sure "everything would be ready."

"My heart sank to my shoes," Elizabeth confessed. During the greater part of her married life she had entertained guests for her husband, some of them expected, most of them otherwise. She was by nature a cordial hostess and as she thought about "fifty-eight people to be lodged, fed and comforted" she got very little sleep that night in the hotel at New Bedford. The fact of "little boys firing crackers under our windows and making night hideous" helped not at all.

The Agassizs had brought Professor B. G. Wilder of Cornell and his wife and child with them. At the hotel they found "a stray lady teacher who had come to the school three days too early, by mistake." They told her she could come along to the island with them; she "might not have a place to lay her head," but she could share whatever lodging there was — and she agreed. They all boarded the *Helen Augusta*, and spent two hours wallowing down Buzzards Bay in the rain. Con Felton, Mrs. Agassiz's nephew, was on the dock at Penikese "looking like a castaway." He said he had managed to get the new dormitory furniture in out of the rain.

As the Agassizs and their party came off the boat, a crowd of workmen piled on board. It was Saturday afternoon and they were leaving. The Agassizs went to the former Anderson house, where they cooked up some ham and eggs for themselves. The rain kept right on pouring down, but it was wonderful how much better they all felt after a good meal. Flanders, the man who had been "in charge of the island" for Mr. Anderson, "got the greater part of the house (in which the carpenters had been living) cleaned and arranged for our habitation" — with Mrs. Agassiz's help.

Not all the carpenters had left, but they planned to leave the next day because it was Sunday. "Flanders made a thrilling address" to them: "told them the object of the building — not for business, not for money," Mrs. Agassiz wrote. They agreed to work all day Sunday, and "before nightfall the first and second floors in the building had nearly all been laid."

"One or two boys and Dr. Wilder, Mrs. Burns [who must have been the stray lady teacher], Mrs. Wilder and I unpacked and washed all the glass and china for the dormitories and dining room," Mrs. Agassiz went on. It was "no light task, for it consisted of twenty-four dozen plates, six dozen cups and saucers, vegetable and meat dishes without end, many dozens of glasses — and fifty-six chamber sets containing all the ordinary pieces." It would seem that they were going to be a few "chamber sets" short, but on this point Lizzie made no comment.

Sunday was a bright summer day. "In the midst of our work, Sunday afternoon, we had a visit from a fashionable New York yacht," Lizzie wrote. "Robert Minturn and Mr. Holyoke came ashore to pay a call. We were all on the piazza washing glass and china, and they seemed to think it quite a delightful picnic. We were able to muster a cup of coffee and tried to be as hospitable as circumstances would permit." Apparently it never occurred to the guests to lend a hand.

On Monday morning "the ladies" unpacked the furniture. On Tuesday they swept up the sawdust and shavings from the second floor of the dormitory, but only one partition had so far been built — the one separating the men's from the women's quarters. The ladies arranged the floor space into "imaginary rooms" by means of "neat sets of furniture."

"When all was done, the large, open rooms, with their fresh pine walls, floors and ceilings, the rows of white beds down the sides and the many windows looking to the sea, were pretty and inviting enough." The place had something the air of a hospital ward, Lizzie thought, but at least no one was ill. The lower floor of the dormitory building was devoted to workrooms, where the students would have tables and specimens. Microscopes, a luxury out of the reach of most of the teachers attending the school, had been supplied from Mr. Anderson's gift of money.

The barn belonging to the Andersons had been cleaned out and a new floor laid. Here, too, there had been time to put up only one partition to separate a lecture room from the kitchen quarters. "The last nails were just being driven on the eighth of July when the steamer with its large company touched the wharf."

It would not have been Agassiz had he forgotten to invite "guests of honor" to the opening of the new school. Here came Mr. Anderson, the donor, and the Governor of Massachusetts along with members of the State Legislature and members of the school board. Agassiz never missed a chance to be dramatic. He never failed to make a donor happy and proud of the way in which his money was spent. It would not have been Elizabeth had she not "arranged the seats and placed a table with flowers where the guests were to sit and Agassiz himself was to stand when all arrived."

Agassiz had prepared no order of exercises, no written address of welcome, trusting to the inspiration of the moment. As he "looked at his pupils gathered there to study nature with him, by an impulse as natural as it was unpremeditated," he asked them to "join silently in asking God's blessing upon their work together." Then he spoke — his address being one of his finest. It was John Greenleaf Whittier who told of the scene in a poem called "The Prayer of Agassiz."

There was "enthusiasm, romance, open air, discomforts, very good food, science, colonies of gulls, hard work and amusement" at Penikese. Agassiz had lost none of his magnetism. "The servants hurry to finish their work to come and hear the lectures." He gave "three of the finest lectures on glaciers" Lizzie ever heard, and she had heard them all. Professor Wilder did some of the lecturing, "an admirable teacher and speaks without notes" while Hawkins, the wonderful draftsman, drew fishes on the blackboard, developing them by degrees from the tail upwards till the spectators are "wild with excitement."

Agassiz's blackboard drawings had always been a popular feature of his lectures. Ernest Longfellow, himself an artist, said that Agassiz "had a wonderful talent for drawing in chalk" and that "it was a real treat to see a perfect fish or skeleton develop under his hand with extraordinary sureness and perfect knowledge, without any hesitation or correcting, like a Japanese drawing in its truth to nature, and it seemed a shame that such beautiful drawings were only in chalk and had to be rubbed out again." The fact that it was now "Hawkins the wonderful draftsman" whose drawings were admired might indicate that Agassiz had not entirely regained control of his hand after his temporary paralysis. This was the only hint that illness was beginning to take toll of him.

There were lectures both morning and afternoon. In the afternoon, the student teachers were sent out "to learn from nature and put into practice methods of study given by Agassiz and Wilder." After climbing around the island, everyone was ready for "chowder, beef or lamb and an excellent pudding" served in the former barn. Carpenters were still at work, and "nice little rooms were emerging one by one" in the big dormitory so that students who woke one morning in what looked like a hospital ward could hope for a certain amount of privacy by nightfall.

The school received a handsome gift, a yacht, presented by Mr. Charles G. Galloupe and especially equipped for dredging — of which Pourtalès took charge. Professor Guyot, Agassiz's old friend from Switzerland, came to give a course of lectures and then stayed on. At sunset, on a little knoll, the two old friends would meet to talk together and the students would gradually gather around Agassiz and Guyot, sitting down to listen. Agassiz had always treated his students as equals and, because of their immaturity, this sometimes had unfortunate results. But this was perhaps the most congenial group of students the professor ever had. They were mature men and women who were giving their lives to that most unselfish of occupations — teaching. Agassiz's pupil teachers provided him with some of his happiest hours; Penikese became a model for future summer schools, and the forerunner of the Woods Hole Laboratories.

Agassiz was aware that he had never really explained his own position in regard to Darwin. Students like Morse, truculent young men who quarreled with earlier scientists primarily because they represented authority, had caused Agassiz to lose his temper and he could never make himself clear when anger got the better of him. The thing to do was to write out a careful statement of his own conclusions arrived at now, in his sixty-sixth year. This kind of writing was something Agassiz hated, but he set to work. "Evolution and Permanence of Type" would be the title of the article.[2]

"The pioneers in the science of Embryology, by a series of investigations . . . have proved that all living beings produce eggs, and that these eggs contain a yolklike substance out of which new beings, identical with their parents, are evolved by a series of gradual changes. These successive stages of growth constitute evolution as understood by the embryologists. . . . The law of evolution, so far as it is understood, is a law controlling development and keeping types within appointed cycles of growth, which revolve forever upon themselves, returning at appointed intervals to the same starting point and repeating through successive phases the same course." Thus the domesticated animals "with all their breeds and varieties have never been traced back to anything but their own species" while "extreme varieties finally degenerate or become sterile."

Agassiz had "found no evidence of a transition between man and his fellow creatures," any more than he had found transition from dog to cat or cow to horse. But a Russian scientist by the name of Kowelvsky had observed a series of cells running longitudinally in the embryo of a soft-shell crab, and this had led him to believe that the crab was the ancestor of a vertebrate — an animal with a backbone. Agassiz, however, cited a German scholar — K. E. von Baer — who had published findings while Agassiz was "preparing for the press" material which concerned the same discovery. The "string of cells does not run along the back at all but is placed on the ventral side of the body," Agassiz explained in corroboration of the German. "To say that the first Vertebrates carried their backbones in this fashion . . . is reversing their whole structure and putting their vertebral column where their abdominal cavity should be." He was indignant when "friends of the transmutation theory" declared that the "transition point was found between the lower and the higher animals and man himself traced to" soft-shelled crabs.

Agassiz was most at home on "the geological side of the question." He spoke of his studies of fossil remains in Silurian and Devonian deposits. He had found "Selachians (sharks and their allies) and Ganoids (garpikes and the like) the highest of all fish, structurally speaking." If evolution were a steady, continuous process, much more primitive forms should have prevailed. And "where do we find . . . fishes that are structurally inferior to all others?" he queried. His answer was that "They come in the latest period of the world's history with what is called the present period, to which we ourselves belong. This certainly does not look like a connected series beginning with the lowest and ending with the highest for the highest fishes come first and the lowest last. . . ."

Agassiz summed up: "It may therefore be said that a great diversity of types has existed from the beginning." He would have rejoiced in the modern methods of determining the age of rock by measuring radioactivity. He would have contrived somehow to get aboard an atomic-powered submarine to explore the vast mountain ranges and deep valleys underneath the icecap. And who could have kept him from exploring space? In 1873 he could only say, "The more I look at the great complexity of the animal world, the more sure do I feel that we have not yet reached its hidden meaning." [3]

In March of 1873, Alexander Agassiz wrote: "Everything seems so prosperous that I feel as if some of us would have to pay a heavy penalty, by and by, for all our happiness. . . ." He and his wife Anna and their three little boys were living on Quincy Street with the senior Agassizs, but a house was being built for them on Commonwealth Avenue — the new, ultrafashionable street in Boston. Ida and Henry Higginson were to share the house, each family having a separate apartment, and they laughed at themselves because they were so excited that they could talk of nothing else. "A house can wait," Alex had said, while he put every cent he could lay hands on into Calumet. He had gambled and won.

In June, Alexander wrote that his father was "rejoicing over his one hundred thousand dollars which he expects to be able to spend" for the museum. And on December 4 — "Father continues very well, works just enough to keep his hand in and is in excellent spirits. . . . He now has a grand idea of applying at Washington for a million of acres of land, more or less, and we shall soon have a Land Script department to peddle out the acres as fast as alcohol is needed."

Alex told of his own plans for the immediate future:

"I am getting ready again to go to Calumet after Christmas. I have got that baby on my hands and Quin absolutely refuses to take it again [and] as he has robbed the poor child of about half a million a year he can afford to let it squeal. I am now looking around for somebody to whom I can transfer my charge and do the signing of the certificates only hereafter and draw my dividends. As to making money for those bloated stockholders any longer, I will not do it. I will rig the machine and run to a depth of 2800 by simply keeping the wheels greased but by then my task is done and I will retire with a pension."

Birthdays were made festive occasions in the Agassiz family. Agassiz's own birthday, May twenty-eight, had several times been a matter of almost public rejoicing. He was one of the charter members of the Saturday Club,[4] that exceedingly convivial group of famous men brought together by Emerson as prime mover. After going to Concord, Emerson had been occasionally lonely for his Boston friends, and those who in after years thought of Emerson as austere should consider the Saturday Club. There were always at least seven courses at the meal, which began at three in the afternoon and sometimes lasted till the first hours of the following morning. There was always sherry, sauterne and claret — everyone smoked cigars, including Emerson, and "Agassiz always sat at the head of the table by native right of his huge good fellowship and intense enjoyment of the scene." Longfellow sat at the opposite end, sometimes also referred to as the "head" of the long table graced by Hawthorne, Oliver Wendell Holmes, Professor Felton, Professor Pierce and assorted wits and scholars. To Agassiz went the credit of teaching the chef at the Parker House, where the meetings were held, to serve mutton rare. There were no set speeches, but no Saturday went by without remarks from almost everyone except Hawthorne and rarely did one of the poets arrive without a line or two — or twenty — in his pocket.

On Agassiz's fiftieth birthday, "the flower of the feast was the reading of three poems by our three poets, for the occasion," at least according to Emerson. "The first [was] by Longfellow, who presided; the second by Holmes and the third by Lowell; all excellent in their way." A birthday of Agassiz's was celebrated in Rio at a men's dinner, with crossed flags of Switzerland and the United States, many toasts and much international company. Agassiz's students often serenaded him on his birthday and there always seemed to be a dinner party for men, whether May 28 fell on a Saturday or not. His little girls wrote of helping their stepmother arrange flowers for him on his desk and a present — a silver inkwell. But their private family celebration would wait till next day.

Another family celebration was always on December 5, Mrs. Agassiz's birthday. It began at breakfast time with presents for her from everyone including the servants. Then there was a dinner at night for as many of the Carys, Feltons and Agassizs as could be gotten together. On December 5, 1873, Elizabeth was fifty-one years old. The Alexander Agassizs were living with her — Anna "in deep mourning for her sister's little girl" but "black was most becoming to her and she had especially her little duchess air." The Shaws came over from their home in Brookline — Henry Higginson was in high spirits, his "droll chaffing" and Ida's good-natured "receiving of it" making everyone laugh. The Cary sisters, Caroline, Sallie and Emma, were there.

Agassiz had been forbidden the cigars which he had smoked so constantly, but in honor of this occasion he smoked one. There was a great deal to eat and good wine to lift the spirits, to make the talk flow freely and to make Alexander's premonition of paying "a heavy penalty" for happiness seem pure nonsense. There was music — for the fine piano given to Elizabeth Agassiz as a wedding gift was never silent on such happy occasions.

Agassiz was sure he would "sleep like a tub" that night. But he woke next morning feeling still "strangely asleep." He went to the museum, but returned long before he was expected and lay down on the couch just to rest a little.

Agassiz went to sleep, recovered consciousness from time to time — but never spoke again. He had been greatly distressed because one of his colleagues had "softening of the brain" and had lived for twelve years without possession of his faculties, but Agassiz was to escape this tragic fate. He lingered only eight days.

Elizabeth's sister Sallie came "to take charge of the household," while Elizabeth stayed by her husband's side. Dr. Brown-Séquard came on from New York, but there was nothing he could do except to order "food by injection," because Agassiz's throat was paralyzed. Elizabeth refused to give up hope, because she had seen her husband rally not once but several times from similar conditions, and the fact that he had lived to be sixty-six was in part due to her care of him. She was sure that she could somehow help him now, and "when she knew that he was dead she was in a state of most unnatural excitement," Sallie said. But next morning, Elizabeth "was like herself again and wanted to see everyone who belonged to her and Agassiz."

Elizabeth dreaded the large funeral which she knew must take place, but somehow she got through it all. "It was a winter afternoon without snow" when she and her children — now hers more than ever — went to Appleton Chapel "that stands among the college elms." "The vice-president of the United States was there, the governor, the ex-governor, Admirals, Major-Generals, poets, naturalists — distinguished ladies, Europeans who came to the United States with Agassiz, members of the faculty and students." It was Jules Marcou, one of the Europeans, who recited the list.

"The students laid a wreath of laurel on his bier and their manly voices sang a requiem; for he had been a student all his life and when he died he was younger than any of them." Theodore Lyman, himself a former student, said this.

Agassiz was buried in Mt. Auburn Cemetery in the Cary plot. A boulder, its surfaces planed by the ice of the Aar glacier, was later brought from Switzerland to be his monument, and his daughter Pauline planted pines around it to make it seem like home.

Almost immediately, Elizabeth received another blow. Alex's wife Anna had been ill. On December 22, "the news from Annie" was very alarming. But "one refuses to believe such a misfortune," wrote Caroline Curtis. It was almost Christmas, and Carrie was "busy all morning" of the twenty-third, "folding and arranging presents for the Cambridge basket." [5] There was something for each of Anna's three little boys, George, Max and Rodolphe — who was just three years old. She was marking little George's drinking cup when her husband came to the door of her room and she could see by his face "that sorrow had come." Anna Agassiz had died of pneumonia.

Elizabeth "made Christmas for the children," and when her sister Carrie went to see her she marveled at the calm atmosphere. The children's "Aunt Carrie" felt that she disgraced herself by bursting into tears. But Elizabeth Agassiz, when Rodolphe climbed into her lap and cuddled against her, knew at last how it felt to have a little child of her own.

Of her husband, Elizabeth wrote:

"It is over, — a life that grew daily fuller and richer in happiness for twenty-three years and was only clouded at last by my anxiety for him. I can never tell anyone how delightful it was to live by the side of a mind so fresh and original, so prodigal of its intellectual capital. There was never a day when I did not feel this powerful stimulus and it seems to me now that I am in danger of mental starvation. And yet were it not for the young life broken at my side in whose desolation my grief is swallowed up, I could be happy, I think, for a long while in my memories.

"My life after Agassiz should be gone had always seemed to me very clear and simple — to gather up the lovely scattered threads of our past, to live on my recollections and to watch over Mother if she should survive him — that was the quiet end I pictured for myself. How little we know what is before us — in less than a week after we followed Agassiz to the grave, Alex and the children were left to my care, and yet when his father died, Annie seemed perfectly well. Alex and I will live together now and a mother never had a more tender, affectionate, delightful son. If I can do something also to comfort him and make his life less desolate, I shall think myself very happy." [6]

Elizabeth Agassiz could see part of what lay before her. She was to mother a family of three little boys. She would never have believed that what most women would call a brilliant career also lay ahead — she was to become one of the founders and the first president of Radcliffe College.

CHAPTER TWENTY–ONE
Our Harvard Girls

FIVE years went by before Alexander Agassiz could bring himself to face the Christmas holidays on Quincy Street in Cambridge without his wife. "Few young men have reached my age and have attained, as it were, all their ambition might desire, and yet the one thing which I crave for and which I want to keep me interested in what is going on, is wanting," he wrote, soon after Anna's death. "How gladly would I exchange all that I have for what I have lost." His custom had been to go to Michigan in January, but now he went in early December — leaving his children with his stepmother.

The season was just as lonely for Elizabeth, but she determined to make it festive for the three little boys. There would be a tree — still considered a German custom, and by no means universal in American homes. Agassiz had loved it. There would be some sort of entertainment, a musical play perhaps, with a part for every child. One year Lizzie "wrote up *Beauty and the Beast*" in dramatic form and made costumes for the cast. Each year the entertainment was different, but the order of events became a family tradition: "tree and presents first" on Christmas afternoon, then supper for the children, and after that the program, reminiscent of Temple Place days. It might be "tableaux from *Lohengrin*" with Emma Cary "playing the music behind the scenes" and Ida's little son, Alex Higginson, "funny and earnest as the Knight drawn by swans." [1] Then there was the year when George Agassiz got a magic lantern for his Christmas gift and "showed beautiful old pictures" while a "quartet of men's voices in another room, sang Christmas carols and hymns."

During 1874, the year after Louis Agassiz's death, his son Alexander felt a returning spark of interest in life when he raised funds for the Museum of Comparative Zoology in his father's memory. In a little over twelve months, $300,000 was collected, $150,000 being given by Pauline and Quincy A. Shaw, $55,000 by Alexander Agassiz, and $50,000 by the Massachusetts Legislature. The rest came from popular subscription and included $1215 from Calumet miners. But Alex had now learned that money, though useful, was not the whole answer to any problem. He could build up a memorial fund but he could not buy remembrance. "Men who have made their mark in the history of science, disappear from the history of the very centers where they have been most active," he said. This was "because their successors are always in a hurry to show how much wiser and more learned they are than their predecessors."

Alex hoped that by administering the museum himself, he might keep his father's memory alive. But Louis Agassiz's significance was first of all as a human being, then as a scientist. His memory was almost lost in the mournful line of brick buildings that eventually rose on Oxford Street, with their locked doors and darkened corridors. He lived again in the small museums that sprang up all over the country both during his lifetime and after his death. In these, Agassiz's enthusiasm, glowing in his students, was kindling a new fire in many a visitor who strayed out of curiosity through hospitable doors — and lingered to find a new field of study.

Louis Agassiz had no money to leave to Elizabeth. His son Alex took over the Quincy Street house, and Elizabeth kept careful accounts so that Alex should not be charged with her personal expenses — such as cab fares and dressmaker's bills. At first she had very little money of her own, but eventually her income from various family trust funds came to about three thousand dollars a year, which was ample for her modest needs.

As hostess for her stepson, it devolved upon Elizabeth to arrange social functions and train a staff of servants. Her way of meeting each new challenge in her life was to think out a plan and then put it into practice. To the many servants, she explained their separate functions lest misunderstandings and jealousies arise. Her "Memorandum for the Laundress" was a case in point. The laundress was to be on special duty every other Sunday. She was to "make the attic beds, empty slops, etc." Alex had remodeled the Quincy Street house, "making it handsome and comfortable," but evidently omitting plumbing facilities for the top floor. On the same Sunday, the laundress would "attend to the beds and the rooms of the family in the evening. In any case of company," she would "attend in the kitchen or pantry as called upon, being sometimes ready to wait at the door."

On the same Sunday, "when the parlor maid goes to church," the laundress would "wash up the breakfast things. When, in case of company, the chamber maid is called to help the waitress, the laundress and the seamstress do the work of the chambermaid, together. The seamstress takes care of her own bed on Sundays." This memorandum is followed by Elizabeth's casual notation, "Had Scientific Society — some hundred people to lunch."

Alexander Agassiz never remarried. His stepmother brought up his children and ran his house in winter, and in summer his wife's mother was his hostess at Castle Hill, the many-gabled house he built in Newport. Alex had taste and the means to gratify it — oriental china and antique English silver being among his collections. Entertaining was on a lavish scale in Newport [2] where he carried his staff, his horses and carriages — while Elizabeth went to Nahant to live the quiet life she preferred.

Alex had his father's charm, when he chose to exert it, and his dinners were notable for wit as well as learning. But Elizabeth was in possession of his secret. After a series of particularly brilliant affairs, "I feel as if I were acting a lie," he told her, "but it is a harmless one which I must make up my mind to keep up for many a long year."

Elizabeth was fifteen years younger than her husband, and she had always expected to live without him someday. But the mind accepts what the heart cannot forget, and she found herself listening for his voice in the hall and his step on the stairs. It was good to have to rearrange the house for the children. A room adjoining her own was furnished for the boys and another for their father. A French nurse was found for "Rodolph" [3] and quarters prepared for her. Soon, Elizabeth was laughing over the boy's struggles with two languages. "I don't want to *me coucher*" he was to declare at bedtime. It was more serious when Max, who was eight, got hold of his father's pistol and "accidentally fired it off." There was no harm done, but Elizabeth admitted that she felt "shakey" for some time afterwards. "I got a large crop of grey hairs, suddenly," she said.

In 1875, Ida Higginson came home to Quincy Street for a long visit. The Higginsons' only child, a little girl named Cecile for Ida's own mother, had died of a fever the summer before. There had been "a perfect terror about bad sewage and malaria in Boston" and "the smell" in Brimmer Street, where the Higginsons had been living, "was sometimes intolerable." Now Ida was expecting another child and she felt sure that this child, too, would die. "The beautiful nursery . . . with the empty chairs drawn up to the low table, the doll's bed and bureau, all the things that Cecile loved and played with" made Ida weep uncontrollably — and to whom should she go for help but to her second mother?

"At first I was very discouraged about her — she seemed somehow beyond my reach, sinking in deep waters," Mrs. Agassiz said, "but before she went away I saw that the change of scene and being forced to see and talk with others had brought back a natural expression to her face, the old tone to her voice . . ."

One caller at Quincy Street was Oliver Wendell Holmes. He found Mrs. Agassiz "at work" on her husband's correspondence and she "talked in a very quiet, interesting way about her married life. What a singular piece of good fortune it was that Agassiz, coming to a strange land, should have happened to find a woman so wonderfully fitted to be his wife!" It seemed to Holmes that Agassiz "could not have bettered his choice if all womankind had passed before him, as the creatures filed in procession by the father of the race."

It was in May, 1874, when Dr. Holmes found Elizabeth beginning the preparation of a biography of Louis Agassiz, but it was probably not until 1876 that she actually began to write. All during her married life, Elizabeth had arranged the household to revolve around her husband's teaching, writing and research. She must now direct a still more complicated establishment and she had no one to help her protect her own hours of work. She resorted to lists and schedules, jotting down in a series of line-a-day diaries items which must not be forgotten. She had written to Agassiz's family in Switzerland and they had gathered together as much of his correspondence as they could find. But the packets of letters were slow to arrive — fellow students and pupils who had been queried slow to answer. On January 24, 1877, Mrs. Agassiz "completed the Munich period, ready for copying."

She always hoped to be in her cottage, high on the cliff at Nahant, by the end of May. This place had always been dear to her, and was now doubly so because of her memories of Agassiz in the laboratory here. It was a place where much work could be accomplished even with a houseful of visiting relatives and friends. Long before it was time to leave Cambridge, she sent orders to Farquhar, the nurseryman, for "variegated honeysuckle" to climb the porch pillars and sprawl over the roof at Nahant; for "blue ageratum for borders and boxes . . . double geraniums and rose geraniums, hollyhocks, marigolds, dwarf and tall oriental poppies." These were for summer; but there must be autumn flowers, too, because Elizabeth would hate to leave Nahant before October. "Perennial golden coreopsis, single dahlias, china asters" — the list was long, and Elizabeth's conscience troubled her about these extravagances, but flowers she could not resist. No gift ever pleased her more than a shipment of rosebushes from Ida.

A niece described "Aunt Lizzie" in her garden at Nahant, wearing "a fresh white morning gown, basket and shears in hand, going leisurely, with her rather stately air, from border to border and then coming back into the porch and arranging flowers in different vases. Lemon verbena and heliotrope she always had in abundance, so that the rooms were fragrant with them. . . . She had a glass tank on the porch in which she kept pond lilies."

It sounded like a life of ease. No one ever noticed that Mrs. Agassiz was always "at work in the morning — but with many interruptions," to quote her own record. No one guessed that "fog and rain" were welcome "in the fall when one is alone at Nahant — with work and a fire" on the hearth. In September, 1877, Mrs. Agassiz went over to see Longfellow to ask if she might read her first chapters aloud. She wanted his criticism, unsure of herself. On October 8, "Began our first reading," she jotted down. "Longfellow is pleased."

The entry in Longfellow's journal for October 8, 1877, shows that he was not merely being polite. "Mrs. Agassiz reads to me the Life of Agassiz she is writing, the beginning only. Very interesting. Childhood."

It was indeed the "beginning only." Elizabeth Agassiz was still struggling for time for her work when a Cambridge neighbor, Mr. Arthur Gilman, came over to see her. He had a daughter for whom he could not find a school exactly to suit him. "Opposed to co-education, we did not care to send our daughter [Grace] to High School," he said. "And we objected also to sending her daily to Boston in the horse-cars." He remembered Mrs. Agassiz's school for girls, where Harvard professors had taught, and he thought something similar ought to be done for Grace.

On February 4, 1879, a group of Cambridge women, meeting at Mr. Gilman's house, 5 Phillips Place, Cambridge, nominated Mrs. Agassiz as a member of a committee to sponsor a school for girls, taught by Harvard professors. Little knowing how far-reaching would be the results, she accepted the nomination.

A circular was "worded with care." Mr. Arthur Gilman later wrote a detailed history of these first stirrings of an idea which led to the founding of Radcliffe College, and he said that the circular avoided "two possible misconceptions, (1) that the plan in any way flavors of or tends to co-education and (2) that Harvard College is in any way responsible for it. . . .[4]

"Mrs. Agassiz expressed the opinion that money sufficient could be had when wanted," said Mr. Gilman. Still intent upon finishing the biography of her husband, Elizabeth never dreamed that, with this simple statement, she had made herself Radcliffe's first President.

From now on, whether or not Rodolphe had "Dyptheretic" sore throat, whether Alex entertained titled European scientists or wanted his "paper on flounder corrected," Mr. Gilman "conferred with Mrs. Agassiz." They decided that "the expense of instruction would probably not exceed four hundred dollars a year" per student, "and may be as low as two hundred and fifty." And "if the scheme should succeed, endowments will no doubt be procured which will reduce the expense." It could not have escaped Mr. Gilman that Louis Agassiz had been past master at securing endowments and that his wife had not only learned the art but was connected either by blood or by marriage with some of the wealthiest people in the area. Together, Mr. Gilman and Mrs. Agassiz drew up a list of Harvard professors to approach on the subject of teaching a few girls in their spare time.

Professor William E. Byerly, Mathematics, said yes — he would charge three dollars an hour. Professor J. P. Cooke said he would teach chemistry but only if he could teach in a laboratory. Professors Benjamin Pierce and F. H. Hedge agreed to teach with no strings attached, but William James believed in wholesale rates. He would teach Psychology and Modern Philosophy, but not for more than four hours a week. He would charge "not less than four dollars an hour" and his price "would probably exclude any solitary pupil." For three pupils, he would charge six dollars, "for four, five and for five or six only $1.50 apiece." For any class larger than six, the charge would be ten dollars an hour.

And now it was seen that this was no "High School" such as Grace Gilman needed, after all. She was sent to Bradford Academy and it was "hoped that in Cambridge young women will pursue a regular College course of four years." The "certificates" which students were to receive for each course successfully followed would then be "merged into one, which will be signed by all the instructors."

Of course the new school had a name. It was called "The Society for the Collegiate Instruction of Women by Professors of Harvard University." "It is probable that a very small number of women will be found at first," said Mr. Gilman, who was not a little astounded at the direction his tentative idea had taken. The school might not do for his daughter Grace, "but it may grow," he said.

Before anything could actually be done, President Eliot had to be consulted. He said that Harvard professors would be allowed this extracurricular activity and he knew very well that they needed the extra money. He remarked that the young women would need a place to live. By March 3, 1879, "three applications had been made to Mrs. Agassiz," and she began to turn over in her mind what to do with "our Harvard girls." But soon it was time to go to Nahant, and Mrs. Agassiz seems to have forgotten the Harvard girls altogether.

The summer of 1879 was a particularly happy one for Elizabeth. "My work gets on," she said. She was progressing with the biography and also preparing a revised edition of *First Lessons in Natural History*. During the bright summer mornings, she sat at her desk within sound of the surf. Out on the piazza were "Quinnie and Robbie," two of Pauline's boys who were visiting their grandmother and taking their first German lessons. Alex's boys were in Newport as usual, but "Alex's chicks arrived in time for Rodolph's birthday on the third of August." He would be nine years old, "seemed very happy and content" although there was stormy weather and he could not have his promised fireworks. The grandchildren were growing up, ready for "lawn tennis and riding," and Elizabeth remarked that she did not seem to find much time to work. And then, all of a sudden, it was September. "The house seems so still," she wrote — for all the children and grandchildren had gone.

On September 4, 1879, by ferry, by narrow-gauge railroad and by horsecar, Mrs. Agassiz traveled from Nahant to Cambridge to a "meeting for the Harvard Girls." This was the day the first entrance examinations were held. Twenty-seven girls were accepted, two left before the end of the year, and out of the remaining twenty-five only three took the regular course. The others rated as special students at the Society for the Collegiate Instruction of Women by Harvard Professors. A girl needed special aptitude just to remember the name of her school, and when the name was jeeringly changed to "Harvard Annex" Mrs. Agassiz herself took it up with gratitude. It suited the pages of her line-a-day diary much better simply to jot down "Annex meeting."

Here was a college class, however, without a dormitory and without classrooms. Mrs. Agassiz found that it was her special duty to go around to Cambridge neighbors and persuade some of them that they wanted to hand over a spare bedroom to a Harvard girl. Two classrooms were hired for the girls at the home of Mrs. J. F. Carret, Number 6 Appian Way, and it was soon decided that two more of the Carret rooms would be needed. The rent for four rooms for four years came to $650.

Elizabeth had been shopping in the spring at R. H. Stearns in Boston, to buy "dimity valances for the beds at Nahant." Now, in the fall, she measured the windows on Appian Way, bought muslin and made curtains which she hung herself. Behind these muslin curtains, the subjects offered were Greek, Latin, Sanskrit, English, German, French, Philosophy, Political Economy, History, Music, Mathematics and Natural History. Some of the professors held classes for the Harvard girls in their own homes, however. Professor Goodwin "opened his study" to the girls, who were free to use his library of Greek texts and the photographs he had brought home from Athens. After class, the girls found Mrs. Goodwin's tea table set for them and good talk, often more valuable than recitations, went on in the living room before the fire. Professor Gurney's history classes were held in his study — his wife, who was a linguist, was interested in education for women, and a member of the "ladies' committee."

Problems soon began to come up which had to be discussed at "a meeting of the ladies" over at Mr. Gilman's house. Mr. Greenough, Latin teacher, appeared and wanted to know if "Miss Gay," who had "dropped Latin 4," would still have to pay for the course. She would. Three other students wanted to take more than four courses, and another was already said to be taking five. Could this be done? Well — not for two hundred dollars, decided the ladies' committee, who had become seven lady managers. Only four of them — Mrs. Agassiz, Miss Alice Longfellow, Mrs. Gurney and Miss Lilian Horsford — had turned up on this particular day, to decide these questions.

Mr. Gilman had been chosen secretary in February, 1879. A treasurer was finally found in June, after "Mr. Henry Lee was chosen . . . and Mr. George Putnam in case he declined," whereupon they both declined. Mr. Joseph B. Warner, a Boston lawyer, consented to serve; and by August, 1879, a subscription amounting to sixteen thousand dollars had been raised. Later, Mrs. Agassiz succeeded in commandeering her son-in-law, Major Higginson, as treasurer. Professor James B. Greenough — who seems to have happened into a ladies' committee meeting because of Miss Gay's troubles with Latin — was for a long time the only faculty advisor to the committee.

No one had thought very much about a library for the students. In fact, no one had really expected very many students anyway, and here were twenty-five — a respectable-sized girls' school. In December, the ladies' committee voted to rent a room at the corner of Appian Way and Garden Street, and to hire a boy "to carry books from the Library and return them as called for by the young ladies." For a dollar a week David Bolger, aged thirteen, was engaged on trial to do this job. The "Library" mentioned here must have been the Cambridge Public Library, because it was not until the following May that Mrs. Agassiz was appointed a committee of one to ask President Eliot if the girls could use books from the Harvard Library.

"Mrs. Agassiz reported a satisfactory interview." She always did. This is not to say that she always got what she asked for, the first time, but she came naturally by the art of leaving the door open for further discussion whenever a request was refused. One of her greatest assets was her mild manner, her seemingly pliant disposition, which concealed infinite perseverence along with faith in ultimate victory. President Eliot, in this case, was satisfactorily interviewed, but the Harvard Corporation viewed the matter with alarm. Suppose a Harvard man wanted a certain book and a girl had it? It was even possible to visualize a time when women might actually want to enter a Harvard Library and sit down to read. The Governing Body of Harvard knew, without question of a doubt, that no Harvard student could concentrate in the presence of females. The Annex sent out an appeal for books and by 1889 their own library had 2886 volumes, a record of which they were extremely proud. Six hundred and seventy-nine were new books; one hundred and three were in either Greek or Latin.

Mr. Arthur Gilman was an unselfish and tireless worker for the Annex. When the school began to grow in spite of his gloomy prognostications, he was understandably overanxious to prove that he was the one who really started it. He was by nature rather dictatorial, and Mrs. Agassiz, the woman whose name had been proposed at a second committee meeting, came to be regarded more and more as the moving force in Annex affairs. Not inconsiderable was her task of keeping Mr. Gilman from antagonizing those whose favor must be gained, and still more difficult was her job of keeping Mr. Gilman from getting his own feelings hurt. "Will you kindly allow me to see you again before you take further steps about raising money?" Mrs. Agassiz wrote to Mr. Gilman, in the spring of 1882. "The more I think of this, the more I fear we shall drift into building up another female college distinct from the University . . ." She feared the "multiplying" of women's colleges, "thus weakening all instead of strengthening those that already exist." [5]

Mrs. Agassiz had Wellesley particularly in mind, and often warned that Radcliffe must not attempt to duplicate or to rival this earlier college. Not that it was as yet "Wellesley" to which she and her Cambridge friends referred. It was "Durant's College." On October 25, 1875, for example, Longfellow made this entry in his diary.

"Drove with the Horsfords and Edith to Wellesley to see Mr. Durant's Female College. A fine building overlooking Lake Woburn. Three hundred pupils.

"After dinner a row on the Lake in the College boat, *Evangeline*, with a crew of eight girls, and the handsome Captain, Miss Emerson. It was like sailing with the nine Muses."

Being only human, Elizabeth Agassiz could not help feeling a twinge of envy, once in a while, where the future Wellesley College was concerned. Professor Horsford, who had gone out there with

Longfellow, had been Professor of Chemistry at the Lawrence Scientific School until 1863, when he went into industrial chemistry and became independently wealthy. Early in his career, he had taught in the Albany Female Academy, was heart and soul in favor of higher education for women, and had now taken Wellesley under his wing, donating money for books and scientific apparatus. To Wellesley went the honor of having "the first laboratories for scientific investigation made available for women in the United States." The wife of Louis Agassiz could not rest until there was a laboratory of some sort for her Harvard girls; but for a long time two small wooden buildings would have to suffice, while she kept right on campaigning for something better.

The Managers and Advisory Board of the future Radcliffe College met on April 25, 1882, and voted to incorporate under the name of "The Society for the Collegiate Instruction for Women," and they left out the part about the instruction being by Harvard professors. But Mrs. Agassiz had determined in her own mind that this was the one thing that would make the Annex unique. Her attachment to Harvard was as strong as her faith in God. All her male relatives and most of her American male ancestors went there, temporarily straitened circumstances being the only excuse for an occasional lapse in favor of a countinghouse. Her husband had labored to help Harvard emerge from the status of a college into that of a university. Mrs. Agassiz disliked the idea of co-education, but a university could include the instruction of women. This was a subtle distinction perfectly clear to feminine logic. And before the Articles of Association were finally signed, on May 22, the words "with the assistance of the instructors of Harvard University" had been added to the legal name of the Corporation.

On July 6, 1882, at the first meeting held after the articles had been signed, Elizabeth Cary Agassiz was elected president. She must have come up from Nahant to attend the meeting, leaving behind her the manuscript of her biography of her husband. She would never have interrupted her work on her book in order to help out the Harvard girls, she told her sister, if it had not been for her own school where Agassiz had taught.

The idea of that little school in the attic room on Quincy Street had been such a good one that Elizabeth could not help but rejoice to see it revived. Now she was president of a college with a name nobody could remember. She had never in her life desired public honors, and she still had no idea that she had embarked upon a career. She was sixty years old.

CHAPTER TWENTY-TWO

"X" College

IT was "a kind of exciting adventure" to start a college. So Mrs. Agassiz told one of the graduating classes at the Harvard Annex, and this was typical of her understatements.[1] For ten years, she solicited from friends and relatives for funds for an institution that might go out of existence at any time. Descendants of Thomas Handasyd Perkins, children and grandchildren of his State Street merchant friends, had a habit of expecting good value for their money. They received satisfaction from contributing not only to worthy causes but to stable organizations, and there were times when Lizzie Agassiz must have felt almost like a swindler. She could never guarantee from one year to the next how long there would be an Annex.

Alexander Agassiz, Quincy Shaw and Major Higginson all made it clear that to underwrite or actually to sponsor a woman's college would be beneath the dignity of Harvard. In 1893, for example, Mrs. Agassiz noted in her diary, "Little talk with Alex about the Annex this morning. He is discouraging and I think he would rather discourage [members of] the Corporation, should he see any of them."

To the outsider, the duties of a College President might seem to be to live in a handsome house, to entertain celebrities properly, to approve or disapprove the work done by a Dean or Deans. But no one needed to tell Mrs. Agassiz that her most important function was to raise money. She organized a series of "parlor meetings" in Boston, in 1883, as one of her first moves. "To Miss Ellen Mason's [in the afternoon] to hear Lizzie speak about raising money for the Annex, which she did most delightfully, interesting to everyone," wrote her sister Caroline, who was inclined to be critical but was evidently impressed. Later, Lizzie spoke in the evening "so men could hear her."

"The so-called 'Annex'" was a name often heard in Boston, Elizabeth said, reading from a carefully prepared manuscript. She doubted if any body knew a great deal about it because "it came into life so quietly." There were now "from thirty-five to forty pupils," most of them teachers in search of further education beyond the Normal School level. She "had to confess" that it was very expensive for them. "The charge per year for a full college course is $200" which was "$50 more than is paid by Harvard students." And there was "the expense of living in Cambridge."

"We have had as yet no flighty students," Mrs. Agassiz remarked cautiously. And she took notice of "certain anxieties respecting the presence of young women in a University town, without constant oversight of their daily lives." This had never worried her, personally, she said. "Our students are scattered by twos and threes in Cambridge families, their lodgings being chosen for them by their friends or by the ladies of the Executive Committee. . . . They quietly pursue their occupations as unnoticed as the daughters of any Cambridge residents." From the point of view of the students, this may have been a sad state of affairs, but the audience in Boston parlors were favorably impressed.

The Annex had been "more nearly self-supporting than we expected and we still have funds enough to carry it on for a year or two longer," Mrs. Agassiz explained during these 1883 spring meetings. She wanted "a large endowment fund, by which means we also hope to commend ourselves to Harvard College and establish a definite relation with the University." The invitations to the "parlor lectures" had been carefully issued and representatives of Boston's higher echelon could be relied on to understand that Annex students "simply want the best education they can get, and they seek it at Harvard because the means to that end exist there . . .

"The school stirs no prejudices, excites no opposition, involves no change of policy for the University," said Mrs. Agassiz, hoping she was right. "Our students themselves manifest no desire for co-education. The element of competition with men does not enter into their aims." She could not help it if her girls worked harder than most of the Harvard men and got better marks. She could not help it if sometimes they rejoiced greatly in these triumphs — but it was not a matter to bring up right now.

Harvard was supposed to be rich, Mrs. Agassiz told her parlor groups. Actually, Harvard's "large deficits for several years past tell us this is not true." Either anticipating arguments or answering those already made, "Harvard needs all she has and more." There would be no asking for money and the Annex would not "come as charity scholars but with full hands." In return for official recognition, a sort of guarantee that Harvard professors would continue to be allowed to teach at the Annex, Mrs. Agassiz wanted to give Harvard "no less than $100,000" because "anything less would make us, financially speaking, an unsafe acquisition for the University. . . .

"Even if we should succeed in raising the whole of this sum, it would not put the education of women on a par with that of men, at Harvard. Indeed, we are advised that for so large a scheme, it would be quite insufficient. But it might give the college the means of continuing on a somewhat broader basis, the work already begun. . . . Good work wins good will, and we cannot but hope that if the College accepts us, we too shall have . . . our bequests and legacies like some departments of the University."

It was as though Harvard were a fortune-hunting bachelor, and as though Mrs. Agassiz were trying to raise a dowry for her deserving daughter, the Annex. But she did not get her money. Times were hard in 1883, and in 1884 even Calumet and Hecla passed their May dividend (a matter which Mrs. Agassiz's sister Caroline referred to privately as "rather a blow"). Harvard had no use for a dowry of only ninety-three thousand dollars, and many of the members of the Corporation breathed a sigh of relief when the vote went against official recognition of the Annex. Of course there was just one thing that everyone underestimated, and that was Elizabeth Agassiz's patience.

The purchase of Fay House in September, 1885, was "a daring experiment" for the Annex. The Carret house on Appian Way was no longer big enough for classes, even though professors helped out by the use of their own homes. And the Fay house was for sale at twenty thousand dollars. This seems a high price for the times, but it was large — almost castlelike with its stone bastions, high ceilings and spacious parlors — a pleasing example of American Gothic. The land was choice, a corner fronting on Garden Street and overlooking Cambridge Common, with Mason Street on one side. The Washington Elm stood in front of the house, and from the garden the whole effect was of romanticism. Having inherited the house in 1856 from her father, Judge Samuel P. Fay, Miss Maria Fay lived there alone in maidenly dignity. In 1885, Miss Fay had come to the conclusion that she would like to see her house occupied by Harvard girls before she died — assuming, of course, that she could get her price.

"A daring expenditure is sometimes wise economy," Mrs. Agassiz said, but she could not bear to touch the endowment fund, now invested and drawing interest, though still short of the goal. "Friends were generous — about half the purchase money" for Fay House "was subscribed — the other half we took from our treasury"

The year 1885 was one of personal achievement, also, for Elizabeth. As William James wrote in October, "Mrs. Agassiz is out with her husband's life in two pretty volumes." James thought it was "a rather short and simplified . . . performance but it gives a beautiful picture of an energetic nature impassioned in one pursuit." It was curious that James should complain about its being short — there were seven hundred and eighty-three pages exclusive of index. If Elizabeth could have written as freely for publication as she did in her private letters, it would have been a better book, but it is interesting and readable, even today. Its preparation, lasting nearly ten years, had formed a sort of inner life for her as day after day she sat at her desk surrounded by her husband's papers. She would miss the work "it was a reward to do," but the reams of foolscap she spoke of buying were evidence of the drudgery now ended.[2]

Four years after the purchase of Fay House, the Annex bought an adjoining piece of land and built a physics and a chemistry laboratory. The two small wooden buildings were "quite pretty and attractive," Mrs. Agassiz said — as though describing summer cottages. She continued to call attention to the fact that at the Annex there was never any "instruction outside of Harvard," and that after ten years of "quiet, unobtrusive existence" — since those first entrance examinations in 1879 — "between fifty and sixty Harvard professors and instructors" gave courses. The students now wanted "academic degrees" instead of the certificates they were given and, since all their courses had been under Harvard instruction, they thought the President of Harvard ought to countersign their diplomas, if and when they passed their courses.

The Annex had "an invested capital of $150,000 with landed estate, buildings etc." Mrs. Agassiz guaranteed that the school was self-supporting, would never cost Harvard a cent, and she wanted to "pass over all our present property" in return for diplomas but "not asking for any rights and privileges" such as Harvard graduates acquire "in the business affairs of the college — as votes for various offices etc., etc."

Elizabeth Agassiz had more luck stalking an iguana in the Galapagos Islands than she did in getting Harvard into anything which looked like an entangling alliance. Her son-in-law, Henry Lee Higginson, recently appointed Fellow of the Harvard Corporation, and her stepson Alex, from time to time Overseer, then Fellow of Harvard, told her how hopeless was her cause. In March, 1893, she wrote anxiously to President Eliot, having heard that he favored granting degrees to Annex girls and that he was "to bring forward our hopes and fears to the Corporation on Monday next . . .": "I am most anxious that we should appear in our true light, as reasonable and not aggressive," she said. It is hard to see how she could have been less "aggressive," but her fears were well founded.

Relying on personal interviews, Mrs. Agassiz tried to see Edward W. Hooper, Treasurer of Harvard, before President Eliot made his official request to the Corporation. Mr. Hooper said he had been away, and could not see Mrs. Agassiz — but his letter was so stiff and self-righteous that it seems unlikely that he would have granted an interview anyway. "It is of course, quite natural that we should have serious doubts about more permanent relations with the Annex," he wrote. He had been talking things over with Mr. Joseph B. Warner, first Treasurer of the Annex, who "showed me quite clearly that there is no reasonable limit to what the Annex might ask of us. The Annex really wants all that the College has, and does not expect to get it except through the College. If we give our degrees we must give instruction necessary to fit women for those degrees, and that means either a duplication of our instruction, or to some extent co-education. I have no prejudice in the matter of education for women. . . . I am quite willing to see Yale or Columbia take any risks they like, but I feel bound to protect Harvard College from what seems to me a risky experiment. . . ."

Mrs. Agassiz replied in a tactful letter designed to keep negotiations alive. This time, however, it seemed as if all doors were shut in her face and that Harvard's "No" was final. So much publicity was given to Harvard's refusal to grant degrees that "some of the friends" of the Annex "who had not spared time or money" began to cool off. Mrs. Agassiz was as close to despair as she had ever been, and she said so when she went to call on Mrs. John E. Gray, wife of the Royall Professor of Law in the Harvard Law School.

Professor Gray heard all about it when he came home to dinner that night. Suddenly he "felt ashamed because he knew little and cared less" about the Annex. He "liked Mrs. Agassiz" and he hated to have her "harassed." Professor Gray turned the matter over in his mind and came up with a lawyer's solution to a difficulty which had been hampering Elizabeth Agassiz's work for fourteen years. The wonder of it was that no one had thought of it before and still more wonderful was the fact that it pleased everybody.

According to English law, all collegiate institutions must have "visitors." These are competant outsiders appointed by the college to check on progress, much as auditors look over the books of a business firm. In English law, "if there is no other visitor provided for by the statutes of the college, then the Crown is the visitor," explained Professor Gray. He had just finished studying a case where "the functions of visitors had been much considered." Why not make Harvard University the Visitor of this women's college that stuck so closely by its side — constantly claiming protection and refusing to disappear?

The idea was delightfully quaint and old-world. Moreover, the Board of Overseers was already the Visitor of Harvard — no breaking a sacred trust here but merely continuing a sacred tradition. Professor Gray wrote to Mrs. Agassiz and she was "truly grateful." Instead of offering to Harvard all the worldly goods which the Annex had, she and Professor Gray put their heads together and decided no such thing was necessary. "It would simplify matters much to retain the present organization, leaving to us the financial responsibility . . . We offered to give all that only because we thought the College might prefer a complete surrender," said Elizabeth — and Professor Gray agreed.

Then came the matter of the degrees. The "form of our diploma should be carefully studied — that it should not be differentiated from the 'A.B.' of Harvard, as a 'ladies degree,' " Mrs. Agassiz announced. And once and for all she put herself on record concerning equality and women's rights. There should be no aping of men, no excessive rivalry, but "Work is work, and must be judged without fear or favor."

Professor Gray proposed that "the Annex Girls have a place in the Harvard catalogue." It would be an important point in our favor, agreed Mrs. Agassiz, thinking what an advantage this would give her when she asked for funds. The lawyer then thought of a point which might help to secure any wavering votes among members of the Corporation of Harvard University. The agreement could be "cancelled by either party on four years notice."

When it came time to write up a "memorandum of agreement" between the President and Fellows of Harvard College and the Society for the Collegiate Instruction of Women, it was evident that no one was going to want to write out the long official name of the

Annex seven times, as required by the seven paragraphs of the document. There had already been discussion concerning a new name. Professor Charles Eliot Norton suggested "Emmanuel" because that was the college from which John Harvard came. But no one liked it very well. Finally, it was decided not to hold up the proceedings for lack of a name. "X College," said the memorandum of agreement.

"X College to be self-supporting in all respects . . . The President and Fellows of Harvard College to be the Visitors of X College; no instructor or examiner to be appointed or retained by X College without the approval of the Visitors . . . The diplomas of X College to be countersigned by the President of Harvard University and to bear its seal; the graduates of X College to have their place in the Catalogues and official publications of this University" — and the whole thing to be "cancelled by either party . . ." should either side repent themselves of the bargain.

It was President Eliot who thought of the name for X College. The Corporation had just revived a scholarship upon information unearthed by Mr. A. Mc F. Davis. The "first woman who ever gave anything to Harvard College" was Lady Mowlson, who gave one hundred pounds in 1641. "Mowlson College" would not do, but fortunately Lady Mowlson had a charming name of her own — she had been Ann Radcliffe before her marriage.

Plenty of people had thought the name should be Agassiz College, but Elizabeth would have none of it. At the next meeting of the Annex council she "put forward President Eliot's suggestion." "It seems appropriate," she said, " 'Radcliffe College' " — dignified and convenient." She was pleased when she found that there was "great enthusiasm among the students, both about their new status in respect to Harvard and about their new name."

In order to incorporate under the name of Radcliffe College and to have the right to confer degrees, an act of the Legislature was necessary. And now, just when it seemed as if there would be smooth sailing, this was opposed on the ground that there was "no guarantee that the new college is able to maintain the high character which it is the duty of the State to require of all its institutions which it charters to grant degrees . . ." The fact that Harvard could withdraw any time was brought up as an argument against a charter, and the much-prized agreement that the President of Harvard should countersign diplomas was brought up as showing that "alone, the new college may not be a competent degree-conferring institution."

The Committee on Endowment of Colleges, from the Association of Collegiate Alumnae, hired a couple of lawyers to set forth these objections and a hearing was ordered for February 28, 1894. President Eliot spoke in behalf of Harvard's plan and J. B. Warner, Treasurer, represented Radcliffe. Four of the most interested of the professors — Norton, Goodwin, Goodale and Byerly — went along to the hearing with prepared speeches in defense of Radcliffe in their pockets.

Elizabeth Agassiz had the responsibility of making the main speech in behalf of the college — just as her husband had so often "gone before the Legislature" in behalf of the Museum. But where Louis Agassiz had delighted in swaying an audience, Elizabeth dreaded all forms of public address. Over the tea cups in her own parlor, she could persuade almost anyone to do almost anything. But public speeches had been for men only, when she was a girl. She wished that things were still ordered that way and that her friends, the suffragists, had not won so many so-called rights.[3] It never occurred to her to refuse to speak, however, or to delegate her duty. Painstakingly, she wrote out her remarks:

"I am aware that our small means have been made a reproach to us, and that our opponents and your petitioners say that we are not rich and well-endowed enough to be trusted with the giving of degrees. It is true that our means are small as compared with certain of the colleges for women. But such as they are, they have been well husbanded; and the fact that we have never been in debt and that we now have pleasant buildings with accommodations for the instruction of three hundred students . . . all this will perhaps reassure you as to the practical management of our affairs. Neither must it be forgotten that if our endowment is small, the active and cordial cooperation of the professors and teachers of Harvard is better than money for us."

Including real estate and "certain legacies" promised but not yet

available, Mrs. Agassiz put Radcliffe's assets at $280,000. A large part
of this sum was the direct result of her own efforts — a point she
never mentioned. As always, she gave all the credit for everything to
Harvard. "But the true builders of the Annex have been and are the
Harvard professors," she said. "They have brought it to its present
prominent position. They represent its true wealth and its strength
— not a bad substitute for endowment funds, though measured by
other standards."

Mrs. Agassiz took a leaf out of her husband's book when she impressed the Legislature with the usefulness of Radcliffe to the Commonwealth of Massachusetts. "Of course our students belong largely
to the class of teachers — young girls who are fitting for a career, or
older women many of whom are experienced teachers. . . No one
can be blind to the advantage for our public education of thus bringing our public schools into more direct contact with our oldest University. . . ."

Of course Mrs. Agassiz declared afterwards that it was President
Eliot and the professors who came with her who really won the day
for Radcliffe. President Eliot said that it was Mrs. Agassiz.

"The Committee on Education is not one of the most distinguished
committees of the Legislature. It ought to be but it is not," said President Eliot. "The ambitious and able members of the Legislature prefer service on the Judiciary Committee or the Committee on Railroads. And so it happens almost every year that the Committee on
Education consists of a number of remarkably plain men. . . ."

The audience which collected in the spacious committee room besides being "singularly hostile" was made up mostly of women, "but
the expression on their faces as I looked at them was not tender,"
Eliot went on. "These women were of two minds: either Radcliffe
should become a college entirely separate from Harvard or Harvard
should take over Radcliffe and let undergraduate women sit in
classes with the men. Radcliffe would reject the first idea and Harvard the second" — as Mrs. Agassiz knew perfectly well. When she
finished reading her paper, she said she was ready to answer questions and this, President Eliot said, "was a terrible ordeal for her."

"Her replies to the questions of the Committee were more effective than her paper. It was an effect produced by her personal bearing, by her speech, and the absolute sincerity and disinterestedness of her petition. It was an effect of personality in public speech as clear and strong as I have ever seen. Before she ceased speaking, the case was won."

President Eliot tried to put into words what Mrs. Agassiz was like. She was "cultivated, well-bred, and in her manner aristocratic," he thought. She was so "modest and unassuming that, at the end of her ordeal with the committee, she had no idea" that she had won them over but was "agitated . . . and felt that she had not succeeded."

As he watched the faces of the committee members, President Eliot felt that he knew what they were thinking. "I am sure those men said to themselves . . . 'I should like to do just what this woman wants me to do. I will vote for the establishment of any college of which this woman is to be the head. I will vote for the establishment of any college which is going to give this woman an opportunity to bring up some women like her.'"

The opposition withdrew objections, and Mr. George Hale, one of the opposition lawyers, sent his fee to Mrs. Agassiz to be added to the Radcliffe fund. The Legislature voted to grant the charter, and Mrs. Agassiz, who had been the only president the Annex ever had, now became the first President of Radcliffe College, according to law.

CHAPTER TWENTY-THREE

Private Life of Madam President

WITH the coming of age of Radcliffe, Mrs. Agassiz became increasingly well known. She herself seemed unaware of all this. But foreign visitors were taking tea on Quincy Street, one day when Caroline Curtis arrived from Winchester. The guests kept asking endless questions about the way in which Radcliffe came into existence — and Carrie was amused to hear her sister give everyone else the credit, leaving herself almost out of the picture. There were endless new demands upon her time, but Mrs. Agassiz made no complaint except to remark that it would be good to be away from the sound of the doorbell once in a while.

Elizabeth had time for few intimate friends, but among them was Sarah Wyman Whitman — whose interest in Radcliffe was almost as strong as her own. Mrs. Whitman was twenty years younger than Mrs. Agassiz, but they called themselves "twins" because they shared December 5 as their birth date. Sally Whitman was an artist, a student of Couture [1] in France and of William Morris Hunt in the United States — a portrait and seven of her landscapes eventually becoming part of the permanent collection of the Boston Museum of Fine Arts. She was said to be the first woman in America to work in stained glass and a memorial window to Mollie Felton was one of her designs. She painted wall decorations, such as "the charming frieze over the study window" for Bishop Phillips Brooks, but she was most in demand as a portrait painter. Elizabeth Agassiz found sitting to Sally a pleasure rather than an ordeal — they so much enjoyed each other's company.

Sally Whitman was better known for her social gifts than as an artist. Her studio at 7 Chestnut Street in Boston was a gathering place like the American studios in Rome of a previous generation, and she had a way of "mingling young and old" — Harvard undergraduates, Radcliffe girls and visiting Tuskeegee students all being invited along with Boston celebrities. Henry Lee Higginson remembered her as a "tall, graceful figure, clad in quaint fashion" and wearing strange jewels. "She was an intense woman, who gave herself and her possessions without stint." Early a member of the ladies' committee who guided the progress of the Annex, Sally Whitman was one of the few people with whom Lizzie Agassiz could talk with perfect freedom.

Now that Radcliffe had a name and a charter, a more formal organization was called for, and Mrs. Agassiz went into conference about it with Sally Whitman. Up to this time there had been only two officials, the president and a secretary. Mrs. Gilman had been "Chairman of the Students' Committee," her husband concerning himself with discipline, while an "Academic Committee" took care of courses and Miss Mary Coes, an early graduate, acted as secretary. The wonder of it was that such a casual arrangement had worked so well, but now Radcliffe must have a Dean.

After much conferring and after all other possibilities had been dismissed, Mrs. Whitman went to Philadelphia to interview Miss Agnes Irwin, who was headmistress of a select girls' boarding school there. On April 7, 1894, Mrs. Agassiz wrote in her diary, "Note from Sally Whitman — returned from Philadelphia, says 'dear Agnes Irwin will come if asked.'" It was now up to Mrs. Agassiz to see that Miss Irwin was asked.

Judging by the order of events jotted down, Elizabeth tackled the hardest job first. She talked with Mr. Gilman "about changes." He and his wife would no longer need to manage student affairs, but he would become "Regent." This was an honorable-sounding title which apparently proved acceptable. The interview with Miss Coes was not entirely a happy one, for Mrs. Agassiz said, "I hope Miss Coes will stay with title of Secretary and $1000 salary."

Entries in Mrs. Agassiz's brief journal for the next three weeks were all of "talks" with members of the Radcliffe Corporation, the Harvard Corporation and the executive board. She even missed a German lesson because of Radcliffe business soon to come up. Never leaving anything to chance, she saw everyone personally in a series of calls or at tea in her parlor on Quincy Street. Finally, the Radcliffe Corporation meeting took place and it was "very pleasant and on the whole amicable" and at "executive meeting" next day Miss Coes's increased salary was "favorably voted; Miss Irwin's invitation officially sent out." When Miss Irwin accepted, Elizabeth wrote on the envelope of her letter, "Acceptance of Deanship, Radcliffe College. A blessed day for me. E. C. AGASSIZ."

Miss Irwin was exactly the person needed as the first Dean of Radcliffe. She was strict to the point of severity, a devotee of pure scholarship, but most of all she was an executive. What had hitherto been a more or less integrated group of girls and women, some of them brilliant, some of them just taking courses in a casual sort of way, now became a well-run institution with rules and regulations. President Eliot told Mrs. Agassiz that "it has been found possible to carry a class of young women at the Annex as fast and as far with two lectures a week, as a parallel class of young men are carried in three lectures a week. . . ." Miss Irwin determined not only that the girls should continue to travel fast and far but that their scholastic prowess should be no secret. And if organization had been lacking, there should be abundance of it now.

To Miss Irwin, Mrs. Agassiz must have seemed a vague, mild-mannered lady, along in years, whose methods were oblique. It was pleasant to be given plenty of authority and to be left alone to do a good job. But when it came to negotiations between Radcliffe and Harvard, Miss Irwin found that Mrs. Agassiz was no figurehead president, after all. She would do things her own way and who could deny that her slow, quiet, tactful way was the one that got results? "The Annex," Mrs. Agassiz was still writing in her diary, and it was a useful reminder that smooth relations might be damaged any time.

The family claimed most of Elizabeth's spare time. There had been deaths, but the ranks were rapidly filled as younger generations formed an ever-expanding circle. The first loss was that of Professor Felton. He died in 1862 of a heart attack and his going was particularly poignant because of his young family and because he was Agassiz's close friend. "How blank a place he left," Elizabeth said. "I remember his constant little visits, half an hour for a chat . . . cheerful, genial, affectionate; he never came that I was not thankful to see him; he never went that I was not sorry to see him go."

Professor Felton had been President of Harvard for the two years just previous to his death. His reputation for scholarship was world-wide in his time, and "as to hospitality, his was almost of the Homeric stamp." He was the intimate friend of Longfellow as well as of Agassiz, and Longfellow's journal entry, written on May 29, 1853, reveals that Felton would have liked to become President of Harvard at that time. His administration is usually passed over as unimportant, but in the two years allotted him he saw the building of a new gymnasium which was "his pride." He was beset with difficulties and was quoted as saying that "there is no more comparison between the pleasure of being professor and president in this college than there is between heaven and hell." [2]

Elizabeth's sister Mollie "looked lovely in her widow's cap," a cousin remarked, mentioning also that Mollie seemed to have overcome the typical Perkins misfortune of overweight.[3] If anxieties could have made Mollie Felton slim, she had plenty of them. Her husband had nothing but his salary to live on, and Homeric hospitality together with journeys to classic lands could not have left much surplus with which to provide for a widow and five children. Two years later, in 1864, Longfellow's journal told of a certain morning call: "*Wednesday, June 1*. A lovely morning. The birds in full song and the lilacs in full bloom. Agassiz comes and says: 'I wish I had better news to bring you. Mary Felton is dead.'" It had been pneumonia — in those days so often fatal.

From now on, Mrs. Agassiz took the Felton children under her wing. Mary, a daughter of Felton's first marriage, was now twenty-five and attempted the care and guidance of a difficult, temperamental family — with help from her aunt Lizzie Agassiz, who was actually no aunt at all. Julia Ward Felton, the other child of Felton's early life, was twenty-two. Mrs. Agassiz's journal gave testimony to an attempt to sell the stories Julia wrote, and later told of regular carriage drives to the sanitarium in Somerville where Julia became increasingly withdrawn until at last there was no use in visiting her any more. Mary Cary Felton's own children were Louisa, known as Lisa and now only fifteen, "Con," his father's namesake, now thirteen, and young Thomas Cary Felton, nine years old. These boys must be educated and given a start in life. Their half-sister, their sister and their aunt Lizzie bent all their efforts to this end and it was for "Con" that Mrs. Agassiz eventually sold shares in Calumet so that he might buy a California fruit ranch. She provided music lessons for his little daughter, Elizabeth — delighted that this child had inherited Mollie Cary Felton's fine contralto voice.[4]

It was a family habit to keep a diary — if not a voluminous one like Elizabeth's Amazon journal or Tom's story of his stay at Maldonado, Uruguay, then a small-page notebook telling of domestic events. Probably Elizabeth had filled a series of such volumes before her marriage, but the earliest available records of this sort begin in 1877 and end in 1906 with a lapse between the years 1880 and 1892 when the little books have disappeared. The interval is bridged by family letters, but there are not many of these — suggesting that related personal papers may have all gone astray together. Perhaps they have been destroyed or perhaps they may someday come to light.

In any case, Mrs. Agassiz's sister Caroline kept much the same sort of record in a series of little leather-bound books which have survived. At about the time of Elizabeth's engagement to Louis Agassiz, young Charles Curtis, lawyer and member of a prominent Boston family, came courting Carrie. They were married in 1851 in King's Chapel, a year after Elizabeth's marriage to Agassiz, and they built a house on the edge of the lake in Winchester. Carrie wrote for the most part of such domestic crises as the departure of her cook, of rowing across the lake to get advice from a neighbor on how to cook a roast of veal, and of tears when the veal was underdone. She was never very domestic, but, under the pen name of "Carroll Winchester," she wrote novels and short stories, her sister Lizzie correcting the proof for her.[5] There was a first little son, Charles, who died, and then a daughter Margaret, born in 1858, and a son Charles, born in 1860. The miles separating Cambridge from Winchester seemed long ones, but eventually Carrie's husband was able to give her a carriage and horses and she often drove over to see her mother and her sisters Sallie and Emma, all of whom lived together, or her sister Lizzie. Her diaries supply much that would otherwise be lost from the private life of Mrs. Agassiz, whose public life as President of Radcliffe is of course a matter of record.

On the sixteenth of January, 1880, Elizabeth was in Winchester "all morning going over" her sister Carrie's story. The book came out in June and there were "pleasant reviews." There was the usual Nahant summer with the Cary family up at the big stone house and Elizabeth in her own, for, since her sister Mollie's death, The Buttery belonged entirely to her. But early in October Elizabeth's mother was taken ill — bronchitis, they called it. Mrs. Cary was eighty-six, and it was notable that no one had ever spoken of her as seeming old. They spoke, rather, of how they would miss her "cheerful, elastic spirit" when, with Elizabeth sitting by her bed, she "turned and settled herself as if to sleep."

During the spring of 1881 Caroline mentioned something that had for some time caused her sister Elizabeth anxiety. It was not Ida now but Pauline who suffered from melancholia. "We drove over to Brookline," Carrie wrote, where, at the Shaws' house, they saw "a whole room full of beautiful Millais pictures. Ida and little Alex [her son who was born in 1876] came out and the day would have been delightful but for the cloud of Pauline's depression." They had "persuaded" Pauline to go to her stepmother for a visit in the hope that this "depression" which had been "coming for some time" would lift, but as they drove from Brookline to Cambridge, "Pauline cried quietly in her corner of the carriage."

The year 1884 was eventful for the Curtis family because their daughter Margaret became engaged to Robert Shaw Russell. "An agitating morning," her mother said when Margaret told her the news. The next day they all went over "to tell Lizzie." Margaret was married in King's Chapel as had been her mother and her Aunts Mollie and Lizzie before her. Her mother mentioned in her diary that the groom's grandfather had once been minister to Russia and that his parents, who lived in Louisburg Square in Boston, were possessed of a "golden dinner service," trophy of Russian diplomatic days.

It was no surprise to read that Margaret went to her Aunt Lizzie Agassiz for a long visit when her marriage ended in tragedy in 1887. Her husband had been away on business and Margaret, anxious because he had not returned, was about to send a telegram when she saw in the evening paper that he was dead. Margaret put her life together again as best she could, becoming interested in "a society called the 'Young Travellers Aid,' " in prison visiting — and in Radcliffe. She soon became an active member of Radcliffe committees, and was the only one of many nieces to take part in Mrs. Agassiz's work.

In 1882, the Cary family sold the house with its big "flower window" on Ware Street in Cambridge and moved to 92 Brattle Street, a pleasant place of many rooms in the brown-shingled "cottage" style. It was a household of women, for here lived the Misses Sallie and Emma Cary, the elderly Miss Lyman, their former governess, and Mrs. Richard Cary, the widowed sister-in-law with her daughter "Georgie." And to this house came their brother Tom, from time to time, much broken in health from his various travels in South America. He suffered fully as much from the harsh medicines given him as he did from bouts of dysentery and malaria, and the family of women where he was obliged to take refuge in his illness exasperated him to a degree. California remained his love, and when he was "ill and out of his head" in Cambridge, he thought his nurse was a man he had befriended in San Francisco. Looking out of the window into the dreary November garden with its dried and withered stalks and dead grass, he thought he saw the bright California sunshine. Time and again, he got well to the surprise of everyone and went back to California. In 1885, while a prisoner of ill health in Cambridge, he wrote a history of California's early days, much of it from his own experience. If he had merely copied off his diary it would have made the most delightful reading; but he was afflicted with self-consciousness when he imagined himself addressing the public, with the result that although several copies of Tom's history in manuscript went to libraries, they languished there unread.

Tom Cary came back to his sisters in Cambridge in 1888, and this time not all the courage in the world could help him to return to California. He had a "swelling in his throat" which the local doctor pronounced nonmalignant, but which returned after an operation and continued to grow until his speech was affected. On Christmas Day, 1888, Caroline spoke of her brother Tom as "sitting up in his sitting room, speechless but very kind." Her widowed daughter Margaret had been with him a good deal, and her son Charles, taking a law degree at Harvard, had become interested in the Far West through his Uncle Tom. Tom had never married, although he had shown a decided interest in pretty girls when he lived in Argentina and vainly awaited the coming of the Agassizs at the port of Maldonardo.

Tom Cary died on the twenty-eighth of December, 1888. No one quite realized how much he must have detested the household of women, most of them growing old, until his will was read. He left one thousand dollars "to each of the Feltons and Georgie — the remainder to Charlie and Margaret." Their mother thought this "in some ways a painful surprise" because "nothing could repay" Tom's sisters, "Sallie and Emma for what they went through." But Carrie could not help rejoicing because "Charlie will not have to go West again" and because her daughter Margaret's bequest would "replace the money Margaret put into her husband's business." As for Mrs. Agassiz, whom her brother had failed to mention, "Lizzie said everything that was delightful about the will."

Mrs. Curtis, in her guise of the authoress Carroll Winchester, loved to collect romantic stories from life within the family. She had nothing to say of the education and future career of her sister Lizzie's three grandsons, but she made entries in her diary when George, the eldest, went to Europe presumably brokenhearted because his fiancé, Nellie Anderson, had jilted him. There was still better story material for Aunt Carrie when George "received a telegram of recall from Nellie, just as he was starting on an African expedition." Now all seemed ready for the happy ending. Mrs. Curtis went to a dinner party early in January, 1889, given for Alexander Agassiz and the table talk was to the effect that Alex had been in Europe "for a couple of months" in order to buy pearls for Nellie Anderson because he was so pleased with his future daughter-in-law that "none good enough for her could be found here."

In the spring, Mrs. Curtis "drove over to Cambridge" where she "had a delightful visit with Lizzie." The talk was all of the approaching wedding — when in came Charlie with news for his mother and his aunt. He had been at a dinner party for the engaged couple the previous evening, but "the guests of honor were not there," and "it was known that the engagement was broken."

Lizzie was "much grieved for the loss of her" and went to see Nellie in the hope of patching up a lovers' quarrel. But after the interview, "Lizzie felt more resigned to the situation," her sister said. George set out for "the West" on what the newspapers called "a dangerous expedition" — and Mrs. Curtis had another plot for one of her novels. The only trouble was that George took Charlie Curtis along — Charlie's sizable bequest from his uncle Tom Cary failing to save him from the Wild West after all. Lizzie went over to try to reassure her sister Carrie.

The young men returned safely, after enough adventures to supply them with anecdotes for years to come. And Mrs. Agassiz, who had so loved to travel with her husband, allowed herself to be talked into a trip to California with Tom and Mollie Felton. Conway was in "Monticelo," overseer on a fruit ranch and hopeful of transplanting his whole family to California, his land of promise. Aside from short excursions — to Lake Champlain with Ida and Pauline, to Niagara with her sister Sallie — Mrs. Agassiz had strayed no farther from Cambridge than to Nahant for the last twenty years. Her trip to California was in 1892, when her own diaries are again available, and her entries sound like notes made by a young girl on the eve of her first journey away from home.

Styles were changing, but a widowed lady still wore a cap. The question, then, was what caps to take to California. Elizabeth listed "morning caps, dinner caps, pins for caps and dress." She was in doubt about what to wear out-of-doors — should it be "bonnet or hat"? Inclined to be daring, she decided upon a hat. There were frivolous items also, "bracelets, brooches" — and a gift from Sallie of "a dear little bracelet watch for my journey."

On March 10, "to the cars at three o'clock," went Elizabeth, with her niece and nephew. There were "many friends and flowers and sugar plums." Next morning "a tremendous blizzard of snow" stopped the train for several hours, but "the cars were comfortable" and Mrs. Agassiz a cheerful traveler as always. There were sightseeing breaks in the journey, and then "Over the Kansas prairies all day — to me most beautiful — these undulating lines and soft coloring — the strange sense of sea, for the surface heaves and breathes like the sea, the long swells hiding the horizon. . . ."

Most exciting was the sight of "snow mountain peaks," and Elizabeth named them off: "Humboldt, Agassiz, Humphreys." [6] It is not every woman who has mountains named for her husband, and Mrs. Agassiz "sat outside on the observation platform" feeling a very special sense of pride in the Western Mt. Agassiz and in watching the peaks which " followed us in varying aspects all the morning till we lost sight of them in Johnson's canyon." Pioneers were still pushing westward, and they "passed a camping ground, half tents, half frame cabins."

This was not just a sight-seeing tour and a family visit for Mrs. Agassiz, however. She addressed various groups in Los Angeles, Pasadena and San Francisco, reading "a paper on the Annex." Western parents in search of an Eastern education for their girls must not be allowed to overlook the superlative attractions of a school taught by Harvard professors. Mrs. Agassiz was gratified by the response and was able to satisfy her conscience that this trip was not pure self-indulgence.

After a pack trip into Yosemite Valley, which was the high light of her vacation, Mrs. Agassiz returned home by way of the Canadian Rockies. The railroad was "wonderful but it seems very dangerous," she said, and she marveled that "men should have said, 'I can do this, and I will.' " There were floods, washouts and delays of which Mrs. Agassiz made no complaint except that she had only three days to spare in order to arrive in time for "Annex Commencement." This was the day when, as College President, she always made a speech — a duty which she greatly dreaded. This year, however, there was pleasure to follow. At the Harvard Commencement she "saw Rodolph come down to take his degree."

In the Quincy Street house, the boys' rooms were now more often empty than occupied, but still theirs none the less. Alex and his three boys were less frequently mentioned in the daily journal but the items concerning them still had a familiar ring. "*August 10.* Working on Alex's report." And at another time, "George and I took tea together and read his manuscript all evening."

Entries concerning "Rodolph," her youngest and so much her own child, were of a different nature. "Rodolph" was "slightly hurt in Polo." He would not be able to play for a while, which was "a shame." He "arrived from Wellesley and said their whole party was coming to lunch." This was entirely unexpected but Mrs. Agassiz and her devoted servants rose to the occasion, and the luncheon "went off very pleasantly."

The diaries were much too brief to do justice to the great event when Rodolphe Agassiz brought to Nahant Maria Dallas Scott of Philadelphia, the girl he was to marry. His grandmother wrote all about it in a long letter to "Sally" — probably her friend Sally Whitman, this time, rather than her sister. Alex had been with her, and he and his stepmother "put roses in the room" that Marie, as they called her, was to occupy. Alex's son "would have been pleased with the part his Father took in it — it seemed to give him so much pleasure to do this first little service for the daughter who is to come."

"With this and a cup of tea," Mrs. Agassiz and Alex managed to pass an hour waiting for a girl they had never seen. "I confess we sank into that agitated state of waiting when the slightest suspicion of a wheel on the driveway makes for a start. Very punctually they arrived and that was the last moment of doubt or embarrassment. I cannot imagine that a daughter could be received with more affection or come into a home (where she did not know a soul) with more simple trust and frankness. Alex and his little daughter were at once at home with each other; it was nice to see and made me happy for him.

"As for myself, she came to me at once as to a friend on whom she had a natural claim. We went to her room together and she was delighted with the welcome of the roses. After that followed a very cheerful teaparty; for we were all hungry; and then followed a happy evening. I felt in a dream as I looked on and saw this young girl the center of the group and Alex, Max and Rodolph surrounding her, while I watched them from my corner by the fireside."

She would always love "little Marie." "My heart is at peace for Rodolph," she said, and added that "the coming of this daughter to Alex seems to me like a blessing."

The following spring, on March 27, Mrs. Agassiz jotted down in her diary that "the marriage" was "the prettiest, the most cheerful and festive, throughout that I have ever seen." And where but to Quincy Street should Marie and Rodolphe come for their first home? They were looking for a place in the country, where Rodolphe could keep the "pretty pony pair" he liked to drive, and his polo ponies, and the saddlehorse that Marie would ride so well. Eventually, they settled in Hamilton, Massachusetts — but there was no need for haste, when it was really such a pleasure for Mrs. Agassiz to have them with her. They were the third young couple to make Quincy Street their first home.

It was the biggest event in Elizabeth's private life since the voyage of the *Hassler* when Pauline and Quincy Shaw asked her to go abroad with them. There was only one regret: she would be away when Marie's first child was born, and little Marie might need her.

This matter of being needed was no delusion on the part of an older woman concerning a younger generation perfectly able to look after itself. In each of Elizabeth's families, whether by blood or by adoption, there was always someone depending on her. At this point, it was her stepdaughter Pauline who needed her most. A

beautiful woman of great wealth, happily married, Pauline nevertheless still suffered from attacks of severe melancholy. Her case was
particularly sad because she tried so hard to overcome her trouble.

Pauline Agassiz Shaw was never self-centered, never idle. Kindergartens were her special activity, and she had come directly under
the influence of Elizabeth Peabody — doubtless through her stepmother. When the Boston School Committee discontinued public
kindergartens in 1879, Mrs. Shaw supported more than thirty schools
in locations where the children most needed to be brought in out of
the streets and given care. She paid for teachers and equipment, even
for food and clothing for some of the children, and many of the
buildings housing the kindergartens belonged to her. All this might
have been done merely by using dividends from Calumet and Hecla
and drawing checks at a desk from time to time. But Pauline supervised personally. She gave herself as well as her money, and she
knew teachers and children. At Christmastime the "great tree"
which Mrs. Agassiz went to see at the kindergarten for the blind
was always loaded with gifts of Mrs. Shaw's own choosing. On the
list of the members of the first American Froebel Society was Pauline Agassiz Shaw and also Elizabeth Cary Agassiz.

Mrs. Agassiz's anxiety about Pauline was reflected by a sentence
or two here and there in her diary. On returning from California,
she wrote, "Pauline seems perfectly well." And again a few days
later: "To Pauline's. All tranquil and cheerful there." During the
summer of 1894, Mrs. Agassiz enjoyed "a perfectly delightful day
with Quin and Pauline" at Nahant — "Pauline cutting and pruning
my trees." But by autumn of that same year, Pauline had suffered
another severe attack of depression, a new doctor with a new "cure"
had failed to help her, and her husband decided to take her abroad
in the hope that a change of scene might be the answer. Two of
their children — young Pauline, known as "Paunnie," and Robert
Gould Shaw — or "Robbie — were to go along. It was a doubtful
experiment, but Quincy Shaw was depending on his mother-in-law
to make it come out right.

CHAPTER TWENTY-FOUR
The Grand Tour

Remember that my European experience consists of one week in England, one in Paris and four in Switzerland," Mrs. Agassiz said when she set out on the Grand Tour with the Shaws. Almost all her male cousins on Temple Place had been sent to Europe to finish their education and most of the girls had gotten there, either with husbands or in search of them. In the matter of mileage, Elizabeth was doubtless the most traveled of all, but letters which she wrote on the Amazon reached her sisters in Europe. Now at last she would have her winter in Italy like all her friends.

For some people, Pauline Shaw's melancholy might have proved contagious — or she might have exasperated a traveling companion. Mrs. Agassiz knew that the best thing she could do for Pauline would be to enjoy the trip herself. Accordingly, when Pauline felt too ill to go out, it was Elizabeth who went with Quincy Shaw to visit the Impressionists whose work he enjoyed so much. Monet, his studies based on the then recent optical discoveries concerning the nature of light, particularly interested Mr. Shaw. "I have to thank Quin, not only for bringing me to see pictures," wrote Mrs. Agassiz, "but for teaching me all these years to enjoy them — for his pictures are really an education," [1] and now she watched him painstakingly deciding which new canvases to add to his collection at home. "I enjoy pictures now as I should not have done in my earlier years," she admitted, but she was not ready to judge the merit of the modern art of her time. It interested her to watch her granddaughter's reactions. "Paunnie takes great pleasure in the galleries; her father has of course awakened and trained her love of art — but for all that she has a very independent opinion."

"Quin, Pauline and I went to breakfast at Versailles," wrote Mrs. Agassiz. "All went well till we reached there and I thought Pauline was enjoying the little excursion. But at breakfast she broke down and the latter part of the day was sad — she went to bed utterly discouraged, poor child." This recognition that Pauline really wanted to be well was the keynote of all Mrs. Agassiz's entries concerning this daughter of hers. Gradually faith in her, on the part of her husband and her stepmother, and her own determination began to show results. Fewer and fewer were the notations of Pauline's recurring depression.

The travelers reached Rome on Mrs. Agassiz's birthday. This trip was "the most beautiful birthday present that Pauline and Quin have ever given me," wrote Lizzie. And a little later, in Venice: "I suppose everyone falls under the enchantment of this place. For myself, I must say that were I seventeen instead of seventy-two, I could hardly feel more romantic."

In any city in the world, Mrs. Agassiz would have found friends or made them; and in Rome, which was to be their winter headquarters, there was still an American colony. All the young artists were now flocking to Paris to study, and the Roman American colony was a little sad, more than a little elderly, and decidedly gone to seed.

The first call that Mrs. Agassiz and her son-in-law made in Rome was at William Story's studio. Elizabeth remembered him from Temple Place days when he had been one of the handsomest of the young men who gathered in those hospitable houses. She knew his wife, the former Emelyn Eldridge of Boston, whose social gifts made the Storys' Roman studio a Mecca for American visitors and where the Brownings were often to be met with. Such was Mrs. Story's success in getting social lions to come to her studio parties that

Julia Ward Howe had remarked that the stone lions carved on the Palazzo Barberini staircase were the only ones who never went inside. She was climbing the stairs herself when she said it — being decidedly a lion or at least a lioness at the time.

But all was now greatly changed. Emelyn Story was dead and William Story "looks sad and has lost all the vivacity of his old manner," Mrs. Agassiz said. He showed her through "his own studio; charmingly arranged and very attractive — and then showed us some of his son Waldo's work, of which he is very proud." Waldo Story "has a great many orders and is very successful. He is doing some very costly work for one of the Rothschilds now." Waldo Story's wife had "renewed the Friday afternoon receptions" which Waldo's mother used to have, but when Mrs. Agassiz went to one, although she admired "the beautiful set of rooms with such enchanting views of Rome," the scene was "peopled with ghosts" for her and she wished she could have been there in earlier days when "Liszt was to be heard (if he chose)" and the Story studio had been so full of enchantment.

Next day Mrs. Agassiz went to Richard Greenough's studio. In her younger days, Richard had been a still more frequent caller than Story and she had kept in touch with him. William Story and Richard Greenough were both of them now seventy-five, having been born in 1819, within a few days of each other. Would Greenough also be "declining fast," as Elizabeth was obliged to say that Story was? She had so looked forward to meeting in Rome the members of her Boston circle who in their youth had escaped the law office or the countinghouse and taken refuge in the world of art. She had half expected that in the enchanted atmosphere of Rome no one grew old and William Story, "losing strength in every way," had been a shock and a disillusionment.

Richard Greenough restored Elizabeth's confidence in the durability of her own generation. He was as brisk as ever, "affectionate" even, and soon began squiring her about to the galleries. Lizzie, a "romantic seventy-two," had the time of her life as she and Richard spent "a whole morning in the Vatican gallery" for a "rapid review" and then returned again and again while he showed her "the world-renowned figures and his own favorites." She thought his own work "seemed to have gained strength in his later years" and she was impressed because he had not abandoned it, as Story had done — even though he certainly seemed willing to set it aside for her sake.

Having promised "dear Julia Howe," Mrs. Agassiz "hunted up Maud Howe Elliott" who, with her artist husband, was still living in Rome. "Across the river" and through narrow stone-paved streets went Lizzie Agassiz, asking her way in English, French and German when her newly acquired Italian failed her. At last, "up five flights of dirty marble stairs" she went, coming to a door with John Elliott's card nailed to it. She rang and soon found herself in "a cozy little parlor with a wood fire burning" and Maud, "looking handsome," was being "brave in her difficulties which are not slight." Maud Howe Elliott was "working hard with her pen" to make things easier "for her boy," as she called her husband, who was "getting on well" with his painting for the Boston Public Library.

Inevitably, Mrs. Agassiz heard all about the decoration.[2] It was a painting containing thirteen winged figures; twelve of them female to represent the hours, and one of them male, representing Time. The Christian centuries were symbolized by twenty horses — there was "Life," "Death," a sun and a moon. The whole thing was called "the Triumph of Time" and until it was done and he got paid, John Elliott would have to depend on his wife's pen. " 'The Triumph of Time' will require time," remarked Mrs. Agassiz, dryly. "It is very large — let us hope it will be great, if it does not find favor." But she rather feared that neither greatness nor popularity would attend it. The picture had been commissioned in 1892 and was finally installed in 1901 in Boston — where the public liked it rather better than Mrs. Agassiz had expected. It was soon forgotten, however, for it was a ceiling painting, and succeeding generations of Bostonians were somewhat stiff-necked.

The discovery of art had not diminished Mrs. Agassiz's enthusiasm for music. Mrs. Stephen Perkins, a family connection, elderly and alone, occupied a small rented room in a convent and "seemed to live on church music." She knew "a member of the Pope's choir and through him has information in advance of all occasions where there is to be music of special interest. . . . She is such a frequenter of churches in her search after music that she knows how to find shelter in corners away from drafts and where there are rests to keep one's feet off the cold floors," Lizzie said. Together, the two ladies from New England rambled all over Rome listening to liturgies. It was great good fortune for the lonely Mrs. Perkins to have so congenial a companion as Mrs. Agassiz, but Elizabeth expressed no regret when she heard her last Roman liturgy and she and the Shaws set out for Florence.

Robbie Shaw, ostensibly traveling with his parents, was absent more often than present during all the sight-seeing. No sooner had they landed and reached Paris than Robbie set out on a trek of his own — "We are so sorry that he did not like being here," remarked his grandmother — but this was a point on which Robbie changed his mind, liking Paris as soon as his family left. He was supposed to join his family in Rome, but failed to appear. His mother grew despondent again when the truth came out — that "Quin has telephoned Robbie that he need not come." Always a bit careful of what went into her journal, Mrs. Agassiz did not say that his father spoiled the boy, but this was a legitimate conclusion. Robbie finally turned up in Rome just in time to go with his family to Florence, which he endured for a week and then left.

His mother "was not well and had a bad night — a great nervous excitement" when her youngest went off again. But to travel with his sister, his parents and his grandmother was not exactly gay for a young man, and perhaps his father hoped that independent European travel would help him mature. It was hard to be named for Robert Gould Shaw, the Civil War hero, at a time when there was no great call for heroism. But neither was it easy to grow up very much while footloose in Europe with too much spending money. Robbie bought experience, doubtless at a fairly high price, but it was not necessarily the kind that would do him much good.

In Florence, Mrs. Agassiz spoke of "lunch with the Alexanders — what a bright old lady! I think it's good for Pauline to be with Fanny A. — they have an affinity for each other." Fanny A., daughter of the "bright old lady," was "Francesca," an American expatriate artist to whom John Ruskin had written innumerable letters, signing them "ever your more than grateful and more than ever loving Fratello." To these she replied as his "Sorella," sprinkling her letters with sisterly affection. No one on earth except Elizabeth Agassiz would have dreamed of referring to the famous Francesca as "Fanny A."

Nevertheless, as Fanny Alexander, "Francesca" had come to Florence with her parents, because of her father's ill health. Her mother was a well-to-do Bostonian and her father a self-taught portrait painter of considerable merit.[3] In Italy, the family became more Italian than the Italians, and Francesca went out among the Tuscan hills where she discovered a young girl strangely gifted in extemporaneous ballad-making. She set down this girl's words and music, then made metrical English translations of her own, engrossing on parchment the Italian on one sheet and the English on another, and illustrating each with designs composed from Italian field flowers. Full page illustrations were drawn in pen and ink in the Pre-Raphaelite manner, with fine detail, originality and real beauty. She achieved a book of arrestingly high quality which she called *Roadside Songs of Tuscany*. Ruskin "discovered" her in 1882 and lectured about Francesca, the "fine gold which has been so strangely entrusted to me, and which before was a treasure hid in a mountain field. . . ."

Ruskin completely changed the tenor of Francesca's life. He made her so famous that her home was scarcely less popular with tourists than the Pitti Palace and the Ponte Vecchio. Francesca bore it well. She thought of Ruskin as a "very pleasant, elderly gentleman with a kind face, a fine voice, and very simple friendly manners." She prepared two more books for which Ruskin found a publisher in England.

Charles Perkins, a cousin of Elizabeth's, had spent many years in Europe, not succeeding as an artist but becoming a connoisseur. He really did more for Francesca than Ruskin ever did, because he saw that her fame was not bringing her a livelihood. Her father was long since dead and her mother's modest fortune exhausted. Perkins paid for the publication in the United States of *Roadside Songs*, under the title *Songs of Tuscany*, and when this beautiful book proved so expensive to produce that there was no hope of any income from it, Perkins gave Francesca an annuity.[4]

Ignoring the Italianized name by which she was known among her admirers, Mrs. Agassiz spoke of Fanny Alexander but said never a word of the paintings and drawings which hung on the walls of the old palace where the Alexanders lived. She was interested only in Miss Alexander's school for Italian children and in the fact that Pauline and Fanny A. arranged to meet every day. There had been many days when Pauline found it impossible to meet and talk to anyone. But now Pauline began to help with the school, and at the end of their stay in Florence she gave the children such a party with such presents that they were "speechless and starry-eyed." Mrs. Agassiz believed that this marked the turning point in Pauline's recovery.

In May, 1895, her niece Mollie Felton and Mollie's friend Isa Gray arrived in Europe, and Mrs. Agassiz joined them to go to Oxford and Cambridge. Elizabeth had seen the places where the friends of her girlhood had gone to find the atmosphere they hoped would make them artists. She had seen elderly widowed friends of ample means wandering aimlessly through foreign churches, keeping out of drafts. Many of her contemporaries had gone to Italy in search of health but the well-populated Anglo-American cemeteries bore mute testimony to the error of this idea. Mrs. Agassiz sent home a long list of the graves of friends and friend's children where she had placed flowers. She was glad to have had her own winter in Italy, but without the slightest regret she set out to visit colleges for women in England so as to have something she could bring home to Radcliffe.

Cambridge, England, came first on the list. Mrs. Agassiz found "a sense of antiquity, a rural quality, suggestive of quiet and scholarly seclusion" which suited her perfectly. Early in the morning, after their late evening arrival, Mrs. Agassiz, Mollie and Isa put in their appearance at Girton. If it was felt in some quarters that Harvard's dignity had been threatened by the proximity of Radcliffe, the attitude of Cambridge University toward its two women's colleges, Girton and Newnham, struck the American visitors as even more pronounced. The impression they received was that the colleges had been pushed as far out of sight as possible, the better to be forgotten.

Radcliffe was a comparative newcomer to the ranks of colleges for women in the United States, but Girton had been founded in 1871, only eight years before Mrs. Agassiz attended her first meeting in behalf of "Harvard Girls." Cambridge did not share its "antiquity" with its women students, and Cambridge degrees were not to be granted to women until 1923. Mrs. Agassiz was astonished to discover that "the instruction in the colleges for women at Cambridge and Oxford is by no means given altogether by the teachers and professors of the University. Much instruction is given by ladies, many of whom have themselves been educated at the colleges where they teach."

"The distance of Girton from the University struck me as objectionable," said Mrs. Agassiz. In fact, she found it downright insulting. "The Chancellor, Masters and Scholars of the University of Cambridge" were happy to have Girton about two miles from their august headquarters and as far as Mrs. Agassiz could tell there were "no tramways or any regular line of coaches." It was part of the function of the college "to provide carriages for driving the students to and from all lectures." She "heard nothing of bicycles here" nor did she see any. At home in America, the young lady cyclist with her high buttoned shoes and her daring shoe-top skirt was becoming very much the style, and Mrs. Agassiz thought that bicycles at Girton "would be not only a quicker but a more economical way of making the short journey."

Mrs. Agassiz did not care very much for people who were "shy." And on visiting Newnham College, she found Mrs. Sidgwick, "Principal at Newnham," to be "a shy, reserved woman." She was "wealthy and gave most generously to the institution," but Elizabeth was obviously hard-pressed to find enough good qualities to balance against the fault of shyness. Mrs. Sidgwick was "fond of lawn tennis" — but this helped only a little.

British college girls were having a good time but in so discreet a manner that even Elizabeth Agassiz, who could not be said to advocate riotous living, was surprised. "Over at Newnham, for recreation after tea," some of the girls "were blowing soap bubbles into the air and over the grass."

There was a luncheon next day for Mrs. Agassiz and her traveling companions, and the visiting Americans asked many questions. After the long battle to allow none but Harvard instructors or professors to teach at Radcliffe, it was surprising to find a system of women instructors along with University Professors tolerated at Cambridge. At both Girton and Newnham, she "felt that the presence of these ladies, their easy, sympathetic companionship with the students, must form no small part of the education" of these girls. Miss Gladstone, "daughter of the statesman," was one of these resident teachers — "an exceptionally pleasant woman of much personal charm." She was evidently not at all shy.

Mrs. Agassiz was invited to take a look at the girls' living quarters. "They have generally at Girton a sitting-room with bed-room adjoining . . ." At Newnham there were bed-sitting rooms where the beds "are broad couches, which when covered by afghans and well cushioned, serve as sofas during the daytime. As for furnishings — they were like college girls' rooms everywhere, made cheerful by the girls themselves, with pretty tables and chairs, with draperies and screens, their favorite photographs etc."

After Cambridge, "to give an account of" the Oxford Colleges for women "would be to go over the same ground as at the Cambridge Colleges," said Mrs. Agassiz. Truth to tell, she had lost her heart to Cambridge with its quiet river overhung with willows, its bridges and its gates. She was "hospitably entertained at Lady Margaret Hall and at St. Hughes" at Oxford, but Cambridge remained her favorite. Although she had come to observe and learn, at venerable Oxford Mrs. Agassiz as first President of Radcliffe found herself the teacher. A great many questions were asked concerning Radcliffe's struggle for recognition from Harvard, no such happy outcome being even in sight where Oxford was concerned. The women would have to wait until 1920 to be admitted to examinations for an Oxford degree, so nothing Mrs. Agassiz could tell them in 1895 was of very much use.

After the visit to Oxford and Cambridge, there was one more European stone unturned. Mrs. Agassiz re-crossed the channel and took the night train from Paris to Lucerne, where she was to see some of her husband's relatives, representing now a second and a third generation. She dreaded it. In fact, she came very close to feeling shy, that state of mind she so deplored. It was "agitating," she said, and she was afraid she would find herself "more or less out of their circle." Of course nothing of the sort happened. The whole "Swiss family" gathered at the old home where Madame Agassiz had spent her last years. There were "hours in the shady garden," where tables stood "always ready for tea or coffee and where the many young people were gay and full of fun, and the older people quietly talked over memories of the past. . . ." Mrs. Agassiz found herself "quite at home."

In mid-June, Mrs. Agassiz went from Switzerland by way of Milan to Venice for one more look at that romantic spot capable of making a woman of seventy-two feel seventeen. This time there was a great gathering of friends and relatives from home. Helen Cary was there, Mollie Felton, and Isa Gray, together with various and sundry Curtises, and Carrie Hall, Julia Ward Howe's granddaughter who was in Europe studying art. They all floated blissfully along the canals, all the happier because of being surrounded by people from home and seeing Venice through strictly New England eyes. "Being all women and all of one mind, we were absolutely irresponsible as to hours," Mrs. Agassiz was glad to say. "Everyone breakfasts when she sees fit and as we have the most amiable of cooks and housekeepers in our *padrona*, she never minds any amount of unpunctualities." After years as a housewife, soothing the nerves of the cook when a scientist husband, son and grandsons were late to meals, the *padrona* seemed an angel. "A life so free from conventionalities and at the same time so sympathetic was never shared I think, by a household of half a dozen people."

Nevertheless, by very reason of the contrast, Venice with its almost currentless canals, its smells not always entirely romantic, reminded Mrs. Agassiz that it was summer at Nahant. There, the breakers were roaring against the cliffs below her house. "But with all the charm of Venice, I think the greatest happiness of my life here is the thought of Nahant. . . . One must allow something for the love of a lifetime, the place where you were almost born . . ." Elizabeth Agassiz would never under any circumstances have become an ex-patriate.

This was the first year that Mrs. Agassiz had ever missed a Radcliffe commencement. It was great news when her cousin, Lilly Cleveland, wrote that the Radcliffe exercises had been held in Sanders Theater, in Memorial Hall. Mrs. Agassiz remembered the time when the graduating class had received their certificates in her parlor on Quincy Street. She had kissed them and given each a rose. Then came graduations at Fay House, still small intimate affairs but more formal. Now the girls would march into the building sacred to the memory of Harvard men fallen in the Civil War, their presence proving that they were "University Women," as Mrs. Agassiz expressed it. In her diary she wrote: "It sets the seal upon our final adoption. The best news I could have heard from Radcliffe."

CHAPTER TWENTY-FIVE
Honorary President

ELIZABETH AGASSIZ arrived in New York on October 25, 1895, and found her grandson Max waiting for her on the dock. Next day they went to Boston by train, and there were her sisters Carrie and Sallie at the station, with a carriage to take her to Cambridge. There was just time to dress and arrange flowers before the family gathered for a big dinner party in honor of her safe return. And then, "coming up to my room at the end of the evening, found the E. C. Agassiz Scholarship." During Elizabeth's absence in Europe, friends and family had subscribed $6150, "given without restriction" save that the scholarship should bear her name. "It was an enchanting joy of my return," Elizabeth wrote before going to bed that night.

Radcliffe affairs were sometimes a source of anxiety as well as "enchanting joy," as Mrs. Agassiz revealed in a few laconic phrases in her diary. "Our dreaded Association meeting over — quite tranquil — no words, great relief." And again, "To Council meeting . . . some of the propositions seemed to me preposterous." The subject was new buildings which Radcliffe greatly needed and Mrs. Agassiz "feared all unity and harmony of plan will be lost sight of."

Radcliffe was entering upon a building phase which would require a great deal of money. To Miss Agnes Irwin, young, ambitious, the future was a challenge and she outlined Radcliffe's requirements. Those pretty little wooden chemistry and physics cottages must go. "Radcliffe needs laboratories of the best sort for teaching purposes," said Miss Irwin, quite rightly — "it needs departmental libraries; it needs a gymnasium and lecture halls of its own; it needs houses, not too large and plenty of them, in which its students may live in a tranquil, wholesome way." Of course this was an appeal to the public, but being addressed to President Eliot, it seemed rather like a demand upon Harvard, and Mrs. Agassiz had always been so careful never so much as to seem to ask Harvard for anything that she was horrified. "Dear Agnes Irwin" would have to spend a few days at Nahant and get a few things very gently put straight in her mind.

Meanwhile, Mrs. Agassiz must make some of those social calls of hers — ask a few people who might have money to give to a good cause to come to tea at Radcliffe. On December 20, 1896, she received a letter from young Mrs. Augustus Hemenway, whose husband, "a student just three years out of Harvard" had given the Hemenway Gymnasium to his college.

"In making a visit to Radcliffe lately, I was struck with the inadequacy of the gymnasium," wrote Harriet Longwood Hemenway. "And in looking across the street and seeing what friends had done to make Harvard what it is, I felt that we are not showing the same appreciation of our women that had been so freely bestowed on the boys.

"I do not know what plans you have for a gymnasium or for the future of Radcliffe, but I am sure you have immediate want for a larger building and I should like to give, if my means permit, a permanent gymnasium to Radcliffe and have the pleasure of seeing it used and enjoyed soon — that is, if your plans are sufficiently matured as to the College's future to allow of its being rightly placed. Will you please mention this to no one, but if things open toward the buildings of it, I shall be ready to begin any time. . . ."

It was a wonderful letter and one which any college president would be extremely lucky to receive. But there were difficulties ahead.

First of all, there was that matter of location. Radcliffe owned

Fay House, with its lawns and gardens, and a small plot adjoining. Once this had seemed ample — and now it was much too small a piece of ground. Cambridge, that pleasant country town of Mrs. Agassiz's early married life, had become a city, and small wooden houses on city lots surrounded the Radcliffe property. It seemed as if the college would have to sell and move farther from Harvard Yard — to the weakening of that still partly intangible tie. Then, just as Mrs. Hemenway's offer made immediate decision necessary, three of the lots "fell into our hands most unexpectedly," Mrs. Agassiz said. Radcliffe was soon able to buy two more small pieces of property and the "somewhat irregular square lying between Garden Street and Brattle Street and bounded" more or less east and west "by Appian Way and Mason street" was in process of being acquired. The decision to stay as near as possible to Harvard was reached before all the land was in Radcliffe's hands, and Mrs. Agassiz was able to write to Radcliffe's new benefactor, on January 3, 1897: "It is now absolutely settled that we remain in our present location. You see, therefore, dear Mrs. Hemenway, that the site may be chosen at any moment . . ."

Hitherto, donors had made their gifts more or less without strings. The gift of a building, as compared to a gift of cash, was a different matter. The elder Mrs. Hemenway, who had died in 1894, had been a forceful lady "of queenly appearance," whose philanthropies had been many and who was particularly interested in the health of girls and women. She established the Boston Normal School of Gymnastics in 1889, which, twenty years later, became the Department of Hygiene and Physical Education at Wellesley. Mrs. Howe, at the time of Mary Hemenway's death, "wondered on whom her mantle would fall." Apparently, it had fallen upon her daughter-in-law along with great force of character. She knew exactly what she wanted to do for Radcliffe.

Harvard's Hemenway Gymnasium had as "Assistant Professor of Physical Training and Director of the Gymnasium" Dr. Dudley A. Sargent. Dr. Sargent was an ardent advocate of gymnastics rather than competitive sports, and he delighted in exhibitions, taking part himself in "aerial acts." His "famous stunt of sitting in a rocking chair on a swinging trapeze" was considered exciting enough to "blanch the cheeks of the ladies." This was in 1881, the same year during which Dr. Sargent organized a private school of physical culture.

After the plans for the Radcliffe gymnasium were well under way, it developed that Mrs. Hemenway would very much like to see Dr. Sargent in charge of it. Certainly he came within the rules for he was an assistant professor at Harvard. Although inspired in his lifework by seeing a circus, and having later joined a circus with his rocking chair, he was a graduate of Bowdoin with an M.D. from Yale.[1]

Miss Irwin believed that her girls should above all be scholarly, while Mrs. Agassiz hoped they would be ladies taking a reasonable feminine interest in rocking chairs — but not on a trapeze. Dr. Sargent also wanted the use of the Radcliffe gymnasium for his private classes, and the whole affair offered a dangerous precedent. A donor ought not to influence the choice of a professor and the professor, once appointed, ought not to ask for private privilege. It was up to Mrs. Agassiz to explain all this to Mrs. Hemenway, without losing the gift to the college. A long correspondence ensued and in the end it was a credit to both ladies that plans went forward to completion.

The gymnasium was opened on December 17, 1898, with appropriate ceremonies, including a speech from Mrs. Agassiz. "Stage fright grows more alarming every time I have anything to do or say in public," she confessed, but "the afternoon was a success — good weather — several hundred people — much interest expressed — and the little entertainment at Fay House afterwards very bright." Later she went to "an exhibition of exercises." "I suppose it is all right," she said, "but I confess that if I were a mother I would not like to see my daughter turn herself inside out or upside down in that fashion. It seems to me as if such unnatural attitudes might be dangerous. However, it is all done under very careful and experienced supervision."

The fact that Radcliffe's donors were apt to be women with too much time on their hands made Mrs. Agassiz's problems no easier.

The fact that Miss Irwin's sympathy with these women could not be relied on made Mrs. Agassiz's patience the more indispensable. In June, at the commencement of 1898, a gift of fifty thousand dollars was announced. It was from Mrs. David P. Kimball, who wanted to build a "Hall of Residence." But nearly a year went by and the location for this first Radcliffe dormitory was still under discussion, with no solution in sight. Mrs. Kimball was "troubled and perplexed," and Mrs. Agassiz appealed to Miss Irwin. "I feel as if longer delay would be discourteous to Mrs. Kimball who must want to see her kindness take tangible shape and be herself in touch with the students' house. . . . I suppose we shall have other Halls or Homes of Residence and why not let Mrs. Kimball's be the first built, within the limits of her gift, (which in the Appian Way would be possible I suppose) and on the spot she prefers? Then the Hall would be wholly hers and we may perhaps carry out some more comprehensive plan for Homes, playgrounds etc. at a future time . . ."

The plan for building on Appian Way failed, and Mrs. Agassiz took defeat with good grace. No one else seemed to realize that a proud and happy benefactor attracts others who would like to enjoy the same satisfactions, but she managed to keep matters moving so that Mrs. Kimball should not be too "perplexed." And at last, with her son-in-law, Henry Higginson, she drove about "over-looking some land for Radcliffe" and they decided, with their Corporation member Mr. Warner's help, that "the Phillips field is best." It is difficult to visualize three hundred thousand square feet of open land between Shepard, Linnaean and Walker Streets — but this was "Phillips field." A month later, "Henry says the contract for the Phillips land is completed and I may tell Mrs. Kimball," Mrs. Agassiz wrote, and although this was not at all the spot the lady had wanted, who could resist Lizzie Agassiz, her face aglow with pleasure, come to announce "good news"?

The first Radcliffe dormitory would be called "Bertram Hall" in memory of Mrs. Kimball's son. It was designed by Alexander Wadsworth Longfellow Jr., nephew of the poet, who with his brother R. K. Longfellow had established a most successful Boston firm. Brick was their favorite medium and heavy stone columns their delight. It was not until 1901 that Mrs. Agassiz jotted down her first mention of Bertram Hall as an accomplished fact. "Two teas in one day," she wrote just after Christmas. "The first at Bertram Hall — it is too delightful — absolutely satisfactory and so cheerful." The following January came the dedication. "The great affair (great for us although very small of course) is well over. The house pronounced perfect for its purpose and also most attractive." One can imagine the scurry of preparation when Mrs. Agassiz "dined with the students" later. "I never saw a happier set of girls; dancing and singing after dinner till 8 o'clock when all went to their studies," she said. Ellen Emerson came in from Concord to another informal dinner. "It was pretty to see her get the girls together and teach them the old-fashioned dances of her girlhood. They all enjoyed it so much and were so gay."

Mrs. Agassiz, seventy-nine when Bertram Hall was completed, needed to be with the girls and see them "so gay." The years after her return from Europe had brought further losses to her circle. Mollie Felton, who had been with her in Oxford and Cambridge, died in 1895 of pneumonia. Three years later, Mrs. Agassiz's journal contained a short notation: "Tom Felton taken ill in a Western town . . . his mind evidently affected and some one must be sent to bring him home." Tom died suddenly in Massachusetts General Hospital soon after arriving in Boston. He had been "as sound a man, as safe from insanity, as lucid as perfect health could make him," and so it was concluded that he must have received an injury, either accidental or intentional; but "the whole thing remains a mystery," Mrs. Agassiz said.

Conway and Lisa were now the only surviving children of Mrs. Agassiz's sister Mollie. Lisa and her aunt Lizzie would eventually become important to each other.

Believing firmly that grief must be put aside and life enjoyed as much as possible within the limits of a New England conscience, Lizzie and her sister Sallie embarked upon a course of action they felt to be justified — but daring and extravagant. They took season tickets to the opera in Boston and reserved a room for themselves at the Adams House on opera nights, rather than returning to Cambridge in a livery stable hack. "These little excursions are so pleasant!" exclaimed Lizzie. It helped her conscience to shop for Radcliffe on the morning after one of these dissipations, for it seemed to be up to Madam President to buy "mats" and dishes, and to visit the New England Cooking School to watch a demonstration of a cookstove.

Sallie Cary had been the beauty of the family, the much-praised leading lady of the Temple Players at the age of eighteen. When she was twenty-two, Otto Dresel, the fascinating young German refugee and concert pianist, had been her music teacher — and perhaps she took his attentions too seriously when he composed songs "just for her" and praised her voice. He composed songs for all the girls, including her sister Lizzie, but he married a pupil who had more money than the Carys.[2] The romantic Caroline thought that Dresel was dangerous to Sallie, but the rest of the family seemed only mildly surprised when Sallie never married. Mollie and Lizzie had been the two Cary sisters who paired off together, but after Mollie's death it was Lizzie and Sallie. There was eight years' difference in their ages and Sallie would always seem young to Elizabeth — young at sixty-eight when she was stricken with pneumonia. In February, 1898, Sallie Cary died after a three days' illness. "Self-possessed and serene," she had "said last loving things" to her sisters, and as Elizabeth wrote out the scene afterwards, she found "the world changed — so different without Sallie, the best, the truest sister, strength and support of us all."

Coming home after parting with her sister, Mrs. Agassiz found Alex just back from his "long journey." He was waiting for her in her sitting room and no one else could have given her more comfort just at that time. Alex had been exploring "the Figi Islands" taking with him apparatus from the Diamond Drill Company. The drills proved somewhat disappointing, but he brought up cores of coral from different levels in order to determine the age, structure and manner of formation of Pacific atolls — his mining experience suggesting this new method. Elizabeth spent quiet evenings with him, discussing his work, reading his reports — and as usual correcting his proofs.

Regardless of what might be happening in her private life, Mrs. Agassiz attended Radcliffe meetings. Patiently she attempted to bring opposing factions into agreement. She disliked but accepted the responsibility of casting the deciding vote when factions remained evenly divided. But the work, which she still loved, had begun to overwhelm her with fatigue as the college year drew toward a close, and her children were worried about her. After Commencement in 1898, she sat down to write a letter for Miss Irwin to present to the Council and Academic Board. "My children agree with me that the time has come when, for their peace of mind and my own, I must withdraw from my official connection with Radcliffe College." She added praise for the work of the Council, the Academic Board and the Faculty of Harvard, with whom she had been "associated for the last twenty years." It was a gracious but brief and firm letter. "I feel like an emancipated woman," said Elizabeth as she settled down to enjoy her summer.

Mrs. Agassiz was staying with Alex at "Castle Hill," the place he had built for himself at Newport, and she enclosed with her letter of resignation a long personal letter to Miss Irwin, outlining her hopes for Radcliffe's future administration. ". . . As I look forward, I think of you as President with a Dean of your own choosing; subject of course to the approval of the Council and the Academic Board. . . ." This mantle of Elija was exactly what Miss Irwin wanted to wear and Mrs. Agassiz's intuition was gravely at fault when she proposed alternative plans.

"Or would you rather retain your place with a sort of representative person as President who would occupy the position very much as I have done? Another possibility has presented itself to me — which is that the Dean should be the highest acting officer of Radcliffe while the President of Harvard should be its nominal head. I wish I could know which of these possibilities commends itself to you? I think Mr. Higginson does not think well of the last possibility — that of merging the Presidency of Radcliffe with that of Harvard; nor am I sure that the President of the University would consider it for a moment, — or that the governing boards of the corporation and overseers would agree to it.

"There is still another possibility — namely to abolish the office of President — leaving Radcliffe College as a department of the University with the Dean as head, — as in the professional schools of Harvard. It is not improbable that whenever the present President resigns, there will be a change of organization giving to the Deans the government of their several departments — the President occupying a position not unlike that of Chancellor of Oxford. This however, is only a matter of conjecture. . . ."

Mrs. Agassiz had attempted once before to resign, and Miss Irwin had talked her into keeping on with the work. Now Major Higginson went around to see Miss Irwin and told her that this time the resignation "must be accepted." In 1890, Major Higginson had given the land called "Soldiers' Field" to Harvard in honor of the Civil War dead. For ten years he had been Treasurer of Radcliffe, as well as a Fellow of the Harvard Corporation. Not without reason, he expected his recommendations to be followed; but Miss Irwin, endowed with remarkable executive ability, was not fond of being told what she was to do. Her intense desire to become President of Radcliffe was not yet revealed, but she could see that in Major Higginson she would have no sort of ally.

Almost in a panic, Miss Irwin wrote to Mrs. Agassiz. "I have been profoundly disturbed by your determination to resign. . . . I know you have earned your repose; still I do feel that we might and could and would take off every one of your burdens if you would consent to remain with us even in name. The Commencement speech is the one black spot, is it not? You need never make one, I think."

Here Miss Irwin failed to appreciate Mrs. Agassiz's sense of duty. If she continued as President of Radcliffe it would not be as a figurehead. She would continue to make that speech, sign and hand out those diplomas — and, above all, she would attend those council meetings, casting her deciding vote whenever necessary. "While all others might exonerate me from all responsibility, I should not exonerate myself," Mrs. Agassiz said. She told Miss Irwin that she thought there could be "a larger provision for the authority of the Dean," which was agreeable news, but she suggested that "if no new President is appointed now, the office, without any appreciable change will naturally merge into that of the President of the University . . ."

Miss Irwin's letter begging Mrs. Agassiz not to resign went to Henry Higginson with a penciled note of enclosure from Elizabeth.[3] It was her "own conviction that Miss Irwin is the best head of the institution that we can have. By her fine judgment, her large scholarship, her high standards and the sympathy which shows itself rarely but is both strong and tender on occasion, she seems to me well fitted for the educational side of the work; and on the other side she is perfectly trained by her familiarity with the world and its ways to meet the social customs as they come up — being self-possessed and ready for any demands of that kind." No one could have written a more cordial recommendation, but Miss Irwin's appointment as "absolute head" of Radcliffe was by no means certain and she continued to plead with Mrs. Agassiz not to resign.

"*September 21, Thursday*. To Cambridge, lunched with Agnes and she is urgent with me to remain at Radcliffe as President," Elizabeth wrote. "I am really too tired and I long to lay down the oars." She ended by accepting the title of "Honorary President" after all, and the usual round of duties from which she could not "exonorate" herself began again.

In 1902, Elizabeth Agassiz's eightieth birthday was approaching and wonderful plans were afoot for her of which she was not to be told. Something had to be told her, of course, and her daughter Pauline was delegated to prepare her for a celebration. Her reactions she jotted down beginning November fourth. She had been at "Mrs. Sargent's luncheon" with Miss Irwin, and Pauline sent word for her to call at the Shaws' on her way home. "It was to hear of Ida and Henry's lovely plan for a concert on my 80th birthday, the 5th of December. It is a lovely plan but I have sworn that I would never have one of these semi-public birthdays. But this time

I must yield, not without dread." And the next day, the entry read, "I went in to see Ida and talk over that suggestion of yesterday. It seems all arranged and how can I think but with gratitude of a thing done for me by my children in such a loving spirit? But to live through one's eightieth birthday quietly seems to me the only way."

People began talking about her concert — which was to be given by the Boston Symphony Orchestra, playing in Sanders Theater in Memorial Hall. After all, Henry L. Higginson was founder and financial supporter of the orchestra and he could have them play for his mother-in-law, if he wanted to. "It makes me shiver," she wrote.

On December 4, the entry read: "Tomorrow is the great day but I feel calmer as it grows nearer. I am trying to be quiet and tranquil." Then Friday, December 5: "The day is here and greetings by telegram and by note and the lovely gifts make it a day in Paradise." Usually it is impossible to keep a secret which is shared by a great many people, but Elizabeth's children had succeeded. The birthday celebration was not to be the Symphony concert alone — that was only part of it. "But a fairy gift — a pure surprise — dropped into my hands, crowned this beautiful day of my life. . . . One hundred and sixteen thousand dollars for Radcliffe College for a Students' Hall — I cannot believe it — it seems too good to be true."

Two years previously, in 1900, Mrs. Agassiz mentioned hearing from President Eliot of "Alex's letter concerning a gift from himself, Quin, Ida and Pauline of $100,000 for completing the façade of the Museum of Comparative Zoology." What a joy it would have been for their father, Mrs. Agassiz wrote. Only once had she ever suggested that she would have liked to see her children interested in Radcliffe. "I had a hope that Ida might come in with me," she remarked, but without reproach. This "fairy gift" was from many donors, but her children had contributed largely and had organized the whole affair.

December 6: "The day I have so feared was one of the most beautiful I have known — not only for its personal happiness but because it brought such a munificent gift to Radcliffe — more than the building for which we have longed as giving new facilities for our work — more than that, because the Students' Hall gives us assurance of stability, of permanence; it consolidates our relation to Harvard and will lead to our completion as one of its recognized departments." And again, for the third day, Elizabeth filled the small pages of her journal with accounts of her birthday.

"The birthday concert was perfect — every one says — as a musical occasion very rare and perfect. After the concert, grandchildren and children, all my dear Curtises and a few neighbors and friends came in. It was very easy and pleasant.

"One of the dearest things was that Alex took me in and led me out" of Sanders Theater. "That made it so much less personal for me — I felt so proud of him and as if the honors were for him, rather than for me." Alex had just received the highest scientific order in Germany, and "I believe that this leaves Alex in possession of all prominent scientific orders in Europe," wrote Mrs. Agassiz, but her friends laughed when she said that the tumultuous applause as she left the hall were for him more than for herself.

A letter of thanks was printed and sent to all the subscribers to the Elizabeth Cary Agassiz fund, but Mrs. Agassiz set to work to answer personally the avalanche of letters that descended upon her. One letter was from William James. When she answered it Mrs. Agassiz was not thinking of the famous Harvard professor whose books she faithfully read, nor of James as one of Radcliffe's most brilliant professors. She remembered a thin, homesick boy on the Amazon — who had recovered from smallpox, to be sure, but whose moods of alternating enthusiasm and misery she had understood better than he realized. "Dear William," she wrote, ". . . Do you remember the afternoon when you and I passed each other in separate boats; as I floated out . . . into the sunset glow . . . and you floated into the hidden water way in the forest? As you went by you said to me, 'Is it real or a dream?' Like a dream it seems now but a dream of what abiding power and strength . . ."

"Indeed I do remember the meeting of those two canoes," James replied. "I remember your freshness of interest, and readiness to take hold of everything, and what a blessing to me it was to have one cultivated lady in sight, to keep the meaning of cultivated conversation from growing extinct. I remember my own folly in wishing to return after the hospital in Rio; my general greenness and incapacity as a naturalist afterwards, with my eyes gone to pieces. It was all because my destiny was to be a 'philosopher' — and the fact is which then I didn't know . . . that if a man's good for nothing else, he can at least teach philosophy.

"But I'm going to write one book worthy of you, dear Mrs. Agassiz, and of the Thayer Expedition, if I am spared a couple of years longer.

"I hope you were not displeased at the *applause* the other night as you went out. I started it — and if I hadn't someone else would a moment later."

"Dear William," wrote Mrs. Agassiz. "Only one line more. . . . I *liked* the applause."

CHAPTER TWENTY–SIX

President Emerita

THE birthday gift of funds for a "Students' Hall" at Radcliffe
had been a fine surprise but there was one thing more that
Mrs. Agassiz wanted and that was to see her successor appointed.
She had been Honorary President for five years and she had worked
hard, especially at fund raising and in matters of policy toward
donors. She had recommended that Miss Irwin become President,
but nothing had come of it. It was clear that there was too much
opposition to Miss Irwin among those men interested both in Harvard and Radcliffe and the thing to do now was to find an alternative.

On May 16, 1903, Mrs. Agassiz wrote in her diary, "I had a note
from Henry [Higginson] on Friday and a visit from Mrs. Whitman
on Saturday." A committee for the "reorganization of Radcliffe"
had been formed and these two hard-working members asked her
if she really wanted to retire. Apparently, they did not think so,
because they wanted to know "what duties she would like to retain." She answered, "None." "All seems going well," she added.
"Mr. Briggs will be asked to take the Presidency. I hope he will
accept."

Le Baron Russell Briggs had been Professor of English at Harvard
and "the only teacher to be mentioned in the same breath with
Copeland," according to one authority. Appointed to "handle stu-

dent relations," Briggs was Harvard's first Dean. He had held that office for eleven brilliantly successful years — so that "Dean Briggs" now seemed to have become his name as though he had never had any other. He was President Eliot's right-hand man and it seemed "presumptuous," Mrs. Agassiz thought, to expect him to become Radcliffe's second President. But she had a way of hoping all things. He had "an attractive personality and was already felt as a power at Harvard."

At a tea which Mrs. Whitman gave at her studio for the Radcliffe girls living at Bertram Hall, Mrs. Agassiz heard that "Mr. Briggs has accepted." She sent a note to Miss Irwin. "I said that I hoped that she, like myself, would consider this an onward and upward movement for Radcliffe" — and with one of her most remarkable understatements, "This is evidently not her feeling," Elizabeth added, in her journal.

Mrs. Agassiz never dreamed that her note, with its "onward and upward" theme, would be the first news Miss Irwin had of the invitation to Dean Briggs. Miss Irwin had been chairman of the committee to decide on his nomination. "I expected to hear from her about it rather than to tell her of it," Mrs. Agassiz said. "I have seen her so little during her frequent absences this spring that I really had no opportunity for a long talk." The committee must have nominated Briggs during one of those absences, but in the heat of the ensuing discussion Miss Irwin accused Mrs. Agassiz "and others too" of "want of openness."

All was not settled by any means. On June first, Mrs. Agassiz left for Nahant, noting that "it is evident that we are to have opposition about the Briggs nomination from Miss Coes and also (I learn from Henry) from Mr. Gilman." Many a time, Mrs. Agassiz had smoothed the ruffled feelings of Mr. Gilman, who worked hard but liked to feel important. Miss Mary Coes had been Secretary since 1894 when Radcliffe received its name. If Miss Irwin should be President, Miss Coes might reasonably expect to become Dean. The opposition now took a long look at the rules.

"Kindest letter from Mr. Briggs, offering to take any function of the Commencement of which I would like to be free, for his own part," noted Mrs. Agassiz a few days later, "but I am afraid he does not know that his election has to be confirmed by the Associate Members. Mary Coes, for one, is in full opposition and she says a unanimous vote is needed. She has it in her power to stop the whole matter, if she chooses. It would be a real misfortune, should we lose this chance of allying ourselves more closely with the educational forces of Harvard." She wrote to the Associates, begging every one to "think what would be best for Radcliffe." On the evening of the Association meeting she was "full of anxiety" — waiting alone at Nahant for news.

Next day Mrs. Agassiz was "in the best of spirits," because she had heard "that the meeting went well at Radcliffe and that Briggs is elected." She was pleased to see that "the papers have full and pleasant articles with regard to the election of Dean Briggs — my successor." In a letter from President Eliot she saw a chance for further good publicity. Eliot proposed to make the Commencement address on June 24, which was about two weeks away. Dean Briggs could give out the degrees and Mrs. Agassiz could "plead the indulgence for her eighty years and stay at Nahant." Nothing could have pleased her better.

The result, however, was a blast from Miss Irwin. "Mr. Eliot wrote to me about the Commencement and I told him that Mr. Briggs does not become President of Radcliffe College until September first and, in your absence, it is my duty to confer the degrees. This you know, happened in 1895, during your absence in Europe; and even if it were not my office, it would be unwise to ask Mr. Briggs to take so unusual a step.

"Please don't think about the Commencement Exercises: it is all settled by our statutes that, in your absence, I am to do your work. After the first of September, it will be different." [1]

Along with Miss Irwin's letter to Mrs. Agassiz came one from President Eliot to say that he had checked up on the matter and that Miss Irwin was entirely within her rights.

Mrs. Agassiz announced that she herself would give out the degrees as usual on this, her last Commencement as Honorary President. Perhaps she might have let Miss Irwin have her little victory, if it had not been such a small one, based on such a literal interpretation of the "statutes." Above all other reasons, however, was the question of what was best for Radcliffe, and of this Mrs. Agassiz had no doubt. Dean Briggs was going to have his work cut out for him and she might as well give him a good start. The Commencement of 1903 "went well. . . . Mr. Eliot's address was strong and fitting, speaking of Dean Briggs as our next President in terms of strongest commendation. The day I had so dreaded is over and was one of the happiest I have ever known in my connection with Radcliffe."

All through the years, the customary note for Wednesdays during term time continued to be "tea at Radcliffe." This was still Mrs. Agassiz's way of becoming personally acquainted with her girls, and it was the last thing she would give up. As the years went by the Freshman girls had to have these teas explained to them and to be brought almost by force by some upperclassman. But by the time they were upperclassmen, they understood the tradition.

How did Mrs. Agassiz look to college girls, during her later years? She seemed a little woman, bright and alert, sitting in her chair by the tea table. She wore a pretty lace cap and a shawl, primarily to keep off the drafts, to be sure, but also because it was becoming to her. "She looked," said one of her girls — hesitating and searching for the right word — "why, she looked like a little fairy Godmother."

On December 4, 1903, just the day before her eighty-first birthday, Mrs. Agassiz went to the "Radcliffe tea," as usual. "Both Mr. and Mrs. Briggs came and it was very pleasant," she said. "They were so nice with the students; the fact that she is a Radcliffe graduate makes it so natural and easy for her. . . ." A few days later, Mrs. Briggs called and Mrs. Agassiz found her "full of sympathy about Radcliffe. I had no idea she would throw herself into its affairs with so much interest. It is very helpful and when I am about again, I hope we shall take part in it together."

The casual reference to being "about again," concerned one of Mrs. Agassiz's severe colds to which she was always susceptible. She was also increasingly a victim of rheumatism which brought forth angry little notations in her journal. She was inclined to be charitable toward everything except her own ailments. "Hobbled like a lame old hen" she would say of herself, but she never took a carriage except in the worst weather or to do honor to some guests — usually younger than herself. "I do not venture upon the electric cars," she wrote when that remarkable invention made the journey from Nahant less complicated. She hired a carriage, which cost her three dollars. "One pays dear for being old in more ways than one."

Only once, she spoke of advancing age with sadness. After guests had gone and left her alone in her Nahant cottage she sat down at the piano, but her fingers had grown stiff. "I made a little music. I wish it were like old wine, the better for keeping, but it gets fearfully broken and musty with the years." A far more characteristic entry in her journal was made at the end of October, 1900, just before leaving Nahant, where she was always so happy. "I am going to sit on the piazza in the sun," she wrote. "Oh how wonderful is this experience of old age! No one knows it till they reach it."

Mrs. Agassiz had been given the title of "President Emerita," which pleased her. She could not have been called "Grandmother Emerita" however, if Emerita means to have served out one's term. She was now at the service of a third generation of children. In March, 1902, she went to Hamilton to stay with her two great-granddaughters, Marie and Anna, while their parents went to Europe. Just as Rodolphe had been the nearest to a child of her own, so these two little girls of his were particularly dear to her. Often they needed her, as now, when their father had gone to England to play on the American polo team against the British and his wife, an ardent horsewoman, had been so pleased to be able to go along.

"A sort of pause has come into my life and it has great charm for me," said Mrs. Agassiz — and this is not the way a great-grandparent might be expected to react, confronted with the care of two lively children. She mentioned that "in the early mornings" she read a book called *Religion and Democracy* which Pauline "likes so much." Mrs. Agassiz did not care for it. "There is a sense of effort about the style — a touch of Emerson without his simplicity." She liked a book Ida sent much better. It was a translation of *The Odyssey* which she read "breathless through the whole morning."

The question arises, what sort of children were they who would let their grandmother read a book all the morning? The answer lies in Rodolphe Agassiz's well-staffed household, where there was a nursemaid and a governess. Nevertheless, Mrs. Agassiz was much in demand, especially when it rained. "We cut out animals and played menagerie and circus with our paper wild beasts," she said. Every night after supper she read aloud from *Rosy's Travels* which was "very tranquilizing."

The papers were scanned for news of the American Polo team, and on May 4, "the American team won . . . Dolph's playing is noticed as good and it is said that the team as a whole played well together." Then the weather in England turned rainy and games were postponed. "Too bad, for all those postponements have a bad effect on our ponies — and their riders have not a fair chance." Some of Mrs. Agassiz's Radcliffe associates might have been surprised to hear that she knew anything about polo, but in the course of bringing up her grandsons she had received a fair amount of education at their hands. She was considerably cast-down when the American team finally lost, but she would enjoy discussing the games when Rodolphe and Marie got home.

Mrs. Agassiz still loved to walk, and every pleasant day she went out with the children — happy when she could say "lengthened my walk a little," although "walking when you are old is a very different thing from walking when you are young. The springiness and elasticity are all gone — an immense pleasure becomes a duty and yet it is better to keep it up if you can." They passed a farmhouse where there were hens and chickens and — just as though she were back in Brazil — Mrs. Agassiz made a call on the farmer's wife, who was "very friendly" and let the children feed the chickens. Then off to Cambridge she went to a "reception for Prince Henry" (son of Edward VII) who was getting a degree from Harvard, "out of season and ordinary rule." There were further festivities Mrs. Agassiz would have liked to attend, but she had promised the children she would come back to them before bedtime and she "could just see their wistful little faces" watching at the window for her.

On July 3, "Dolph and Marie," the childrens' parents arrived with "immense rejoicings" and the next day their great-grandmother left "with a grateful heart" because she had been "three months and a half in charge of the children and never an hour of illness." Before long came a present from Rodolphe. It was a low carriage which his grandmother could get into without difficulty in spite of her lameness — to be kept for her in Cambridge for use with Alex's horses.

Mrs. Agassiz had often been anxious because her grandsons would inherit more money than was good for them.[2] "Had a talk with Quin about Rodolph," she wrote, several years previously, when he was first married. The talk was "chiefly about Rodolph's new plans, which make me anxious — not from any doubt of him but because I think his Uncle Henry and his father are putting him in the way of large affairs which, even if successful, offer prosperity rather than happiness — these two do not always go together."

The "large affairs" concerned "Colorado mines." The Calumet copper mines reached "vast proportions" with "fully two hundred miles of passages" by 1909, but in 1898, when Mrs. Agassiz had her talk with her son-in-law, the Calumet directors had been acquiring other mining interests — not all of them successful. In 1880, there were the silver mines in Mexico, promoted by Clarence King, for example. They incurred a million dollar loss instead of the gains expected, and Alexander Agassiz always blamed himself for the fiasco. He had been injured in a fall at Calumet some years before and suffered chronic disability. He started out on the long mule-trek to investigate the mines King had painted in such glowing colors but was obliged to turn back, unable to finish his journey. There had been silver enough — but transportation difficulties and cost of labor caused the failure. Alex knew he could have foreseen and probably could have overcome these handicaps. It would be good to have a son to send out on future missions — a son who would wring success out of failure by sheer force of personality, as his father had done. But Rodolphe was not the man for it.

With no burning desire to make discoveries in natural science, and never having remembered a serious lack of money, Rodolphe nevertheless knew what he wanted. He "grew quite interestd in his occupations as a landowner, sowing and planting, setting out trees and so on." He "looked very fine in his pinks" when he came in from hunting, his grandmother said. Although he eventually became President of Calumet and Hecla, Director of the State Street Trust Company and of numerous other firms, he could count on Mrs. Agassiz's support when he advocated the life of a gentleman farmer.

Among the three boys left in Mrs. Agassiz's charge upon the death of their mother, Maximilian was the only one consistently to join his father on scientific expeditions. Much as she regretted their leaving, Elizabeth was always happy to see her stepson and her grandson setting out together. George seems to have been the temperamental member of the trio. In 1901, Mrs. Agassiz gave a luncheon for George "before the great Harvard and Yale game," as she put it with a touch of the sardonic. "It was a pretty and a pleasant lunch, but George was much displeased with our new maid, Julia — thought her awkward, stupid and no waitress. I, on the contrary, thought her very satisfactory and it seemed to me the waiting was prompt, quiet and intelligent. So folks differ."

Although George's home was Quincy Street, he was away a good deal — to Madeira — to Alaska. His grandmother thought him lonely as well as "fastidious," and George's second engagement was a complete surprise. "With George, it is the unexpected that happens," Mrs. Agassiz said. She was "very very glad" because she was afraid his first broken romance was to be his last. Of George's fiancée, Mabel Simpkins,[3] she wrote, "Her personal charm, her fine character, make this a delightful event for us all." She went right over to Boston to buy Mabel a gift, and found a fine gold chain "with two topaz hearts" which Mabel liked. "She told me afterwards that George liked it too — I was so glad . . . I never know whether he will be pleased."

It was only natural that Alexander Agassiz's three sons should be Elizabeth's chief interest, but news of an engagement among the other grandchildren sent her first to the jeweler's for a present and then to the family gathering where the new and future member was to be met and welcomed. "A lovely day at Pauline's," she wrote in February, 1897. Both Pauline "and Quin were well and seemed cheered immensely by Robbie's engagement." This was their young-

est son, Robert Gould Shaw, and he was to marry Miss Nancy Langhorne, one of the beautiful Langhorne sisters of Virginia. Two years
earlier, her sister Irene had married Charles Dana Gibson, to be
known forever, though inaccurately, as the "original Gibson Girl."
If Mrs. Agassiz had been a reader of society columns, or if she had
looked at illustrated magazines, she might have recognized Nancy
Langhorne — the girl taking the five-barred gate at a hunt club, or
dancing at the Cotillion in New York, or visiting Bar Harbor. At
"Mirador," the Langhorne estate in Virginia, Nancy, her four sisters
and her three brothers, practically lived on horseback — the girls
always riding sidesaddle, at their father's insistence. They made
yearly excursions to Hot Sulphur Springs, where their reputation
for beauty was early established — with Nora, the youngest, being
given a prize for "most beautiful baby" at the age of two. It was
said to be Ward McAllister, cousin of Sam Ward, who made them
famous in New York Society.

After the engagement reception in June at Pride's Crossing,
Mrs. Agassiz wrote of her future granddaughter-in-law: "She is
most attractive, this young girl who brings such a new element into
the family." Nancy Langhorne was "only eighteen, very small, very
bright, very fond of horses, rides splendidly, loves the country and
farm life and seems altogether well adapted for Robbie and his way
of life." With a view to making her feel accepted in her new family,
Mrs. Agassiz had an heirloom amethyst brooch copied for her.

In 1898, Mrs. Agassiz went from Nahant to Beverly "to see
Nancy's baby. The new R. G. Shaw — the dearest, wellest baby
possible." And thereafter she went each year to spend a day with
"the child-mother and her boy." But this marriage came to an end in
1903. In 1906, the former Nancy Langhorne married Vincent Astor.
Eventually the Vicountess Astor became the first woman member of
the British parliament. Her jewels, as Mrs. Agassiz noted, were often
the subject of newspaper comment. There was the coronet set with
the famous Sancy diamond which was worn by Louis XV at his
coronation; then there were the three long strings of matched pearls.
Mentioned only in Mrs. Agassiz's journal, doubtless, was a repro-
duction-antique amethyst brooch.

CHAPTER TWENTY-SEVEN
The Great Question

BORN in 1822, Mrs. Agassiz was living in a rapidly changing world by 1903. Most of what she saw she liked. There was the automobile, for example. "Rodolph and Marie came over (to Nahant) in their new automobile — an hour and a half from Hamilton. That brings us very near," she said. The distance, by whatever road they took, could hardly have been much over fifteen miles, so here was twentieth-century speed. But for her own pleasure, Mrs. Agassiz executed her "pet plan" and drove to Concord to see Ellen Emerson, using her son Alex's carriage and pair. "We drove two hours and a half . . . and returned in the same pleasant and peaceful fashion to Cambridge the next afternoon in the delicious spring weather through a world of blossoms."

Ellen was living in the square white house that had been her father's and she had filled the many comfortable bedrooms with permanent and *non*paying guests. "I never saw a more quaint and peculiar household," said Mrs. Agassiz. There were seven elderly ladies with a nurse "who was a member of the family" to look after them. Elizabeth mentioned "two old dames of 86 and 88" — evidently unwilling to concede that her own 80 years might entitle her to be called an "old dame" herself.

As a mater of fact, Elizabeth Agassiz, though over eighty, was neither quaint nor peculiar. Her engagements were those of a much younger woman: a luncheon, a tea, dinner in Boston followed by the theater — and on the following day no mention of fatigue in Mrs. Agassiz's journal, but instead some comments on Mansfield as Julius Caesar — "stilted, posing — with no distinction."

With the beginning of her years of retirement, there was more time for reading and more space in her journals for Mrs. Agassiz's reactions. William James remained her favorite among the brilliant men at the beginning of the new century. Mrs. Agassiz read *The Varieties of Religious Experience*, which came out in 1902, but she was not sure that some of the people he interviewed on their psychic experiences had not fooled him. However, "his wit has always a literary refinement and a certain elegance in turn of phrase that is perfectly spontaneous and natural."

William's brother, Henry James, did not fare so well at Mrs. Agassiz's hands. She had been reading his biography of her old friend William Story, the sculptor. "Henry James's intricacies of style render it somewhat difficult of interpretation, but happily the people of whom he treats are simpler than he is . . ."

Elizabeth was indignant in behalf of Cambridge. "He characterizes our Cambridge society as 'bourgeois' — it contained Longfellow and his wife, a very distinguished and charming person, Lowell and his very beautiful and refined wife, Story himself, Holmes and the Norton family, Prescott, Motley and so on. Perhaps H. J. does not admit of nobility in the social sense, without a title."

Elizabeth read the life of Phillips Brooks and a book on Huxley — noting that the men were poles apart. She somewhat favored the scientist above the clergyman. To please her daughter Ida, she read "a pleasant article on the raising of beagles," which Ida's son Alexander had written. Along with clergymen, scientists and beagles comes "Miss Crawford's account of John Eliot and his Indians." Mrs. Agassiz thought that the author was "entirely mistaken" and that the Indians could never have been Christianized: "The whole history is a story of failure — a failure which makes the volume in Harvard Library containing John Eliot's translation of the Bible into the Indian tongue one of the saddest sights in the world. One of the

noblest and at the same time one of the most futile efforts . . . ends
in a volume that no man can read."

Radcliffe had by no means been crowded out of Mrs. Agassiz's
life, even though it occupied less space in her journal since her retirement. First came the matter of the hall to be built with the funds
raised for her birthday. "My candidate for architect is Mr. Longfellow," said Mrs. Agassiz, but Miss Irwin told her "how neglectful
he was about the kitchen department at Brooks House. This will
never do for us, for luncheons will make an important feature of
our new Hall." However, Mr. Longfellow was made aware of his
shortcomings and promised to be more careful about kitchens. He
then came in with a plan which Mrs. Agassiz thought "admirable
and very ingenious considering the uses the new Hall is to be put
to." But his estimate was $280,000 which was much too high. They
could have everything on a smaller scale, he suggested, and for a
while it seemed that this idea would go through. Then Henry Higginson informed his mother-in-law that "our building at this time
would involve a loss of about $20,000 on account of the high price
of material and labor." This might be the twentieth century, but
the time had not come when buildings were put up regardless of
cost and ability to pay. Mrs. Agassiz was "disappointed" but never
dreamed of doing anything but wait. A year later, it was time to go
ahead. "Elizabeth Agassiz Hall" they were going to call it. "A large
mouthful," she commented.

Sarah Wyman Whitman, as an artist and member of the Radcliffe
council, always had a great deal to do with the interior decorating
and furnishing of Radcliffe's new buildings. Since their birthdays
fell on the same day of the month, Elizabeth and her "twin" Sally
often had a birthday tea together — just a private festival all by
themselves. In many ways, Sally Whitman had taken the place of
her sister Sallie in Mrs. Agassiz's life, and one of the great pleasures
of the new hall was in planning details for it together. Mrs. Whitman's portrait of Elizabeth Agassiz was to hang in the new building.

On June 22, 1904, Mrs. Agassiz was in Nahant when she wrote in
her journal: "Bad news from Sally Whitman — dear, dear Sally —

is she going where all the mysteries are solved — the great secrets?"
And on the twenty-sixth, the entry read: "Sally Whitman died yesterday at the Hospital.[1] How impossible it seems. No more ever
again but silence — a last farewell to such a friend as is rarely found."
Her diary for 1904 was uncompleted because Mrs. Agassiz was herself taken very ill.

"Lizzie seems really aged by her sorrow for Mrs. Whitman," wrote
Caroline Curtis, after visiting her sister at Nahant on the second of
July. "Two apparently slight attacks of the heart" caused the doctor
to suggest that "if there is anything needing decision in her affairs
it should be brought to her attention." Mrs. Agassiz's nephew,
Charles Curtis, now a lawyer, had taken charge of many complicated Perkins and Cary family bequests and trust funds so he came
down to Nahant prepared to deal with a last will and testament. But
doctors and relatives alike reckoned without Elizabeth Agassiz's
indomitable spirit. Seven days later she was "able to walk across the
room and get out of her chair without help."

Mrs. Curtis's account of her sister's illness suggests, however, that
Elizabeth may have had a series of rather severe shocks or cerebral
hemorrhages. In August, Mrs. Curtis "found Lizzie had become
much weaker — the depression and trouble with her speech has returned, the whole condition very sad." Mrs. Agassiz, who had forced
back her tears when the death of her husband and her son's wife
changed all their lives, and who had given her much-loved sisters
and her one close friend a brave, even a smiling last farewell, now
wept and "struggled to speak" but could not. She seemed "exhausted
and strange, almost wandering," her sister said, who had never seen
Lizzie other than in full possession of her faculties. On the third of
September "a telephone message came from Nahant that Lizzie was
failing" and her sister, who hurried to her, felt there was "little
hope of her lasting many days." The children came and went; Ida,
Pauline; the grandchildren and their wives whom Elizabeth had
loved. Time and again she had gone to them when they needed her
and now they stood around helplessly, trying to think of something
they could do.

It was all a dream to Mrs. Agassiz. Nurses arranging her flowers suddenly carried her back to Brazil, and she tried to explain that it was a flower "festa" given by her servants — a "partly religious ceremony." Then, on September 5 — "To Nahant," Carrie wrote, "where there was a curious change. Lizzie has recovered her voice and speech, and taking more food, is stronger."

The explanation, in her own words, came when Mrs. Agassiz resumed her diary in January, 1905. The whole summer had been "a perfect blank" to her. This she knew, however: "Alex came," and said, " 'Take her home and she will get well.' " At first the various doctors who had been called in refused to move her but by the end of the month, on a cold, rainy Friday, she went back to Cambridge. "It is true," said Elizabeth, "that I began to mend at once. I have continued to improve, but it was slow."

Casting back, she recalled her eighty-second birthday. "What a day was that! — What a beautiful day with its lovely expressions of affection and its gifts ending with a gorgeous lemon tree for my flower window." Christmas had been "difficult" — but only because "it is not easy to shop from one's chamber." Elizabeth had "limited" her "gifts to the children" — meaning that she and her faithful maid, Amelia, had selected, ordered and wrapped only about forty presents. She was reading "Morley's 'Gladstone,' a life of John Andrew, Civil War Governor of Massachusetts, and 'Roma' by Maud Eliot, to the last degree entertaining." This was the woman whose mind was "astray" even in October, according to her sister, and who had been given at one point only a few days to live!

By March, Mrs. Agassiz was well enough to send "a somewhat anxious note" to Radcliffe because there was a paragraph in the paper "about the misconduct of some girls at Memorial Hall." A member of the Council called on her at once to reassure her that "these disturbers" had nothing to do with Radcliffe. They were agitating for womens' rights and Radcliffe girls would be "incapable of such ill-judged rudeness."

Through sheer determination, Mrs. Agassiz recovered much of her ability to walk. But Dr. Taylor and Dr. Wolcott spoke darkly of "rheumatism" and said that Nahant would be no place for her during the coming summer. They recommended a higher altitude, and favored her niece Lisa Felton's home at Arlington. The altitude of the town of Arlington is thirty feet and the Heights, where Lisa's house was, could not have been much more than twice that — but Mrs. Agassiz had always been able to accept anything above sea level as "high" and both her doctors seemed to agree. She sent for her nephew Charlie Curtis to see about renting her Nahant house. "Charlie advises against the bathrooms and thinks we shall get but a small rent out of my Nahant house anyway," noted Mrs. Agassiz. But she told Charlie to have the bathrooms put in and the subsequent returns justified her judgment. She insisted upon being a paying guest at her niece Lisa's house for Lisa could use the extra money. She sent for her "nice cabinetmaker" and had awnings made for Lisa's windows and a railing for the porch steps.

Just before it was time to leave for Arlington, the "new Radcliffe Hall" was opened. Mrs. Agassiz's doctor said she could go to see it — but she refused. "Decided it would be too exciting," she wrote — but all through her journal of these days ran the thread of her desire to "walk better." Although she found a "wheeling chair" waiting for her at Arlington, the gift of Ida and Pauline, she walked every day and reported progress. She had always been able to walk well, with that dignity and grace of which her nieces spoke — and she was not going to be seen tottering into Elizabeth Agassiz Hall if she could help it.

When she returned to Cambridge in the fall, Mrs. Agassiz wrote that she "quite astonished" her sister Emma by her "capital walking." And by spring came the triumphant notation: "Pauline came and took me over the Hall, named after me." Mrs. Agassiz mounted the broad granite steps with very little assistance, and walked about not at all "like an old cripple" as she had once called herself. "We had a lovely morning together," she and Pauline. "It is a beautiful building, without and within. . . ."

Arlington was again to be the summer retreat, and Mrs. Agassiz observed with satisfaction that her Nahant cottage had been rented "to some people from Ohio for $1200." She was happy about going to Arlington, but there were two things she would miss. One was the sound of the bell at Nahant, as the long rolling swells lifted the buoy below the cliffs. And she missed music within the house, for always a piano had been sent down for the summer. It would seem that Lisa had no piano — perhaps had no room for one in her little house, which was so " modern and convenient." Mrs. George Agassiz, Elizabeth's granddaughter-in-law, had tried to fill this deficiency the first summer. The "musical machine" duly arrived, but Elizabeth had been bitterly disappointed in it.

"So kind in Mabel," she said, "but to tell the truth, I cannot endure it. It is called 'Victor' and is understood to reproduce the musical sounds of the human voice. But the reproduction seems to me a hideous mockery. . . .

"I long to see my Emma — to hear her play Chopin — so full of passion and sweetness as his music always is, — with a touch all her own."

But Miss Emma Cary was in Nahant. Now seventy-three, she had spent her life in the service of music, playing before distinguished private audiences, studying constantly, working with children in music — and befriending musicians. She often arranged the music for Radcliffe Commencements.[2] She gave musical parties, "so gracious, so easy, so simple that all the guests seemed at home." When Elizabeth was no longer able to come to these concerts Emma sent music to her on Quincy street — by asking her protégés to go there to sing.

There was to be one more return to Cambridge, and Elizabeth would hear her sister Emma play again. There would be another birthday — her eighty-fourth — with "flowers coming in all day," a "splendid Azalea plant from Rodolph and Marie" and then "a little watch from Mabel" — more acceptable, it seemed, than a phonograph. Amelia, Mrs. Agassiz's faithful attendant, would "go Christmasing" for her — that favorite word still part of her private vocabulary. She would prepare "some seventy presents, not counting charities."

In one of her rare moments almost of petulance, Mrs. Agassiz complained of winter weather. "I am so weary of staying indoors." And when a mild day came along there would be no walking. "I am going to drive. I wish that I liked it; but I hate it. I never liked to drive." But when she got home, Elizabeth added another line to her journal for the day. "After all, the drive was delightful."

During the long winter, "the Planet Mars has occupied me," Lizzie said. She had been reading the new book, *Mars and Its Canals*, by Percival Lowell, and she was as excited over the idea of life on another planet as her husband would have been. Her grandson George Agassiz dampened her enthusiasm. "Had a bit of a talk with George about Mars," she wrote. "I don't think he is much impressed with the 'canals.'" But of course she had already decided that George was a pessimist.

A "golden day" was one when a letter came from Alex — from Easter Island — from Acapulco — wherever he might be. "How well I remember the trumpets . . . which by old tradition, they used to blow over the forests at Acapulco," Elizabeth said. "There is a kind of wild pathos about it. At least it was so, in my time." And then there was the letter which Alex wrote to a daughter-in-law "which spoke of our relations, his and mine, and which I could hardly read without emotion." Once, soon after she became his second mother, she had spoken of him as undemonstrative. Now she knew he loved her.

Alex was at home during the winter of 1906–1907. Year after year, since his father's death, Elizabeth had watched him go out the door — to visit distant mines, to dredge deep seas. Never more than once or twice had she been absent on the day of his return. And then what talks they had! Almost the only woman to whom Alexander Agassiz ever talked about his scientific work was Elizabeth. She knew what he had done and what he was trying to do, and she read everything he wrote — even now.

"Alex came and sat with me awhile before his club dinner," she said. This dinner was the formal affair she had supervised for him each year, all through the years, attending to every perfect detail, greeting his guests — then withdrawing to her sitting room, where she knew that some of the eminent scientists would come to speak with her before the evening was over. And now no more. With deep dismay, Elizabeth realized that one of those "compulsory naps" had overtaken her, from which she "came with unusual or occasional difficulty about speaking." The clock showed that only a few minutes had gone by. Elizabeth straightened herself, as for a moment she felt humiliated. But it had been beautiful to wake and find Alex there, silently watching over her. It would be good to tell him all that he had meant to her during the lonely years without his father. But there was the "difficulty about speaking" and the thing to do was to force her tongue to say, clearly, just the usual "Good night."

To her niece Lisa's "hospitable and dear roof" Mrs. Agassiz returned for the summer of 1907. She could not hear very well, and "Dr. Blake sent out an ear trumpet," but she said scornfully that her faithful Amelia "Can roll a piece of stout paper so as to make a better 'Acousticon' than any of their advertised machines."

Elizabeth Agassiz had enjoyed a cloudless faith when she was a young girl. She pictured her friends, when she lost them, as taking tea together in Heaven as they had on Temple Place or Beacon Street. Marriage to a natural scientist changed her point of view, but did not leave her without hope. Louis Agassiz had been a religious man, following the faith of his fathers more than his fellow scientists thought his own findings justified. With Alexander, science came first and everything he failed to prove by his own methods must of necessity go into the discard.

It was so much Mrs. Agassiz's habit to go to church that only absence from church was worthy of mention in her journals. She sometimes thought the minister had little to say and, because of her musical background, she sometimes complained mildly of the quality of the church music in Cambridge. But in her last years, Mrs. Agassiz felt regretful that she could no longer occupy the pew in the Unitarian church which seemed somehow a part of home. She had always been accustomed to think for herself and on one of the final pages of her journal she wrote, "If there is a life after death, we will know the great secret."

Elizabeth's last journal entry was written in a somewhat unsure hand. She was evidently quoting from memory, a trifle haltingly, with a word or two crossed out:

"And he said, go forth and stand upon the mount before the Lord.

"And behold the Lord passed by and a great and strong wind rent the mountains.

"And after the fire a still small voice."

On Monday, June 24, Lisa Felton telephoned to Caroline Curtis from Arlington. Mrs. Agassiz had "suffered a stroke of paralysis and was unconscious." This time there was no chance of recovery, and on June 27, 1907, she died without regaining consciousness. "She looked like herself — but sleeping," they said.

More than thirty years had passed since the day of Louis Agassiz's great public funeral at Appleton Chapel in Harvard Yard. Now "one hundred people of Radcliffe in cap and gown, headed by Dean Irwin and President Briggs" marched to Appleton Chapel to honor Mrs. Agassiz. She had never asked for more than the one greatest gift life has to offer a woman — the love of her husband and family. She had received this gift, and six grandsons and three great-grandsons attended this childless woman who had greatly loved her husband's children.

But out of sheer generous-heartedness, Elizabeth Agassiz had also given herself to a cause that came unasked to her door and which she could easily have brushed aside as too much trouble. She could hardly have wanted a public funeral, but if "Radcliffe people" wanted to march in solemn procession she would never have refused them. It was she, more than anyone else, who gave them the right to appear in cap and gown in Harvard's precincts.

Elizabeth Cary Agassiz was buried in Mt. Auburn Cemetery, where Louis Agassiz's glacial stone from the Aar stood in the Cary plot, and pines from Switzerland watched over it.

Acknowledgments

I wish first of all to express my gratitude to MRS. GORDON C. PRINCE, *great-granddaughter of Louis Agassiz. Her knowledge of Agassiz from within the family helped me to visualize him as a human being, while her actual recollections of Elizabeth Agassiz were also of great value. Mrs. Prince placed at my disposal all family photographs and other material in her possession and explained my aims as a biographer to members of the previous generation so that in respect to certain restricted manuscripts my path was made smooth.*

MR. CHARLES P. CURTIS, *grandson of Caroline Cary Curtis, was equally kind, and I owe him an equal debt of gratitude. He gave his permission for my use of his grandmother's and his great-uncle's diaries, which not only filled the gap caused by the missing Elizabeth Cary Agassiz diaries but gave a picture of the Boston Agassizs as seen through the eyes of younger members of the Cary family.*

PROFESSOR EDWARD LURIE *had completed his doctorate on Louis Agassiz and was at work on his forthcoming biography when we met in Cambridge, Massachusetts, in 1957. I have never encountered more generous co-operation from anyone working in the same field as myself. Of great value to me were his notes made at the Smithsonian Institution and at the Gray Herbarium, Harvard University, where he had discovered much Agassiz correspondence.*

The most important source of manuscript material for this book was the Women's Archives, Radcliffe College. I wish to thank MRS. RICHARD BORDEN, *Director,* MISS MARY E. HOWARD, *Archivist, and* MRS. DOROTHY C. FASS, *Assistant to Mrs. Borden, for their help. The Women's Archives has been established only comparatively recently but it is already a treasure house for the biographer. Further important material is at the Radcliffe Library, and I wish to thank the staff for their kind co-operation.*

Houghton Library of Harvard University contains more than 700 letters in the Agassiz collection and much related material. I wish to thank PROFESSOR WILLIAM A. JACKSON, Director, and MISS CAROLYN E. JAKEMAN, and her staff, who are always indefatigable in their search for contemporary letters and journals, such as the William James papers which shed so much light on my subject. I wish to thank MR. STEPHEN T. RILEY, Director of the Massachusetts Historical Society, for calling my attention to the Thomas G. Cary, Jr. diary and other valuable material. The Museum of Comparative Zoology, Harvard University, contains many Agassiz family papers. I was fortunate in meeting DR. ALFRED SHERWOOD ROMER, Director, who gave me permission to read manuscripts.

I wish to thank MR. DAVID McKIBBEN, Art Director of the Boston Athenæum, who was most helpful in the matter of illustrations, and who told me of the Sargent drawing of Ida Agassiz Higginson. At the Bostonian Society, MRS. ROPES CABOT, Curator, discovered the drawing of the "Hourly" omnibus to Cambridge and other scenes.

My husband and I visited the Agassiz house in Nahant, now owned by MR. WALTER L. HOBBS, who very kindly showed us around. He introduced us to MRS. MILTON M. HOAG, whose house nearby was the one owned by Thomas Handasyd Perkins. The original monochrome wallpaper is still to be seen. DR. RAYMOND CALKINS of Cambridge, Massachusetts, gave me a copy of his mother's account of Mrs. Agassiz's school, where she was a pupil. For much unpublished information and many letters, I am indebted to the late MARGARET FAYERWEATHER. For particularly gracious permission to quote printed material, I wish to thank WILBUR K. JORDAN, President of Radcliffe, MISS MARGARET S. PERRY and HOWARD DOUGHTY. My lifelong friend, the late MRS. HENRY C. HART, gave me her personal recollections of Elizabeth Cary Agassiz as President of Radcliffe.

Chapter Notes

CHAPTER ONE

1. For descriptions of Temple Place, see *King's Handbook of Boston; The History and Genealogy of the Cabot Family*, by L. Vernon Briggs (Boston: privately printed, 1927) and *Memories of Fifty Years in the Last Century*, by Caroline Gardiner Curtis (Boston: privately printed, 1947).

2. Colonel Perkins's house on Temple Place was sold in 1854 for $52,500 to the Provident Institution for Savings. The inside was remodeled in 1906, so that little save the "bow front" with its curved windows remains to remind the passer-by of the vanished glories of a street now lined with shops.

3. *Annals of King's Chapel*, by Henry Wilder, gives J. Elliot Cabot's eulogy of Thomas G. Cary. Pew numbers are from the same source.

4. The story of Mrs. Cary's choice of husband for her daughter Lizzie is told in *The Proper Bostonians*, by Cleveland Amory (New York: E. P. Dutton and Company, 1947). I quote from *Memories of Fifty Years*.

5. Description of Agassiz by Bronson Alcott is to be found in *Pedlar's Progress* by Odell Shepard (Boston: Little, Brown and Company, 1937).

6. Just outside of Harvard, Massachusetts, is "Fruitlands," a house occupied by the Alcotts and now preserved as a museum. In one of the rooms is a Thoreau manuscript dated 7 July, 1851, which reads:

"The moon is now more than half full. I have been tonight with some company to look through Perez Blood's telescope a second time. A dozen of his neighbors were swept along in the stream from curiosity. . . . I was amused to see what sort of respect this man with the telescope had obtained from his neighbors — something akin to that which savages award to the civilized man."

7. All quotations from William James are from letters and fragments of diaries of William James (Houghton Library, Harvard University).

CHAPTER TWO

1. For the early adventures of the Cary family and the Perkins family I am indebted to *The Cary Letters*, edited at the request of the family by C. G. C. (Caroline Gardiner Curtis), and *Memories of Fifty Years in the Last Century* by Caroline Gardiner Curtis (cf. Chapter 1, Note 1). *The Cary Letters* were privately published in 1891 and are most delightful. Both volumes were the gift to me of Charles P. Curtis, grandson of Caroline Gardiner Cary Curtis, and have proved of great value.

2. The late Margaret Fayerweather, descendant of James Perkins, gave me the story of "Moussa," the Perkins slave, as she heard it as a child. She showed me a "Corner" or "Roundabout chair" of mahogany in Queen Anne style which had been the one allotted to Moussa when he "sat on the door."

3. See *Memoir of Thomas Handasyd Perkins Containing Extracts from his Diaries and Letters,* by Thomas Graves Cary (Boston: Little, Brown and Company, 1855).

4. For letters concerning the Perkins interest in the slave trade and in importation of opium see *The History and Genealogy of the Cabot Family* (cf. Chapter 1, Note 1).

CHAPTER THREE

1. A series of fine photographs at the New-York Historical Society show what an attractive place St. John's Park used to be.

2. *The Cary Letters* (cf. Chapter 2, Note 1) supply details of boat races, LaFayette, and the theater, and of the little Carys at their "deal-board table" in the nursery.

3. New York City directories give the addresses of the Cary brothers and the New-York Historical Society has the volumes showing real estate transactions.

4. Elizabeth Peabody mentioned "the Cary girls" and their governess, Miss Lyman, in her letters to her sister Sophia in Cuba, known as "Cuba Journal" and now in the Henry W. and Albert A. Berg Collection in the New York Public Library. Miss Peabody and Miss Lyman were friends, and her name occurs frequently in the Peabody sisters' correspondence.

5. "We always had our dear Miss Lyman with us," wrote Caroline Gardiner Curtis in *Memories of Fifty Years in the Last Century*. I find no

record of any school attended by the older Cary children in New York, but there might have been a school the younger children forgot.

6. I am indebted to my friend the late Mrs. Margaret Fayerweather for the story of the pirates on Temple Place, which is from a letter from Sarah Perkins, granddaughter of James Perkins, to her cousin John Forbes, headed "Pearl Street November 23, 1834." The Fayerweather papers are now part of the New York Public Library manuscript collections and the Berg Collection.

CHAPTER FOUR

1. Tom Cary's story of the Temple Place Players is in typescript at the Radcliffe Archives. It appears to have been prepared in this form at the time when *Memories of Fifty Years in the Last Century* was being written and it was used, evidently, although not quoted. It was also used by Lucy Allen Paton in her *Elizabeth Agassiz, A Biography* (Boston: Houghton Mifflin Company, 1919). I have made many inquiries concerning the original, but in vain. If it ever comes to light there may be further entries; and the whole thing would make good reading, for Tom had a sense of humor and very little reverence for some of his Boston contemporaries.

2. *Famous Families of Massachusetts*, by Mary Caroline Crawford (Boston: Little, Brown and Company, 1930).

3. *Famous Families of Massachusetts*, by Mary Caroline Crawford (Boston: Little, Brown and Company, 1930).

4. The "black schooner . . . among the haycocks" is from Longfellow's diaries. (Houghton Library, Harvard University).

5. *The History and Genealogy of the Cabot Family*, by L. Vernon Briggs (Cf. Chapter 1, Note 1).

CHAPTER FIVE

1. Material on Agassiz's early life in this chapter is from *Louis Agassiz, His Life and Correspondence* edited by Elizabeth Cary Agassiz (Boston: Houghton, Mifflin and Company, 1886).

2. Agassiz's correspondence, after his arrival in the United States, is sprinkled with criticism of American scholarship. When he spoke of a young man who "works like a German student" this was high praise, rarely accorded.

CHAPTER SIX

1. While preparing the biography of her husband, Mrs. Agassiz wrote to Joseph Denkel, who was living in Germany. He replied, giving her a long account of his years of acquaintance and work with Agassiz. This manuscript is at Houghton Library, Harvard University. Mrs. Agassiz had other sources of information and used this account little or not at all. She probably felt that in some ways it was not sufficiently respectful; but today it seems truthful, naïve and intimate.

2. "Recollections of Agassiz," by Theodore Lyman (*Atlantic Monthly*, Vol. XXXIII, February, 1874).

3. This was the price paid by the Boston Public Library during Agassiz's lifetime.

4. "'Alexander von Humboldt centennial' with text of Agassiz's address copied from The Boston Advertiser" (*Living Age*, Vol. CIII, 1869).

5. In 1832, Neuchâtel had "five or six thousand inhabitants," according to Jules Marcou. Louis de Coulon, father and son, were "two of the most devoted and at the same time most modest naturalists." See *Life, Letters and Works of Louis Agassiz*, by Jules Marcou (New York: The Macmillan Company, 1896).

6. This drawing is sometimes attributed to Cécile, and sometimes not attributed. The style is certainly similar to examples of her signed work.

CHAPTER SEVEN

1. Ida Agassiz Higginson visited Europe with her husband, and went to the British Museum to see her mother's drawings; and the curator, not knowing that the initials C. A. represented Cécile Agassiz, made this comment while showing them. See *Letters and Recollections of Alexander Agassiz*, edited by G. R. Agassiz (Boston: Houghton Mifflin Company, 1913).

2. "Recollections of Agassiz," by Theodore Lyman (*Atlantic Monthly*, Vol. XXXIII, February, 1874).

3. *Letters and Recollections of Alexander Agassiz*, edited by G. R. Agassiz.

4. *Life, Letters, and Works of Louis Agassiz*, by Jules Marcou (New York: The Macmillan Company, 1896) was published ten years after the appearance of Mrs. Agassiz's *Louis Agassiz, His Life and Correspondence*. "Odious as it is and painful for us, I think on the whole silence from the family is best," she wrote to her son-in-law, Henry Higginson. "Now that omissions have been made about family matters at Ida's request, it seems to me that the second vol. is by far the worst."

Professor Edward Lurie, in the course of his research on Agassiz, found these deleted pages among the Agassiz manuscripts at the Museum of Comparative Zoology. By modern standards, they are perfectly harmless, although occasionally unsympathetic. I have corrected certain of Marcou's outright misstatements, by means of letters in Radcliffe Archives, and have indicated in text where I think Marcou should be taken with a grain of salt. Since Marcou knew Agassiz in Switzerland, he remains a useful source.

CHAPTER EIGHT

1. This description of Desor is from Marcou. Most of the information concerning Desor is from this source, as I have indicated in text.

2. See *Theodore Parker*, by Henry Steele Commager. (Boston: The Beacon Press, 1947).

3. Charles Lucien Jules Laurent Bonaparte, Prince of Canino, was an ardent naturalist. His special interest was ornithology and he was of great assistance to Audubon. He planned to go with Agassiz to the United States but was prevented by ill health. He was born in 1803 and died in 1857.

4. Diaries, Julia Ward Howe (Houghton Library, Harvard University). Also Fayerweather papers (New York Public Library).

CHAPTER NINE

1. *Louis Agassiz, His Life and Correspondence*, edited by Elizabeth Cary Agassiz (Boston: Houghton, Mifflin and Company, 1886). Agassiz to Élie de Beaumont; Boston, August 31, 1847. Monsieur Elie de Beaumont placed "fossil fishes from the collection at the Mining School" in Paris at Agassiz's disposal in 1832. Their friendship continued.

2. In the course of his research for his forthcoming biography of Agassiz, Professor Edward Lurie found much valuable correspondence at the Gray Herbarium, Harvard University. I am greatly indebted to him for allowing me to read his notes.

3. Marcou wrote of the Desor affair, giving himself a hero's role as mediator between Agassiz and Desor. I have a feeling that he was considerably carried away by his sense of drama.

In 1851, Édouard Desor sued Charles H. Davis, Captain of the *Bibb*, and had the proceedings printed in a small pamphlet. I am indebted to Professor Lurie for the use of his microfilm of this pamphlet, a copy of which is at Harvard Archives.

In 1856, Thomas B. Curtis returned to Agassiz papers and letters concerning the Desor affair. These are now at Houghton Library and I am deeply grateful to Mrs. Gordon C. Prince for making arrangements for me to see these papers. Although the story can be pieced together from other sources, these papers are essential for the complete vindication of Agassiz.

4. I have no evidence of the exact nature of the "acts of levity" in Agassiz's past. He was decidedly afraid of the Boston puritanical point of view, and he was never wealthy enough to cut a very wide swathe — so I picture his levities as comparatively innocent. Let the reader decide.

5. *Lake Superior: Its Physical Character, Vegetation and Animals Compared with Those of Other and Similar Regions, by Louis Agassiz, with a narrative of the tour by J. Elliot Cabot and contributions by other scientific gentlemen. Elegantly illustrated.* (Boston: Gould, Kendall and Lincoln, 1850.)

CHAPTER TEN

1. The plural of words ending in *z* should be formed by adding an apostrophe, according to *Words into Type: A Guide in the Preparation of Manuscripts . . . based on studies by Marjorie E. Skillin, Robert M. Gay and other authorities* (New York: Appleton-Century-Crofts, 1948). The name Agassiz is given as an example. However, since the name is pronounced by the family as though ending in *y*, it seems to me more logical to apply the rule for the name Mary, also given as an example, and add *s*, as in regular plural forms.

2. Sonrel became a successful Boston photographer, and the best of the many photographs of Agassiz carry his name.

3. These stories, with variations, are to be encountered in almost all reminiscences of Agassiz; but I am indebted to Agassiz's great-granddaughter, Mrs. Gordon C. Prince, for what I consider the best versions.

4. *Life, Letters and Works of Louis Agassiz,* by Jules Marcou (Vol. II, p. 4). Cf. Chapter Seven, Note 4.

5. Landscapes painted on windowshades may be seen at Old Sturbridge Village, Sturbridge, Massachusetts. Where nineteenth-century interiors are being recreated, doubtless more will appear. Perhaps Jacques Burkhardt's signature may be found on some linen shades with its castle on the Rhine or Alpine scene.

6. Agassiz wrote a report of his exploration of the Florida reefs for Professor Alexander Dallas Bache, Superintendent of the United States Coast Survey, who published extracts from it in his annual report for 1852. Congress appropriated money to publish a detailed report, and

Sonrel prepared plates; but Louis Agassiz never found time to write a complete text. Alexander Agassiz and Pourtalès finished it in 1882.

7. These letters are all undated; but with the help of Miss Mary E. Howard, Archivist at the Women's Archives, Radcliffe College, I have arranged them in chronological order to the best of my ability.

CHAPTER ELEVEN

1. The Agassiz house on Quincy Street was burned in 1917. At this time, President Emeritus Charles W. Eliot wrote an article about the house for the *Harvard Alumni Bulletin*. He placed the snake story on Quincy Street, but the original letter in the Radcliffe Archives, though undated, contains this mention of Oxford Street.

2. See *Home by the River, The Story of Hampton Plantation*, by Archibald Rutledge (Indianapolis: Bobbs-Merrill Co., Inc.), for fine photographs of present-day Hampton.

3. *The Edge of the Sea*, by Rachel Carson (Boston: Houghton Mifflin Company, 1955), makes an excellent companion for the present-day collector of shells in this region, where the tides and currents still fling ashore these treasures.

4. Thackeray said that Louis Agassiz was "a delightful *bonhommious* person as frank and unpretending as he is learned and illustrious." See *Thackeray, the Age of Wisdom, 1847–1863*, by Gordon N. Ray (New York: McGraw-Hill, 1958).

5. *Seaside Studies in Natural History*. I have quoted from the revised edition "by Elizabeth C. Agassiz and Alexander Agassiz" (Boston: 1865).

6. Longfellow's journal.

7. Caroline Curtis diary; Nahant, 1904. The landscape wallpaper was put on when Caroline "was very little." The wall was "formerly plain yellow," and "the workmen made mistakes and Father and Mary climbed on the dining room table and painted in India ink clouds to cover."

CHAPTER TWELVE

1. Longfellow's personal comments on the situation at Harvard are from his journals at Houghton Library, Harvard University. *Three Centuries of Harvard*, by Samuel Eliot Morison (Cambridge: Harvard University Press, 1936) also proved a valuable source of information for this chapter.

2. See *The Autobiography of Nathaniel Southgate Shaler* (Boston: Houghton, Mifflin Company, 1909). The sandy-haired, full-bearded

Shaler became almost as popular a professor at Harvard as Agassiz. In 1902 he was immortalized in "Harvard Celebrities," verses by Henry Ware Eliot, Jr., and in caricatures by Edward Revere Little. The verses follow:

This is Shaler
Fairy-taler.
Scientific mountain-scaler,
Penetrator
Of each crater
From the poles to the equator.
Tamer of the hurricane,
Prophet of the wind and rain,
Hypnotizer
Of the geyser,
Wizard of the frozen plain.
Hark! What is that deep and distant subterranean roar,
Arising near Memorial and reaching out to Gore?
'Tis the rumble of applause
When the speaker makes a pause
In relating an adventure from his fund of earthquake lore.

3. Marcou, Vol. II, Appendix calls this work *North American Testudinata.*

4. The original manuscript of this letter was presented by Charles P. Curtis, Jr. to the president of Harvard, and I am told that it occupies a place of honor in the president's office.

5. These figures are from an article by Alexander Agassiz in the Harvard Graduates Magazine for June, 1907.

6. From "The Saturday Club" by Oliver Wendell Holmes. The description of Agassiz as a member of the Saturday Club is in part as follows:

The great Professor, strong, broad-shouldered, square,
In Life's rich noon-tide, joyous, debonair,
His social hour no leaden care alloys,
His laugh rings loud and mirthful as a boy's —
That lusty laugh the Puritans forgot, —
What ear hath heard it and remembers not?

7. It seems to have become necessary to explain that the Museum of Comparative Zoology, or "Agassiz," is the place where "the glass flowers" are. The "Ware Collection of Blaschka Glass Models of Plants" is doubtless unique. It was made near Dresden, Germany, between 1887 and 1936.

CHAPTER THIRTEEN

1. "The Agassiz House on Quincy Street," by Charles W. Eliot, '53, President Emeritus. (*Harvard Alumni Bulletin,* March 29, 1919.) "The house was designed by Henry Greenough and the college made it possible for Professor Agassiz to build it by taking a large mortgage on it." There was "only one bathroom and the tub was not infrequently occupied by turtles."

2. Elizabeth Cary Agassiz's correspondence with her father is from the Radcliffe Women's Archives.

3. Agassiz's "daily lecture" was "during the last hour of the morning." See "The Agassiz House on Quincy Street" (Note 1).

4. Estimate by Professor Edward Lurie.

CHAPTER FOURTEEN

1. All direct quotations from Morse are from his diary in *Edward Sylvester Morse, a Biography,* by Dorothy G. Wayman (Cambridge: Harvard University Press, 1942).

2. Verrill diary, Harvard Archives, Widener Library.

3. Alexander Agassiz's letters to Theodore Lyman, Museum of Comparative Zoology, tell of student difficulties. I have condensed these stories and omitted the Henry James Clark controversy as being repetitious. Clark claimed co-authorship of *Contributions to the Natural History of the United States,* published a pamphlet called "A Claim for Scientific Property" which angered Agassiz, and was dismissed as "adjunct professor of Harvard" — according to Marcou.

4. Richard Cary Curtis, namesake of Richard Cary and great-grandson of Caroline Cary Curtis, was killed while serving in the American Air Force in Italy in 1945.

5. Ware Street, Cambridge, is now almost entirely lined with small brick apartment houses. One or two old homes remain, and at the side of one of them is a curious circular window which may well be the "flower window" added by Mrs. Thomas Graves Cary. Below it there is no garden but a black-topped parking area instead.

6. Diary of Caroline Cary Curtis.

7. "Parkman's Dark Years: Letters to Mary Dwight Parkman," edited by Howard Doughty (*Harvard Library Bulletin,* 1950).

CHAPTER FIFTEEN

1. *Uncle Sam Ward and His Circle,* by Maude Howe Elliott (New York: The Macmillan Company, 1928).

2. *Random Memories,* by Ernest Wadsworth Longfellow (Boston: Houghton Mifflin Company, 1922).

3. Longfellow journals (Houghton Library, Harvard University).

4. *Old Cambridge,* by Thomas Wentworth Higginson (New York: The Macmillan Company, 1900).

5. William James' Brazilian journals (Houghton Library, Harvard University). These papers also include pencil sketches of fellow assistants, of Brazilian types, and of a small monkey.

6. In 1878 William James married Alice Howe Gibbens, "distinguished by the serenity of her disposition, as well as by her wit and beauty," according to the *Dictionary of American Biography.*

CHAPTER SIXTEEN

1. As in the previous chapter, I have used Mrs. Agassiz's letters in preference to the text of *A Journey in Brazil.*

2. In some cases the names of river towns mentioned by Mrs. Agassiz have been changed and in many cases the modern spelling differs from that in *A Journey in Brazil.* It is Teffé, according to Mrs. Agassiz, for example.

3. I think that the results of Hunnewell's efforts at photography must be at the Museum of Comparative Zoology. I realize that these particular studies might prove unsuitable for illustrations, but I hope that someday pictures of the Agassizs in Brazil may be brought to light. Meanwhile, I am most grateful for the use of the group photograph of Agassiz's assistants which is part of a display in the outer office of the director.

CHAPTER SEVENTEEN

1. *Life and Letters of Henry Lee Higginson,* by Bliss Perry contains much of Ida's story and supplements letters to her stepmother. Her water color sketch is one of the illustrations.

2. Federal Guide Series, *Georgia.*

3. For general information concerning Calumet and Hecla and for figures on output, profit and so on, I am indebted to *Michigan Copper and Boston Dollars,* by William Gates, Jr. (Cambridge: Harvard University Press, 1951). This source gives the name as Edwin J. Hurlbert.

4. The Alexander Agassiz correspondence, Museum of Comparative Zoology, gives the first-hand story. Hurlbert's name here appears as John.

5. At the time of their marriage, Major Henry Lee Higginson's gift to his bride was a pearl cross. Ida Agassiz Higginson mentioned this

"wedding present from my husband" in her will — and also "my necklace of 96 pearls which I have used as a bracelet" and "my necklace of 73 pearls."

CHAPTER EIGHTEEN

1. The diary of Thomas Graves Cary, Jr., is full of "Perkins drollery." I regret that there is not space to quote more of it.

2. Agassiz's assertion that he found glacial evidences in Brazil was scoffed at, and I have seen it stated that there never was ice in Brazil. I went therefore to the Museum of Natural History, New York City, with my question — was Agassiz wrong when he said he "followed morainic soil"? I was most kindly and courteously treated by the attendant whom I approached and directed to the library where no pains were spared to help me. In the Handbook of South American Geology edited by William F. Jenks (Geological Soc. of Amer., 1957), an article on glaciation in Brazil by Avelino Ignacio de Olivera mentions "scattered vestiges of glaciation extending 1200 kilometers from central Bahia to northwestern Parana. . . ." It is still "not known whether these vestiges are the result of alpine or continental glaciers" . . . but "there seems to be a correlation between this Brazilian glaciation and those noted in the Congo, Angola, West Griqualand, Transvaal, Southern Rhodesia . . . Canada and the United States. . . ."

3. So far as I know, Agassiz went on only three scientific journeys alone after his marriage to Elizabeth. One of these was to the Adirondacks in 1858. Longfellow was invited but said, "Is it true that Emerson is going to take a gun?" On being told that it was true, "Then somebody will be shot," Longfellow said, refusing to go along. So reported William James Stillman, artist and organizer of the expedition and of the "Adirondack Club." Stillman painted a picture of the party which now hangs in the Concord Library, and Emerson wrote a long poem entitled "The Adirondacs, a Journal." Nobody was shot.

CHAPTER NINETEEN

1. Again it is Elizabeth Agassiz's letters at the Women's Archives, Radcliffe College, that form the basis for this chapter, rather than her published articles of the voyage of the *Hassler*.

2. The Alexander Agassiz correspondence at the Museum of Comparative Zoology provides the human touch.

3. Emerson's journal (*The Heart of Emerson's Journals*, edited by Bliss Perry — Boston: Houghton Mifflin Company, 1909): "*October, 1854.*

When someone offered Agassiz a glass of water, he said that he did not know whether he had ever drunk a glass of that liquid before he came to this country."

CHAPTER TWENTY

1. It was with great regret that Alexander Agassiz and other trustees decided that Penikese must be given up. After the death of Agassiz there was no one with the necessary enthusiasm to keep this far too expensive project going, and in 1907 Massachusetts took over the island and established a leper colony there. This too was abandoned. See American Guide Series, *Massachusetts*.

2. *Atlantic Monthly*, Vol. XXXIII, January, 1874.

3. Headline in the *Springfield Union*, August 5, 1958, *SKELETON MAY PROVE MAN EXISTING 10 MILLION YEARS*, tells of a discovery in an Italian soft-coal mine; a case in point.

4. *The Early Days of the Saturday Club*, by Edward Waldo Emerson (Boston: Houghton Mifflin Company, 1918).

5. Caroline Curtis diaries.

6. This letter from Elizabeth Agassiz to her uncle William H. Gardiner is a recent acquisition of the Women's Archives, Radcliffe College; the gift of Sister Geraldine Mary, St. Anne's Convent, Denver, Colorado.

CHAPTER TWENTY-ONE

1. Accounts of Christmas festivities are from both Elizabeth Agassiz's and her sister Caroline Curtis's diary. Alex Higginson was born in 1876.

2. Julia Ward Howe often mentioned attending a dinner at Alexander Agassiz's. Her nickname for him was "dear Zoo."

3. Spelled by Mrs. Agassiz in her journals RODOLPH. In *Elizabeth Cary Agassiz* by Paton and in *Who's Who in America*, the name is spelled RODOLPHE.

4. Radcliffe Library archives.

5. *Elizabeth Cary Agassiz, A Biography*, by Lucy Allen Paton (Boston: Houghton Mifflin Company, 1919), is an invaluable source of information about Radcliffe's early years. Manuscript material at the Radcliffe Library and in the Women's Archives provides a glimpse a little more behind the scenes.

CHAPTER TWENTY-TWO

1. Mrs. Agassiz's Commencement addresses were always carefully written out, and among the Agassiz papers at the Women's Archives at Rad-

cliffe are notebooks and loose pages of rough drafts of speeches, evidence of careful preparation.

2. Miss Slack, Louis Agassiz's former secretary, faithfully typed handwritten manuscript. Before her book was finally completed, Mrs. Agassiz hired a room in a nearby house where she could work without interruption. She was unsure of herself as an author and wrote anxiously to her editor for advice.

3. Julia Ward Howe was among the friends who thought that Radcliffe ought to demand more "rights" from Harvard. In reading Mrs. Howe's journals, one gathers that she felt that "dear Lizzie Agassiz" was insufficiently aggressive.

CHAPTER TWENTY-THREE

1. Thomas Couture, French historic and genre painter, 1815–1879. In *Random Memories*, Ernest Wadsworth Longfellow gives an interesting chapter on his studies with Couture. This artist was popular in the United States and several of his paintings now hang in the Metropolitan Museum of Art in New York.

2. *Three Centuries of Harvard*, by Samuel Eliot Morison (Cambridge: Harvard University Press, 1946).

3. Aunt Caroline Perkins Gardiner — not always noted for tact.

4. This teacher was Mrs. Marie Gallison. She was a German musician who wrote an account in German, *My Life in Two Continents*, an English translation of which has recently been added to the Women's Archives at Radcliffe. Mrs. Gallison was a protégée of Miss Emma Cary's, but also indebted to Mrs. Agassiz for much assistance.

5. *From Madge to Margaret*, by Carroll Winchester, was published by Lee, Shephard in 1880; *The Love of a Lifetime* was published by Cupples, Upsham and Company in 1884.

6. This peak would appear to have been named for Major Andrew Atkinson Humphreys, engineer, scientist and Civil War officer, who was commissioned to "ascertain the most practicable and economic route for a railway from the Mississippi River to the Pacific Ocean."

CHAPTER TWENTY-FOUR

1. Mrs. Agassiz's diary is the chief source of information concerning her European tour.

2. I am indebted to Dr. Milton Edward Lord, Director of the Boston Public Library, for this description of the Elliott ceiling painting.

3. Francis Alexander, father of Francesca, was born in Killingly, Con-

necticut, in 1800 and died in Florence in 1881. At the museum of Primitive American paintings at Harvard, Massachusetts, collected by Miss Clara Endicott Sears, there is a fine example of Alexander's work. Although for the most part self taught, his style has none of the stiffness usually associated with "primitives."

4. I am indebted to the late Mrs. Margaret Fayerweather for the story of Francesca. While visiting Mrs. Fayerweather, I saw many of Francesca's paintings and a copy of *Songs of Tuscany*.

CHAPTER TWENTY-FIVE

1. *Dictionary of American Biography*.

2. Otto Dresel was born in Germany in 1826. He came to the United States in 1848, settling in New York and then, after a visit to Germany, he returned to Boston, which he made his home until his death in 1890. He married Anna, only child of Ellis Gray Loring.

3. Most of the correspondence between Mrs. Agassiz and Miss Irwin concerning the presidency of Radcliffe College are at the Radcliffe Library in an envelope bearing the notation "Papers given by Charles Curtis."

CHAPTER TWENTY-SIX

1. This letter was included in those sent to the Radcliffe College Library by Charles Curtis. They seem not to have been taken into account in *Elizabeth Cary Agassiz, a Biography*, by Lucy Allen Paton (See Chapter 21, Note 5.) and may not have been among the papers available in 1919, when Miss Paton's book was completed.

2. When Quincy Adams Shaw died in 1908, the newspapers referred to him as "the reputed richest man in New England." He gave to his wife, Pauline Agassiz Shaw, "$800,000 to be paid to her at such times and in such amounts as she shall call for same . . ." This was Mrs. Shaw's fund for her many charities. She was to receive "in addition, $40,000 per annum." But sons, daughters and grandchildren were not to receive "more than $12,000 per annum until the age of 25."

3. Mabel Simpkins of Yarmouthport, Massachusetts. They were married in 1902 when the bridegroom was forty years old.

CHAPTER TWENTY-SEVEN

1. Mrs. Sarah Wyman Whitman left no immediate relatives. To Radcliffe she gave a bequest of one hundred thousand dollars.

2. Mrs. Agassiz arranged for Mrs. Marie Gallison, the German musician and singing teacher, to "form a large chorus at Radcliffe." "Every girl who wished to sing in the chorus" was to be accepted "whether she had a voice or not." Mrs. Gallison was to "educate" the girls "to love the very best music ever written" and to "behave like ladies on the stage," according to her own account in *My Life in Two Continents*.

Index

Index